A Taste of the Country

Editor: Julie Schnittka
Food Editor: Mary Beth Jung
Assistant Food Editor: Coleen Martin
Assistant Editor: Sherri Congleton
Art Director: Ellen Lloyd
Cover Design and Illustrations: Jim Sibilski
Food Photography: Mike Huibregtse, Judy Anderson
Directors of Food Photography: Judy Larson, Sue Myers, Linda Dzik

©1994, Reiman Publications, L.P.
5400 S. 60th Street, Greendale WI 53129
International Standard Book Number: 0-89821-120-4
Library of Congress Catalog Card Number: 94-66234
All rights reserved.
Printed in U.S.A.

Pictured on front cover. Clockwise from the top: Fresh Vegetable Casserole (page 27), Chili Verde (page 13), Wild Rice Quiche (page 46) and Spicy Stuffed Peppers (page 42).
Pictured on back cover. Clockwise from the top: Creole Jambalaya (page 12), Apple Danish (page 56), California Fresh Fruit Dip (page 6) and Maple Pecan Corn Bread (page 52).

Appetizers, beverages and sauces are important additions to any get-together. Pictured here, the Three-in-One Cheese Ball, is a great appetizer. And you'll want to keep plenty of Sugar 'n' Spice Nuts on hand for *year-round* nibbling.

TASTY TREATS. Clockwise from the top: **Fruitcake Cookies** (p. 61), **Sugar 'n' Spice Nuts** (p. 5), **Praline Sundae Topping** (p. 5), **Cheery Cherry Loaf** (p. 56) and **Three-in-One Cheese Ball** (p. 5).

Appetizers, Beverages & Sauces

THREE-IN-ONE CHEESE BALL
Mary Anne Marston, Almonte, Ontario
(PICTURED ON OPPOSITE PAGE)

    1 package (8 ounces) cream cheese, softened
    4 cups (16 ounces) shredded cheddar cheese, room temperature
    2 tablespoons milk
    2 tablespoons minced onion
    2 tablespoons Worcestershire sauce
Coarsely cracked black pepper
    1/2 cup (2 ounces) crumbled blue cheese
Minced fresh parsley
    1/4 teaspoon garlic powder
Finely chopped pecans
Assorted crackers

In a mixing bowl, beat cream cheese, cheddar cheese, milk, onion and Worcestershire sauce until mix is fluffy. If a smoother spread is desired, process in a food processor until creamy. Divide into thirds (about 1 cup each). Shape first portion into a ball; roll in cracked pepper. Add the blue cheese to the second portion; mix well. Shape into a ball; roll in parsley. Add garlic powder to the remaining portion; mix well. Shape into a ball; roll in nuts. Cover and refrigerate. Let stand at room temperature 1 hour before serving time. Serve with crackers. **Yield:** 3 cheese balls.

CONTINENTAL CHEESE SPREAD
Mrs. Thomas Wigglesworth
Absecon, New Jersey

    1 package (8 ounces) cream cheese, softened
    1 tablespoon milk
    3 tablespoons grated Parmesan cheese
    1 tablespoon minced fresh parsley
    1 tablespoon minced green onion
    1 garlic clove, minced
    1/2 teaspoon dried thyme
    1/8 teaspoon pepper

In a bowl, beat cream cheese and milk until fluffy. Add Parmesan cheese, parsley, onion, garlic, thyme and pepper. Mix until well blended. Spoon into a small container. Cover and refrigerate at least 1 hour. Store in refrigerator. **Yield:** 1 cup.

SUGAR 'N' SPICE NUTS
Debbi Baker, Green Springs, Ohio
(PICTURED ON OPPOSITE PAGE)

    3 cups lightly salted mixed nuts
    1 egg white
    1 tablespoon orange juice
    2/3 cup sugar
    1 tablespoon grated orange peel
    1 teaspoon ground cinnamon
    1/2 teaspoon ground ginger
    1/2 teaspoon ground allspice

Place nuts in a large bowl. In a small bowl, beat egg white and orange juice with a fork until foamy. Add sugar, orange peel, cinnamon, ginger and allspice; mix well. Pour over nuts and stir to coat. Spread into an ungreased 15-in. x 10-in. x 1-in. baking pan. Bake at 275°, stirring every 15 minutes, for 45-50 minutes or until nuts are crisp and lightly browned. Cool completely. Store in an airtight container. **Yield:** 4 cups.

CRUNCHY CHEESE DIP
Deborah Hill, Coffeyville, Kansas

    1 can (8 ounces) pineapple tidbits
    2 packages (8 ounces *each*) cream cheese, softened
    1 can (8 ounces) water chestnuts, drained and chopped
    3 tablespoons chopped fresh chives
    1 teaspoon seasoned salt
    1/4 teaspoon pepper
    1 cup chopped pecans
Fresh chopped parsley
Assorted crackers

Drain pineapple, reserving 1 tablespoon juice. In a small bowl, combine pineapple, cream cheese, water chestnuts, chives, salt, pepper and pecans. Stir in reserved juice; mix well. Garnish with parsley. Cover and chill. Serve with crackers. **Yield:** about 3-1/2 cups.

SALMON APPETIZERS
Evelyn Gebhardt, Kasilof, Alaska

    1 can (15 ounces) salmon *or* 2 cups cooked salmon, flaked
    1 package (8 ounces) cream cheese, softened
    4 tablespoons mild *or* medium salsa
    2 tablespoons chopped fresh parsley
    1 teaspoon dried cilantro
    1/4 teaspoon ground cumin, optional
    8 flour tortillas (8 inches)

Drain salmon; remove any bones. In a small bowl, combine salmon, cream cheese, salsa, parsley, cilantro and cumin if desired. Spread about 2 tablespoons of the salmon mixture over each tortilla. Roll each tortilla up tightly and wrap individually with plastic wrap. Refrigerate 2-3 hours. Slice each tortilla into bite-size pieces. **Yield:** about 48 appetizers.

PRALINE SUNDAE TOPPING
Valerie Cook, Hubbard, Iowa
(PICTURED ON OPPOSITE PAGE)

    1/4 cup butter *or* margarine
    1-1/4 cups packed brown sugar
    16 large marshmallows
    2 tablespoons light corn syrup
Dash salt
    1 cup evaporated milk
    1/2 cup chopped pecans, toasted
    1 teaspoon vanilla extract
Ice cream

Melt butter in a saucepan. Add brown sugar, marshmallows, corn syrup and salt. Cook and stir over low heat until marshmallows are melted and mixture comes to a boil. Boil for 1 minute. Remove from the heat; cool for 5 minutes. Stir in evaporated milk, pecans and vanilla; mix well. Serve warm or cold over ice cream. Store in the refrigerator. **Yield:** 2-1/2 cups.

FIRESIDE CHEESE SPREAD
Debbie Jones, California, Maryland

- 1 container (16 ounces) cheddar cheese spread, softened
- 2 packages (one 8 ounces, one 3 ounces) cream cheese, softened
- 3 tablespoons butter *or* margarine, softened
- 1 teaspoon Worcestershire sauce
- 1/2 teaspoon garlic powder
Paprika
Snipped fresh parsley
Assorted crackers

In a medium bowl, combine cheese spread, cream cheese, butter, Worcestershire sauce and garlic powder. Blend thoroughly. Chill at least 3 hours or overnight. Sprinkle with paprika and parsley. Serve with crackers. **Yield:** about 3-1/2 cups.

SALMON SPREAD
Carolyn Stewart, Anchorage, Alaska
(PICTURED ON PAGE 58)

- 2 cans (15 ounces *each*) salmon, drained, boned and flaked
- 1 tablespoon minced onion
- 1 tablespoon prepared horseradish
- 1 tablespoon lemon juice
- 1 package (8 ounces) cream cheese, softened
- 2 to 3 tablespoons mayonnaise
- 1-1/2 teaspoons dried dill weed
- 1/2 teaspoon salt
- 1 cup (8 ounces) sour cream
Fresh dill *or* parsley, optional
Toasted bread rounds *or* crackers

In a mixing bowl, combine first eight ingredients; mix well. Spread on a serving platter and shape into a loaf or ball. Top with sour cream. Chill. Garnish with dill or parsley if desired. Serve with bread rounds or crackers. **Yield:** 8-10 appetizer servings.

LEMONY ICED TEA
Sharon Emery, New Burnside, Illinois

- 8 cups water
- 3/4 cup sugar
- 1/2 cup lemon juice
- 1/2 cup white grape juice
- 1/4 cup unsweetened lemon-flavored instant tea mix
Ice
Lemon slices

In a large pitcher, combine water, sugar, lemon juice, grape juice and tea mix. Stir well to dissolve the sugar. Serve on ice with lemon slices. **Yield:** 8 servings.

CALIFORNIA FRESH FRUIT DIP
Nancy Cutright, San Jose, California
(PICTURED ON BACK COVER)

 This tasty dish uses less sugar, salt and fat. Recipe includes *Diabetic Exchanges*.

- 1 cup plain low-fat yogurt
- 2 tablespoons honey
- 2 tablespoons lime juice
- 1 teaspoon grated lime peel
- 1/4 teaspoon ground ginger

In a small bowl, combine all ingredients. Serve with fresh fruit. Cover and refrigerate leftovers. **Yield:** about 1 cup. **Diabetic Exchanges:** One serving (2 tablespoons) equals 1/4 fruit, 1/4 skim milk; also, 33 calories, 22 mg sodium, 1 mg cholesterol, 7 gm carbohydrate, 2 gm protein, trace fat.

RHUBARB PUNCH
Eleanor Martens, Rosenort, Manitoba

- 3 quarts diced fresh *or* frozen rhubarb
- 4-1/2 cups sugar
- 3 quarts water
- 1 can (6 ounces) frozen orange juice concentrate, thawed
- 3 tablespoons lemon juice
Lemon-lime soda

In a heavy saucepan, bring rhubarb, sugar and water to a boil. Boil for 15 minutes; cool and strain. Stir in orange and lemon juices. Refrigerate until well chilled. To serve, combine 1/2 cup rhubarb syrup to 1 cup soda. **Yield:** 24 servings (12 ozs. each).

CRANBERRY CHUTNEY
Alease Case, Summerland Key, Florida

- 1 pound fresh *or* frozen cranberries
- 2-1/4 cups packed brown sugar
- 1 cup raisins
- 1 cup water
- 1/2 cup chopped pecans *or* walnuts
- 1/4 cup candied ginger, chopped
- 1/4 cup lemon juice
- 1 teaspoon salt

- 1 teaspoon grated onion
- 1/4 teaspoon ground cloves

Combine all the ingredients in a Dutch oven; bring to a boil. Reduce heat and simmer for 20-30 minutes or until slightly thickened, stirring occasionally. Pour into hot sterilized jars, leaving 1/4-in. headspace. Adjust caps. Process in a boiling-water bath for 10 minutes. If not processed, store chutney in the refrigerator. **Yield:** 4-1/2 cups.

BASIL BUTTER
Emily Chaney, Penobscot, Maine

- 1-1/2 cups loosely packed fresh basil leaves
- 3/4 pound butter (no substitutes), softened
- 1-1/2 teaspoons lemon juice
- 1-1/2 teaspoons white pepper

In a food processor, chop basil. Add butter, lemon juice and pepper; blend until smooth. Drop by half-tablespoons onto a cookie sheet; freeze. Remove from cookie sheet and store in freezer bags. Use to flavor chicken, fish or vegetables. **Yield:** 4 dozen butter balls.

ORANGE TEA
Sally Mueller, Loveland, Colorado

- 7 cups water
- 1 can (12 ounces) frozen orange juice concentrate
- 1/2 cup sugar
- 2 tablespoons lemon juice
- 5 teaspoons instant tea
- 1 teaspoon whole cloves

In a large saucepan, combine water, orange juice concentrate, sugar, lemon juice and tea. Tie the cloves in a small cheesecloth bag; add to saucepan. Simmer, uncovered, for 15-20 minutes. Remove spice bag. Serve hot. Store leftovers in glass container in refrigerator. **Yield:** 8 servings (2 quarts).

SPICED RHUBARB
Paula Pelis, Rocky Point, New York
(PICTURED ON PAGE 74)

- 10 cups diced fresh *or* frozen rhubarb
- 4-1/2 cups sugar
- 1 cup cider vinegar
- 2 teaspoons ground cinnamon
- 1/2 to 1 teaspoon ground cloves
- 1/2 to 1 teaspoon ground allspice

In a large Dutch oven or kettle, combine all ingredients. Bring to a rapid boil;

reduce heat and simmer for 60-70 minutes. Pour into pint jars and refrigerate. Serve as a glaze for ham or spread on biscuits. **Yield:** about 4 pints.

GAIL'S HOMEMADE SALSA
Gail Michalski, Amsterdam, New York

1 can (28 ounces) peeled
   tomatoes with liquid, cut up
1 can (28 ounces) crushed
   tomatoes
1 can (4 ounces) chopped
   green chilies
1 medium onion, chopped
1 tablespoon cider vinegar
2 teaspoons salt
1/2 teaspoon onion powder
1/2 teaspoon garlic powder
Tortilla chips

In a large bowl, combine first eight ingredients. Cover and refrigerate for 8 hours or overnight. Serve with tortilla chips. **Yield:** 7 cups.

SWEET-AND-SOUR MUSTARD
Cheri White, Richland, Michigan

1 cup packed brown sugar
1/2 cup cider *or* raspberry vinegar
1/3 cup dry mustard
2 tablespoons water
2 eggs, lightly beaten

In a saucepan, whisk together all ingredients. Cook over low heat, stirring constantly, until thickened. Pour into small jars. Cover and refrigerate. **Yield:** 1-1/2 cups.

RASPBERRY CHOCOLATE SAUCE
Linda Gronewaller, Hutchinson, Kansas

1 package (12 ounces)
   unsweetened frozen
   raspberries, thawed
3/4 cup baking cocoa
3/4 cup whipping cream
1-1/2 cups sugar
1/3 cup light corn syrup
1/4 cup butter (no substitutes),
   softened

Puree raspberries in a food processor or blender. Press through a fine sieve; set aside. In a saucepan, combine cocoa and cream. Add sugar, corn syrup, butter and raspberries; mix well. Bring to a boil over medium heat, stirring often. Boil for 8 minutes without stirring. Remove from the heat. Cool at least 15 minutes before serving. Spoon over ice cream, pound cake or brownies. Re-

frigerate leftovers in a covered container for up to 1 month. **Yield:** 3-1/4 cups.

CORN RELISH
Karen Smock, Girard, Pennsylvania
(PICTURED ON PAGE 44)

10 cups fresh whole kernel corn
1 small head cabbage, shredded
6 medium onions, chopped
4 medium green peppers,
   chopped
2 medium sweet red peppers,
   chopped
1 quart cider vinegar
4 cups sugar
2-1/2 teaspoons ground turmeric
2-1/2 teaspoons dry mustard
2 teaspoons celery seed
2 teaspoons salt

In a large Dutch oven, combine corn, cabbage, onions and peppers. In a bowl, stir together remaining ingredients. Pour over vegetables. Bring to a boil; reduce heat and simmer for 10 minutes. Ladle into hot sterilized jars, leaving 1/4-in. headspace. Adjust caps. Process in a boiling-water bath for 10 minutes. Let stand for at least 1 week to blend flavors. **Yield:** about 14 jars (12 ozs. each).

CORNCOB JELLY
Marge Hagy, Brewster, Washington

12 large corncobs
4 cups water
1 box powdered fruit pectin
4 cups sugar
Yellow food coloring

Cut corn kernels from cobs and reserve for another recipe. In a large kettle, place corncobs and water; bring to a boil. Boil for 10 minutes. Remove and discard the cobs; strain liquid through cheesecloth. Liquid should measure 3 cups. Add additional water if necessary. Return to the kettle and stir in pectin. Bring to a full rolling boil. Add sugar and bring back to a boil. Skim foam and add a few drops of food coloring. Pour into hot jars. Cool and refrigerate until ready to use. **Yield:** about 4 pints.

DOUBLE HOT HORSERADISH MUSTARD
Madeline Cole, Willow, Alaska

1/4 cup cider vinegar
1/4 cup dry mustard
3 tablespoons white wine
   vinegar

2 tablespoons mustard seed
1 tablespoon prepared
   horseradish
1-1/2 teaspoons honey

Combine all ingredients in a blender container. Process on high until smooth. Transfer to a small jar and cover tightly. Store in the refrigerator. **Yield:** 1/2 cup.

RHUBARB CHUTNEY
Mrs. Selmer Looney, Eugene, Oregon
(PICTURED ON PAGE 75)

4 cups diced fresh *or* frozen
   rhubarb
2 cups diced peeled apples
1 orange
1 lemon
2 cups packed brown sugar
1 cup raisins
1 cup currants
1/2 cup diced candied citron
1/2 cup apple juice
1/2 teaspoon ground nutmeg
1/2 teaspoon ground allspice
1/2 teaspoon ground cloves
1/2 teaspoon ground cinnamon
1/4 teaspoon salt

Place rhubarb and apples in a large Dutch oven or kettle. Grate the rind of the orange and lemon; add to kettle. Peel and section orange and lemon. Discard the seeds. Cut fruit into small pieces; stir into kettle. Add remaining ingredients. Bring to a boil. Reduce heat and simmer, uncovered, for 30-40 minutes or until thickened, stirring occasionally. Pour into half-pint jars and seal. Freeze or process for 15 minutes in a boiling-water bath. **Yield:** about 6 half-pints.

HOT CHOCOLATE MIX
Margery Richmond, Winnipeg, Manitoba

4 squares (1 ounce *each*)
   semisweet chocolate, grated
1/2 cup baking cocoa
1/2 cup confectioners' sugar
1/4 teaspoon ground cinnamon
Dash salt

In a bowl, combine all ingredients. To use, add 2 tablespoons mix to 3/4 cup hot milk. **Yield:** 1-1/2 cups dry mix.

BETTER BUTTER

For a delicious change, try spreading herb butter on your corn on the cob. Simply combine 2 sticks of butter softened to room temperature with 1 teaspoon chopped fresh sweet basil or 1/2 teaspoon dried basil.

Soup is such a *versatile* menu item...from hearty main meals to light first courses. For a quick but satisfying meal, try Cheesy Vegetable Soup. Fresh Fruit Soup is a great cool down after spicy Mexican dishes. And Chicken and Barley Soup is so delicious you'll want to share it with friends.

SOUPS ON! Clockwise from the top: **Hungarian Goulash Soup** (p. 9), **Cheesy Vegetable Soup** (p. 9), **Fresh Fruit Soup** (p. 9) and **Chicken Barley Soup** (p. 9).

Soups, Stews & Chili

CHICKEN BARLEY SOUP
Diana Costello, Marion, Kansas
(PICTURED ON OPPOSITE PAGE)

 This tasty dish uses less sugar, salt and fat. Recipe includes *Diabetic Exchanges*.

- 1 broiler-fryer chicken (2 to 3 pounds), cut up
- 2 quarts water
- 1-1/2 cups diced carrots
- 1 cup diced celery
- 1/2 cup barley
- 1/2 cup chopped onion
- 1 chicken bouillon cube, optional
- 1 teaspoon salt, optional
- 1 bay leaf
- 1/2 teaspoon poultry seasoning
- 1/2 teaspoon pepper
- 1/2 teaspoon dried sage

In a large kettle, cook chicken in water until tender. Cool broth and skim off fat. Bone the chicken and cut into bite-size pieces; return to kettle along with remaining ingredients. Simmer, covered, for at least 1 hour or until vegetables and barley are tender. Remove bay leaf. **Yield:** 5 servings (about 1-1/2 quarts). **Diabetic Exchanges:** One serving (prepared without bouillon and salt) equals 2-1/2 lean meat, 1 starch, 1 vegetable; also, 259 calories, 127 mg sodium, 89 mg cholesterol, 22 gm carbohydrate, 31 gm protein, 5 gm fat.

CHEESY VEGETABLE SOUP
Amy Sibra, Big Sandy, Montana
(PICTURED ON OPPOSITE PAGE)

- 3 tablespoons butter *or* margarine
- 3 tablespoons all-purpose flour
- 2 cans (14-1/2 ounces *each*) chicken broth
- 2 cups coarsely chopped broccoli
- 3/4 cup chopped carrots
- 1/2 cup chopped celery
- 1 small onion, chopped
- 1/2 teaspoon salt
- 1/4 teaspoon garlic powder
- 1/4 teaspoon dried thyme

- 1 egg yolk
- 1 cup heavy cream
- 1-1/2 cups (6 ounces) shredded Swiss cheese

Melt butter in a heavy 4-qt. saucepan; add flour. Cook and stir until thick and bubbly; remove from the heat. Gradually blend in broth. Add next seven ingredients; return to the heat and bring to a boil. Reduce heat; cover and simmer for 20 minutes or until vegetables are tender. In a small bowl, blend egg yolk and cream. Gradually blend in several tablespoonfuls of hot soup; return all to saucepan, stirring until slightly thickened. Simmer for another 15-20 minutes. Stir in cheese and heat over medium until melted. **Yield:** 8-10 servings (2-1/2 quarts).

HUNGARIAN GOULASH SOUP
Betty Kennedy, Alexandria, Virginia
(PICTURED ON OPPOSITE PAGE)

- 3 bacon strips, diced
- 1 small green pepper, seeded and chopped
- 2 medium onions, chopped
- 1 large garlic clove, minced
- 1-1/2 pounds beef stew meat, cut into 1/2-inch cubes
- 2 tablespoons paprika
- 1-1/2 teaspoons salt
- Pepper to taste
- Dash sugar
- 1 can (14-1/2 ounces) stewed tomatoes, chopped
- 3 cups beef broth
- 2 large potatoes, peeled and diced
- 1/2 cup sour cream, optional

In a large kettle, cook bacon until almost crisp. Add green pepper, onions and garlic; cook until tender. Add beef cubes and brown on all sides. Sprinkle with paprika, salt, pepper and sugar; stir and cook for 2 minutes. Add tomatoes and broth. Cover and simmer for about 1-1/2 hours or until beef is tender. About 1/2 hour before serving, add the potatoes and cook until tender. Garnish each serving with a dollop of sour cream if desired. **Yield:** 8 servings (about 2 quarts).

FRESH FRUIT SOUP
Jenny Sampson, Layton, Utah
(PICTURED ON OPPOSITE PAGE)

- 1 can (12 ounces) frozen orange juice concentrate, thawed
- 1-1/2 cups sugar
- 1 cinnamon stick (2 inches)
- 6 whole cloves
- 1/4 cup cornstarch
- 2 tablespoons lemon juice
- 2 cups sliced fresh strawberries
- 2 bananas, sliced
- 2 cups halved green grapes

In a large saucepan, mix orange juice with water according to package directions. Remove 1/2 cup of juice; set aside. Add sugar, cinnamon stick and cloves to saucepan; bring to a boil. Reduce heat and simmer for 5 minutes. Blend cornstarch and reserved orange juice to form a smooth paste; stir into pan. Bring to a boil; cook and stir until thickened, about 2 minutes more. Remove from the heat and stir in lemon juice. Pour into a large bowl; cover and chill. Just before serving, remove the spices and stir in fruit. **Yield:** 8-10 servings (about 2-1/2 quarts).

TURKEY WILD RICE SOUP
Doris Cox, New Freedom, Pennsylvania

- 1 medium onion, chopped
- 1 can (4 ounces) sliced mushrooms, drained
- 2 tablespoons butter *or* margarine
- 3 cups water
- 2 cups chicken broth
- 1 package (6 ounces) long grain and wild rice mix
- 2 cups diced cooked turkey
- 1 cup heavy cream
- Chopped fresh parsley

In a large saucepan, saute onion and mushrooms in butter until onion is tender. Add water, broth and rice mix with seasoning; bring to a boil. Reduce heat; simmer for 20-25 minutes or until rice is tender. Stir in turkey and cream and heat through. Sprinkle with parsley. **Yield:** 6 servings.

BARLEY BROCCOLI SOUP

Gloria Porter, Grandin, North Dakota

 This tasty dish uses less sugar, salt and fat. Recipe includes *Diabetic Exchanges*.

3 cups water
3 beef bouillon cubes
1/2 cup medium pearl barley
2 cups fresh *or* frozen chopped broccoli *or* asparagus, cooked and drained
4 cups milk
5 slices American cheese
1/4 teaspoon ground nutmeg
1/4 teaspoon pepper
4 bacon strips cooked and crumbled, optional

In a saucepan, bring water, bouillon and barley to a boil. Reduce heat; cover and simmer for 50-60 minutes or until barley is tender and nearly all liquid is absorbed. Stir often but do not drain. Add broccoli or asparagus. Stir in milk, cheese, nutmeg and pepper. Add bacon if desired. Heat through, stirring often, until soup is hot and cheese is melted. **Yield:** 8 servings. **Diabetic Exchanges:** One serving (prepared with skim milk and without bacon) equals 1 meat, 1/2 skim milk, 1/2 starch; also, 145 calories, 620 mg sodium, 15 mg cholesterol, 17 gm carbohydrate, 9 gm protein, 5 gm fat.

POTATO SOUP WITH SPINACH DUMPLINGS

Rosemary Flexman, Waukesha, Wisconsin
(PICTURED ON PAGE 55)

2 cups cubed peeled potatoes
1/2 cup chopped onion
1/2 cup chopped sweet red pepper
2 tablespoons butter *or* margarine
3 cans (14-1/2 ounces *each*) chicken broth
1 package (10 ounces) frozen chopped spinach, thawed
1 cup seasoned dry bread crumbs
1 egg white, lightly beaten
Chopped fresh parsley

In a large saucepan, combine potatoes, onion, red pepper, butter and chicken broth; bring to a boil. Reduce heat; cover and simmer about 10 minutes or until the potatoes are tender. Remove from the heat. In a small bowl, combine the spinach, bread crumbs and egg white; let stand for 15 minutes. Shape into 1-in. balls; add to soup. Return to a boil; re-

duce heat and simmer 10-15 minutes or until dumplings are firm. Sprinkle with parsley. **Yield:** 4 servings.

QUICK & EASY

HARVEST CORN CHOWDER

Carolyn Lough, Medley, Alberta

1 medium onion, chopped
1 tablespoon butter *or* margarine
2 cans (14-1/2 ounces *each*) cream-style corn
4 cups whole kernel corn
4 cups diced peeled potatoes
1 can (10-3/4 ounces) condensed cream of mushroom soup, undiluted
1 jar (6 ounces) sliced mushrooms, drained
3 cups milk
1/2 medium green pepper, chopped
1/2 to 1 medium sweet red pepper, chopped
Pepper to taste
1/2 pound bacon, cooked and crumbled

In a saucepan, saute onion in butter until tender. Add cream-style corn, kernel corn, potatoes, soup and mushrooms. Stir in milk. Add green and red peppers. Season with pepper. Simmer for 30 minutes or until vegetables are tender. Garnish with bacon. **Yield:** about 12 servings (3-1/2 quarts).

CHILI CON CARNE

Janie Turner, Tuttle, Oklahoma

2 pounds ground beef
2 tablespoons olive oil
2 garlic cloves, minced
2 medium onions, chopped
1 green pepper, chopped
1-1/2 teaspoons salt
2 tablespoons chili powder
1/8 teaspoon cayenne pepper
1/4 teaspoon ground cinnamon
1 teaspoon ground cumin
1 teaspoon dried oregano
2 cans (16 ounces *each*) tomatoes with liquid, chopped
3 beef bouillon cubes
1 cup boiling water
1 can (16 ounces) kidney beans, undrained

In a large kettle, brown ground beef. Drain and set aside. In the same kettle, heat oil; saute garlic and onions over low heat until onions are tender. Stir in green pepper, salt, chili powder, cayenne pepper, cinnamon, cumin and oregano. Cook for 2 minutes, stirring

until well mixed. Add beef and tomatoes with liquid. Dissolve bouillon in water and add to soup. Simmer, covered, for about 1 hour. Add kidney beans; simmer 30 minutes longer. **Yield:** 8-10 servings (about 2-1/2 quarts).

BEEF AND BARLEY SOUP

Phyllis Utterback, Glendale, California
(PICTURED ON OPPOSITE PAGE)

1 tablespoon cooking oil
2 pounds beef short ribs
2 medium onions, coarsely chopped
3 large carrots, sliced
3 celery ribs, sliced
1 can (28 ounces) whole tomatoes with liquid, chopped
2 quarts water
4 chicken bouillon cubes
1/3 cup medium pearl barley

In a large Dutch oven or kettle, heat oil over medium-high. Brown beef. Add onions, carrots, celery, tomatoes, water and bouillon; bring to a boil. Cover and simmer for about 2 hours or until beef is tender. Add barley; simmer another 50-60 minutes or until the barley is done. **Yield:** 10-12 servings (3-1/2 quarts).

ASPARAGUS LEEK SOUP

Anne Landers, Louisville, Kentucky
(PICTURED ON PAGE 58)

3 large leeks, sliced into 1/2-inch pieces
1 large onion, chopped
3 tablespoons butter *or* margarine
4 medium potatoes, peeled and diced
3 medium carrots, thinly sliced
1 teaspoon salt
2-1/2 quarts chicken broth
1/2 cup uncooked long grain rice
1 pound fresh asparagus, cut into 1-inch pieces
1/2 pound fresh spinach, chopped into 1/2-inch pieces
1/4 teaspoon pepper
1 cup heavy cream

In a saucepan, saute leeks and onion in butter until tender. Add the potatoes, carrots, salt, broth and rice. Cover and bring to a boil; reduce heat and simmer for 25 minutes. Stir in asparagus. Cover and simmer for 10 minutes or until vegetables are tender. Add spinach, pepper and cream; heat through. **Yield:** 12-16 servings (4-1/2 quarts).

When chilly winds blow, warm your family's hearts and stomachs with a robust meal. For starters, serve savory Beef and Barley Soup. Meat and potato lovers will want to prepare the New England Lamb Bake or Sweet-and-Sour Pork Chops. And for dessert, what could be more appealing than old-fashioned Apple Crisp!

SOUPER STARTER. Clockwise from the top: **Beef and Barley Soup** (p. 10), **Apple Crisp** (p. 73), **Sweet-and-Sour Pork Chops** (p. 46) and **New England Lamb Bake** (p. 38).

GAZPACHO
Sharon Balzer, Phoenix, Arizona

2 cans (14-1/2 ounces *each*)
tomatoes with liquid, minced
2 cups vegetable juice
2 tablespoons red wine vinegar
1 garlic clove, minced
1 teaspoon salt
1/2 teaspoon pepper
8 to 10 drops hot pepper sauce
1 package (6 ounces) seasoned
croutons
1 medium cucumber, peeled
and diced
1 medium green pepper, diced
1 bunch green onions with
tops, sliced

In a large bowl, combine first seven ingredients. Cover and refrigerate overnight. Stir well; ladle into soup bowls and
garnish as desired with croutons, cucumbers, peppers and green onions.
Yield: 6-8 servings.

CREOLE JAMBALAYA
Ruby Williams, Bogalusa, Louisiana
(PICTURED ON BACK COVER)

 This tasty dish uses less sugar, salt and
fat. Recipe includes *Diabetic Exchanges.*

3/4 cup chopped onion
1/2 cup chopped celery
1/4 cup chopped green pepper
2 garlic cloves, minced
2 tablespoons butter *or*
margarine
2 cups cubed fully cooked ham
1 can (28 ounces) tomatoes
with liquid, cut up
1 can (10-1/2 ounces)
condensed beef broth
1 cup uncooked long grain
white rice
1 cup water
1 teaspoon sugar
1 teaspoon dried thyme
1/2 teaspoon chili powder
1/4 teaspoon pepper
1-1/2 pounds fresh *or* frozen
uncooked shrimp, peeled
and deveined
1 tablespoon chopped fresh
parsley

In a Dutch oven, saute onion, celery,
green pepper and garlic in butter until tender. Add next nine ingredients; bring to
a boil. Reduce heat; cover and simmer
until rice is tender, about 25 minutes. Add
shrimp and parsley; simmer, uncovered,
until shrimp are cooked, 7-10 minutes.
Yield: 8 servings. **Diabetic Exchanges:**
One serving (prepared with margarine

and low-sodium tomatoes and beef
broth) equals 3 lean meat, 1-1/2 starch, 1
vegetable; also, 310 calories, 464 mg
sodium, 154 mg cholesterol, 28 gm carbohydrate, 31 gm protein, 8 gm fat.

SPICED TOMATO SOUP
Lois DeMoss, Kingsburg, California

2 cups water
5 pounds fresh tomatoes,
quartered
3/4 cup sugar
2 tablespoons salt
1 tablespoon mixed pickling
spice, tied in a cheesecloth
bag
3 large onions, chopped
1 bunch parsley, chopped
1 celery rib, sliced
2 tablespoons butter *or*
margarine
2 tablespoons all-purpose flour
5 bacon strips, cooked and
crumbled
Unsweetened whipped cream
Toasted slivered almonds

In a large kettle, bring first eight ingredients
to a boil. Reduce heat and simmer for
1-1/2 to 2 hours or until vegetables
are soft. Remove from the heat and cool
slightly; discard spice bag. Press mixture through a food mill; return juice to
kettle. In a small saucepan over medium
heat, melt butter. Add flour and cook, stirring, until browned and bubbly; stir into
soup. Add bacon and heat through. Top
individual servings with a dollop of
whipped cream and sprinkle with almonds.
Yield: 8-10 servings (2-1/2 quarts).

BEEF RAVIOLI SOUP
Marian Platt, Sequim, Washington

1 cup sliced celery
1/2 cup chopped onion
1 cup sliced carrots
2 tablespoons vegetable oil
4 cups beef broth
1/8 teaspoon pepper
1/4 teaspoon crushed red
pepper flakes
1 can (15 ounces) beef ravioli
1/4 cup chopped fresh parsley
Grated Parmesan cheese

In a large kettle, saute celery, onion and
carrots in oil for 3 minutes; add broth and
seasonings. Bring to a boil; reduce heat
and simmer, covered, about 15 minutes
or until the vegetables are tender. Stir in
the ravioli and heat through. Garnish with
parsley and Parmesan cheese. **Yield:** 4-
6 servings (1-1/2 quarts).

SOUTHWESTERN
CHICKEN SOUP
Joe Greenough, Bedford, Texas

 This tasty dish uses less sugar, salt and
fat. Recipe includes *Diabetic Exchanges.*

1 can (10-1/2 ounces)
condensed beef broth
1 can (12 ounces) tomato paste
1 can (15-1/2 ounces) kidney
beans, rinsed and drained
1 can (11 ounces) Mexicorn,
drained
1-1/2 cups diced cooked chicken
3 green onions, sliced
2 to 3 tablespoons chili powder
1 can (4 ounces) chopped green
chilies
1-2/3 cups water

In a large saucepan, combine beef broth
and tomato paste. Add remaining ingredients. Cover and simmer for 20 minutes. **Yield:** 6 servings. **Diabetic Exchanges:** One serving (prepared with
low-sodium beef broth and salt-free
tomato paste) equals 1-1/2 starch, 1-1/2
lean meat, 1 vegetable; also, 224 calories, 631 mg sodium, 21 mg cholesterol,
32 gm carbohydrate, 20 gm protein, 3
gm fat.

CLAM CHOWDER
Rosemary Peterson, Archie, Missouri

2 cans (6-1/2 ounces *each*)
minced clams
6 potatoes, peeled and diced
6 carrots, diced
1/2 cup chopped onion
1/2 cup butter *or* margarine
1-1/2 cups water
2 cans (10-3/4 ounces *each*)
condensed cream of
mushroom soup, undiluted
2 cans (12 ounces *each*)
evaporated milk
1 teaspoon salt
1/2 teaspoon pepper

Drain clams, reserving liquid. Set the
clams aside. In a large kettle, combine
clam juice, potatoes, carrots, onion, butter and water. Cook over medium heat
for 15 minutes or until the vegetables are
tender. Stir in soup, milk, salt and pepper; simmer until heated through. Stir in
clams. **Yield:** 10-12 servings (3 quarts).

CHOWDER CHANGE

*For clam chowder, try omitting the
flour and some or all of the potatoes.
Thicken the chowder with instant
mashed potatoes for a smooth base.*

CHUCK WAGON CHOW
Ed Jones, Baker City, Oregon

1/2 cup all-purpose flour
1 teaspoon salt
1/4 teaspoon pepper
2 pounds beef round steak (1/2 inch thick), cut into 1/2-inch cubes
1/4 cup cooking oil
1 medium onion, chopped
1 green pepper, chopped
1 garlic clove, minced
1 tablespoon chili powder
1 teaspoon dried oregano
1 can (16 ounces) kidney beans, juice drained and reserved
1 can (16 ounces) whole kernel corn, juice drained and reserved

Combine flour, salt and pepper in a large plastic bag. Place beef cubes in bag and shake to coat evenly. In a Dutch oven or large skillet, brown beef in oil. Add onion, green pepper and garlic; cook until peppers are crisp-tender. Stir in chili powder, oregano and reserved vegetable liquid; bring to a boil. Reduce heat and simmer, covered, until meat is tender, about 45-50 minutes. Stir in beans and corn; simmer 10 minutes or until heated through. **Yield:** 6-8 servings.

MOM'S CHICKEN NOODLE SOUP
Marlene Doolittle, Story City, Iowa

1 broiler-fryer chicken (2 to 3 pounds), cut up
2 quarts water
1 onion, chopped
2 chicken bouillon cubes
2 celery ribs, diced
2 carrots, diced
2 medium potatoes, peeled and cubed
1-1/2 cups fresh *or* frozen cut green beans
1 teaspoon salt
1/4 teaspoon pepper
NOODLES:
1 cup all-purpose flour
1 egg, beaten
1/2 teaspoon salt
1 teaspoon butter *or* margarine, softened
1/4 teaspoon baking powder
2 to 3 tablespoons milk

In a large kettle, cook chicken in water. Cool broth and skim off fat. Skin and bone chicken and cut into bite-size pieces; add to broth with remaining ingredients except noodles. Bring to a boil. Reduce heat and simmer, uncovered, for 50-60 minutes or until vegetables are tender. Meanwhile, for noodles, place flour on a bread board or countertop and make a well in the center. In a small bowl, stir together remaining ingredients; pour into well. Working the mixture with your hands, fold flour into wet ingredients until dough can be rolled into a ball. Knead for 5-6 minutes. Cover and let rest for 10 minutes. On a floured surface, roll dough out to a square, 1/16 to 1/8 in. thick, and cut into 1/4-in.-wide strips. Cook noodles in boiling salted water for 2-3 minutes or until done. Drain and add to soup just before serving. **Yield:** 4-6 servings (1-1/2 quarts).

SPLIT PEA VEGETABLE SOUP
Maureen Ylitalo, Wahnapitae, Ontario

1-1/2 cups dry split peas, rinsed
2-1/2 quarts water
7 to 8 whole allspice, tied in a cheesecloth bag
2 teaspoons salt
1/2 teaspoon pepper
6 large potatoes, peeled and cut into 1/2-inch cubes
6 carrots, chopped
2 medium onions, chopped
2 cups cubed cooked ham
1/2 medium head cabbage, shredded

In a large kettle, combine peas, water, allspice, salt and pepper; bring to a boil. Reduce heat; cover and simmer for 1 hour. Stir in potatoes, carrots, onions, ham and cabbage; return to a boil. Reduce heat; cover and simmer for about 30 minutes or until vegetables are tender, stirring occasionally. Discard allspice. **Yield:** 16-20 servings (about 5 quarts).

CHILI VERDE
Sherrie Scettrini, Salinas, California
(PICTURED ON COVER AND PAGE 26)

4 tablespoons cooking oil, *divided*
4 pounds boneless pork, cut into 3/4-inch cubes
1/4 cup all-purpose flour
1 can (4 ounces) chopped green chilies
1/2 teaspoon ground cumin
1/4 teaspoon salt
1/4 teaspoon pepper
3 garlic cloves, minced
1/2 cup chopped fresh cilantro *or* parsley
1/2 to 1 cup salsa
1 can (14-1/2 ounces) chicken broth
Flour tortillas, warmed

In a Dutch oven, heat 1 tablespoon oil over medium-high. Add 1 pound of pork; cook and stir until lightly browned. Remove and set aside. Repeat with remaining meat, adding more oil as needed. Return all of the meat to Dutch oven. Sprinkle flour over meat; mix well. Add chilies, cumin, salt, pepper, garlic, cilantro or parsley, salsa and chicken broth. Cover and simmer until pork is tender and chili reaches desired consistency, about 1-1/2 hours. Serve with warmed tortillas. **Yield:** 6-8 servings.

QUICK & EASY

PRONTO POTATO SOUP
Elaine Rutschke, Spruce View, Alberta

8 bacon strips, cut into pieces
1 small onion, chopped
1-1/2 to 2 cups leftover mashed potatoes
1 can (10-3/4 ounces) condensed cream of chicken soup
1 to 2 soup cans of milk
1/2 teaspoon salt
Dash pepper
2 tablespoons chopped parsley

In small frying pan, brown bacon until crisp. Remove and let drain on paper towel. Add onion to drippings in pan and saute 2-3 minutes. Drain fat off. Meanwhile, in a 3-qt. saucepan, mix cold mashed potatoes and soup until smooth. Add milk gradually to desired consistency, stirring constantly. Add bacon and onions. Season with salt, pepper and parsley. Heat through. **Yield:** 3-4 generous servings.

WILD RICE SOUP
Elienore Myhre, Balaton, Minnesota

1/3 cup uncooked wild rice
1 tablespoon vegetable oil
1 quart water
1 medium onion, chopped
1 celery rib, finely chopped
1 carrot, finely chopped
1/2 cup butter *or* margarine
1/2 cup all-purpose flour
3 cups chicken broth
2 cups light cream
1/2 teaspoon dried rosemary
1 teaspoon salt

Rinse rice; drain. In a medium saucepan, combine rice, oil and water; bring to a boil. Reduce heat; cover and simmer for 30 minutes. Meanwhile, in a large kettle, cook onion, celery and carrot in butter until vegetables are almost tender. Blend in flour; cook and stir for 2 minutes. Add broth and *undrained* rice. Bring to a boil; cook and stir until slightly thickened. Stir in cream, rosemary and salt. Reduce heat and simmer, uncovered, for about 20 minutes or until rice is tender. **Yield:** 8 servings (about 2 quarts).

*T*ake control of your week-day meals by having a kettle of satisfying Chunky Chili simmering on the back burner and a refreshing Mexican Salad chilling in the refrigerator. After enjoying that great combination, nibble on delicious Spiced Almond Cookies.

CHILI WARM-UP. Clockwise from the top: **Chunky Chili** (p. 15), **Spiced Almond Cookies** (p. 66) and **Mexican Salad** (p. 21).

PUEBLO GREEN CHILI STEW

Helen LaBrake, Rindge, New Hampshire

 This tasty dish uses less sugar, salt and fat. Recipe includes *Diabetic Exchanges*.

2 pounds lean boneless pork, cut into 1-1/2-inch cubes
1 tablespoon cooking oil
3 cans (12 ounces *each*) whole kernel corn, drained
2 celery ribs, chopped
2 medium potatoes, peeled and chopped
2 medium tomatoes, coarsely chopped
3 cans (4 ounces *each*) chopped green chilies
4 cups chicken broth
2 teaspoons ground cumin
1 teaspoon dried oregano
1 teaspoon salt, optional

In a large Dutch oven, brown half of the pork at a time in oil. Add remaining ingredients. Cover and simmer for 1 hour or until pork is tender. **Yield:** 10 servings. **Diabetic Exchanges:** One serving (prepared with low-sodium chicken broth and without added salt) equals 2 lean meat, 1 starch, 1 vegetable; also, 196 calories, 561 mg sodium, 52 mg cholesterol, 25 gm carbohydrate, 13 gm protein, 7 gm fat.

MUSHROOM/ONION SOUP

Nancy Kuczynski, Holmen, Wisconsin

 This tasty dish uses less sugar, salt and fat. Recipe includes *Diabetic Exchanges*.

2 cups (8 ounces) fresh mushrooms
3 tablespoons butter *or* margarine
2 medium onions, chopped
2 tablespoons all-purpose flour
5 cups chicken broth
1/2 teaspoon salt, optional
Dash pepper
1/3 cup uncooked long grain rice
1 bay leaf
2 tablespoons chopped fresh parsley

Trim mushroom stems level with the caps; finely chop stems and thinly slice caps. in a large saucepan, melt butter; add mushrooms and onions. Cook and stir over low heat for 5 minutes. Blend in flour; add broth, salt and pepper. Cook, stirring constantly, until mixture boils. Reduce heat. Add rice and bay leaf; cover and simmer for 15-20 minutes or until the rice is tender. Discard bay leaf. Sprinkle with parsley. **Yield:** 4 servings (about 1-1/2 quarts). **Diabetic Exchanges:** One serving (prepared with margarine, low sodium broth and no added

salt) equals 1 vegetable, 1 fat, 1/2 starch; also, 118 calories, 126 mg sodium, 1 mg cholesterol, 10 gm carbohydrate, 8 gm protein, 5 gm fat.

CHUNKY CHILI

Verna Hofer, Mitchell, South Dakota
(PICTURED ON OPPOSITE PAGE)

 This tasty dish uses less sugar, salt and fat. Recipe includes *Diabetic Exchanges*.

1-1/2 pounds lean chuck *or* round steak, cut into bite-size pieces
1 tablespoon cooking oil
2 garlic cloves, minced
2 green peppers, chopped
1 large onion, chopped
1 to 3 tablespoons chili powder
2 teaspoons ground cumin
1 teaspoon dried oregano
1 can (28 ounces) tomatoes with liquid, chopped
1 can (16 ounces) kidney beans, rinsed and drained
Crusty round French rolls, optional

In a large heavy saucepan, cook meat in oil until lightly browned. Add remaining ingredients except kidney beans; bring to a boil. Reduce heat and simmer, covered, for 2-1/2 to 3 hours or until meat is tender. Stir in beans during the last 30 minutes of cooking. If desired, serve in "bread bowls" by hollowing out rolls and spooning chili into center. **Yield:** 6 servings. **Diabetic Exchanges:** One serving (without roll) equals 3 meat, 2 vegetable, 1 starch; also, 361 calories, 663 mg sodium, 66 mg cholesterol, 27 gm carbohydrate, 27 gm protein, 17 gm fat.

BUTTERY ONION SOUP

Sharon Berthelote, Sunburst, Montana

2 cups thinly sliced onions
1/2 cup butter *or* margarine
1/4 cup all-purpose flour
2 cups chicken broth
2 cups milk
1-1/2 to 2 cups (6 to 8 ounces) shredded mozzarella cheese
Salt and pepper to taste
Croutons, optional

In a large kettle, saute onions in butter over low heat until tender and transparent, about 20-30 minutes. Blend in flour. Gradually add broth and milk; cook and stir over medium heat until bubbly. Cook and stir for 1 minute more; reduce heat to low. Add mozzarella cheese and stir constantly until melted (do not boil). Season to taste with salt and pepper. Serve with croutons if desired. **Yield:** 6 servings (about 1-1/2 quarts).

BEEF LENTIL SOUP

Constance Turnbull, Arlington, Massachusetts

 This tasty dish uses less sugar, salt and fat. Recipe includes *Diabetic Exchanges*.

1 pound ground beef
1 quart water
1 can (48 ounces) tomato juice
1 cup dried lentils, rinsed
2 cups chopped cabbage
1 cup sliced carrots
1 cup sliced celery
1 cup chopped onion
1/2 cup diced green pepper
1/2 teaspoon pepper
1/2 teaspoon dried thyme
1 bay leaf
1 teaspoon salt, optional
2 beef bouillon cubes, optional
1 package (10 ounces) frozen chopped spinach, thawed

In a large kettle, brown ground beef. Drain. Add water, tomato juice, lentils, cabbage, carrots, celery, onion, green pepper, pepper, thyme and bay leaf. Also add salt and bouillon if desired. Bring to a boil. Reduce heat and simmer, uncovered, for 1 to 1-1/2 hours or until the lentils and vegetables are tender. Add spinach and heat through. Remove bay leaf. **Yield:** 6 servings (2-1/2 quarts). **Diabetic Exchanges:** One serving (prepared without bouillon and salt) equals 2 meat, 2 vegetable, 1-1/2 starch; also, 317 calories, 128 mg sodium, 45 mg cholesterol, 38 gm carbohydrate, 28 gm protein, 7 gm fat.

CORNY GOOD CHILI

Mary Wolfe, LaCrete, Alberta

1 pound ground beef
1 medium onion, chopped
1/4 cup chopped celery
1 can (16 ounces) pork and beans, undrained
1 can (15-1/2 ounces) kidney beans, rinsed and drained
1 can (12 ounces) whole kernel corn, undrained
1 can (10-3/4 ounces) condensed tomato soup, undiluted
1 can (10-3/4 ounces) condensed vegetable soup, undiluted
1/4 cup water
1/4 cup packed brown sugar, optional
1 tablespoon vinegar
2 to 3 tablespoons chili powder

In a Dutch oven, brown ground beef, onion and celery; cook until tender. Drain. Add remaining ingredients; simmer until heated through. **Yield:** about 6-8 servings.

ITALIAN VEGETABLE SOUP

Janet Frieman, Kenosha, Wisconsin
(PICTURED ABOVE)

QUICK
& EASY

1 pound bulk Italian sausage
1 medium onion, sliced
1 can (16 ounces) whole tomatoes with liquid, chopped
1 can (15 ounces) garbanzo beans, drained
1 can (14-1/2 ounces) beef broth
1-1/2 cups water
2 medium zucchini, cut into 1/4-inch slices
1/2 teaspoon dried basil
Grated Parmesan cheese

In a 3-qt. saucepan, cook sausage and onion; drain fat. Stir in tomatoes, beans, broth, water, zucchini and basil. Bring to a boil. Reduce heat and simmer 5 minutes or until the zucchini is tender. Sprinkle each serving with cheese. **Yield:** 6-8 servings (2 quarts).

SAUSAGE BROCCOLI CHOWDER

Donald Roberts, Amherst, New Hampshire

1 pound bulk Italian sausage
1 medium onion, chopped
3 garlic cloves, minced
8 ounces fresh mushrooms, sliced
2 tablespoons butter or margarine
2 cups broccoli florets
2 to 3 carrots, diced
2 cans (14-1/2 ounces each) chicken broth
1 can (10-3/4 ounces)

condensed cream of mushroom soup, undiluted
9 ounces cheese tortellini, cooked and drained
1/2 teaspoon pepper
1/2 teaspoon dried basil
1/2 teaspoon dried thyme
2 quarts light cream
1/2 cup grated Romano cheese

In a skillet, cook and crumble sausage until no longer pink. Remove to paper towels to drain; set aside. In the same skillet, saute onion, garlic and mushrooms in butter until tender; set aside. In a Dutch oven, cook the broccoli and carrots in chicken broth until tender. Stir in sausage and the mushroom mixture. Add soup, tortellini, pepper, basil and thyme; heat through. Stir in cream and Romano cheese; heat through. **Yield:** 12-16 servings (4 quarts).

QUICK
& EASY

KENTUCKY CHILI

Tina Sullivan, Corinth, Kentucky

1-1/2 pounds ground beef
1 medium onion, chopped
2 cans (32 ounces each) tomato juice
1 cup water
1 can (15 ounces) chili beans, undrained
1 tablespoon chili powder
1 teaspoon salt
1/2 teaspoon pepper
8 ounces uncooked spaghetti, broken in half

In a skillet, brown ground beef and onion; drain and set aside. In a large kettle, combine the tomato juice, water, chili beans, chili powder, salt and pepper. Bring to a boil; reduce heat and simmer 10-15 minutes. Stir in beef mixture; simmer an additional 10 minutes. Meanwhile, cook spaghetti according to package directions. Drain and stir into chili. **Yield:** 10-12 servings (3 quarts).

TURKEY SOUP

Carol Brethauer, Denver, Colorado

 This tasty dish uses less sugar, salt and fat. Recipe includes *Diabetic Exchanges*.

1 turkey carcass
3 quarts water
2 cans (10-1/2 ounces each) low-sodium chicken broth
1/2 cup uncooked long grain rice
1 medium onion, finely chopped
4 celery ribs, finely chopped
2 carrots, grated
1 bay leaf
Dash poultry seasoning
Salt, optional

Pepper
Onion powder
Garlic powder

Place turkey carcass, water and broth in a large soup kettle. Simmer over low heat for 4-5 hours. Remove carcass from stock. Remove any meat and dice. Return to stock along with rice, onion, celery, carrots, bay leaf and poultry seasoning. Add remaining seasonings to taste. Simmer over medium-low heat until the rice is cooked. **Yield:** 8 servings (3 quarts). **Diabetic Exchanges:** One serving (prepared without salt; turkey meat estimated at 1 oz.) equals 1 lean meat, 1/2 starch; also, 95 calories, 54 mg sodium, 21 mg cholesterol, 9 gm carbohydrate, 10 gm protein, 2 gm fat.

QUICK
& EASY

MOM'S MONDAY LUNCH POTATO SOUP

Evelyn Bonar, Pensacola, Florida

8 bacon strips, diced
1 small onion, chopped
1-1/2 cups leftover mashed potatoes
1 can (10-3/4 ounces) condensed cream of chicken soup, undiluted
2 cups milk
1/2 teaspoon salt, optional
1/8 teaspoon pepper
2 tablespoons chopped fresh parsley

In a 3-qt. saucepan, cook bacon until crisp; remove to paper towels to drain. Saute onion in the drippings until tender. Add the potatoes and soup and stir until smooth. Gradually stir in milk. Cook over medium heat, stirring constantly. Stir in bacon, salt if desired and pepper. Cook until heated through. Garnish with parsley. **Yield:** 3-4 servings.

QUICK
& EASY

CHILLED RHUBARB SOUP

Laurel Anderson, Pinole, California

1 pint fresh strawberries, sliced
3 cups sliced fresh or frozen rhubarb (1/2-inch pieces)
1-1/4 cups orange juice
1/2 to 1 cup sugar
Sliced oranges, kiwifruit and/or additional strawberries, optional

In a 3-qt. saucepan, bring strawberries, rhubarb and orange juice to a boil. Reduce heat; cover and simmer for 10 minutes. Remove from heat; stir in sugar to taste. In a blender or food processor, blend half the fruit mixture at a time until smooth. Chill. To serve, spoon into soup bowls and, if desired, garnish with oranges, kiwi and/or strawberries. **Yield:** about 1 quart.

CORN AND SAUSAGE CHOWDER
Joanne Watts, Kitchener, Ontario
(PICTURED ON PAGE 18)

3 ears fresh corn, husked and cleaned
4 cups heavy cream
2 cups chicken broth
4 garlic cloves, minced
10 fresh thyme sprigs
1 bay leaf
1-1/2 medium onions, finely chopped, *divided*
1/2 pound hot Italian sausage links
2 tablespoons butter *or* margarine
2 teaspoons minced jalapeno peppers with seeds
1/2 teaspoon ground cumin
2 tablespoons all-purpose flour
2 medium potatoes, peeled and cut into 1/2-inch cubes
Salt and pepper to taste
1-1/2 teaspoons snipped fresh chives

Using a small sharp knife, cut corn from cobs; set corn aside. Place the corncobs, cream, broth, garlic, thyme, bay leaf and one-third of the onions in a large saucepan. Heat almost to boiling; reduce heat and simmer, covered, for 1 hour, stirring occasionally. Remove and discard corncobs. Strain cream mixture through a sieve set over a large bowl, pressing solids with back of spoon; set aside. Meanwhile, brown sausage in a large skillet. Cool and cut into 1/2-in. slices. In a large saucepan, melt butter. Add jalapenos, cumin and remaining onions; cook 5 minutes. Stir in flour; cook and stir 2 minutes. Gradually add corn stock. Add sausage and potatoes. Cover and cook until potatoes are tender, about 25 minutes. Add corn and cook just until tender, about 5 minutes. Remove bay leaf. Season with salt and pepper. For a thinner chowder, add additional chicken broth. Sprinkle with chives before serving. **Yield:** 8 servings (2 quarts).

BRUNSWICK STEW
Alyce Ray, Forest Park, Georgia

2 pork chops (about 1 pound)
2 whole chicken breasts
1 pound round steak, cut into bite-size pieces
1-1/2 quarts water
1 can (8 ounces) tomato sauce
2 teaspoons hot pepper sauce *or* to taste
1/2 cup vinegar
1/4 cup sugar
2 cups chopped onion
4 to 5 garlic cloves, minced
2 cans (16 ounces *each*) tomatoes with liquid, chopped
2 cans (16 ounces *each*) cream-style corn
2 cans (16 ounces *each*) whole kernel corn, drained
1 cup toasted bread crumbs
Salt and pepper to taste

In a Dutch oven or soup kettle, place pork chops, chicken breasts and round steak; cover with water. Cook, covered, for about 1-1/2 hours or until meat is tender. Strain stock into another large kettle; refrigerate overnight. Remove bones from meat; dice and place in a separate bowl. Cover and refrigerate overnight. The next day, skim fat from stock; add tomato sauce, hot pepper sauce, vinegar, sugar, onions, garlic and tomatoes. Simmer, uncovered, for about 45 minutes. Add cream-style and kernel corn, reserved meat and chicken; simmer for about 15 minutes or until thoroughly heated through. Stir in bread crumbs; season with salt and pepper. **Yield:** 6 quarts.

BASQUE VEGETABLE SOUP
Norman Chegwyn, Richmond, California

3/4 pound Polish sausage, sliced
1 broiler-fryer chicken (2 to 3 pounds)
8 cups water
2 leeks, sliced
2 carrots, sliced
1 large turnip, peeled and cubed
1 large onion, chopped
1 large potato, peeled and cubed
1 garlic clove, minced
1-1/2 teaspoons salt
1/2 teaspoon pepper
1 tablespoon snipped fresh parsley
1 teaspoon dried thyme
1 cup shredded cabbage
2 cups cooked navy *or* great northern beans

In a skillet, cook the sausage until done. Drain on paper towels; set aside. In a large Dutch oven, cook chicken in water until tender. Remove chicken; let cool. Strain broth and skim off fat. Return broth to Dutch oven. Add leeks, carrots, turnip, onion, potato, garlic, salt, pepper, parsley and thyme. Bring to a boil. Reduce heat; cover and simmer for 30 minutes. Meanwhile, remove chicken from bones and cut into bite-size pieces; add to the Dutch oven. Add cabbage, beans and cooked sausage. Simmer, uncovered, for about 30 minutes or until vegetables are tender. **Yield:** 10-12 servings.

CONFETTI CHOWDER
Rose Bomba, Lisbon, New Hampshire

3 tablespoons butter *or* margarine
1 cup diced carrots
1 cup diced zucchini
1 cup broccoli florets
1/2 cup chopped onion
1/2 cup chopped celery
1/4 cup all-purpose flour
1/2 teaspoon salt
1/2 teaspoon pepper
1/4 teaspoon sugar
3 cups milk
1 cup chicken broth
1 cup whole kernel corn
1 cup diced fully cooked ham
1/2 cup peas
1 jar (2 ounces) sliced pimientos, drained
1 cup (4 ounces) shredded cheddar cheese

Melt butter in a Dutch oven. Add carrots, zucchini, broccoli, onion and celery; cook and stir for about 5 minutes or until crisp-tender. Sprinkle flour, salt, pepper and sugar over vegetables; mix well. Stir in milk and chicken broth; cook and stir until thickened and bubbly. Add corn, ham, peas and pimientos; cook and stir until heated through. Remove from the heat; add cheese and stir until melted. Serve hot. **Yield:** 6-8 servings (2 quarts).

CALIFORNIA CHEESE SOUP
Darla Dockter, Fargo, North Dakota

1 quart water
2 chicken bouillon cubes
1 cup diced celery
1/2 cup diced onion
2-1/2 cups diced peeled potatoes
1 cup diced carrots
1 bag (16 ounces) frozen California Blend vegetables
2 cans (10-3/4 ounces *each*) condensed cream of chicken soup, undiluted
1 pound process American cheese, cut into cubes

Bring water to a boil in a large kettle; add next six ingredients. Reduce heat and simmer, covered, until all vegetables are tender, about 30 minutes. Stir in soup and cheese; cook until soup is heated through and the cheese is melted. **Yield:** 10-12 servings (3 quarts).

*S*alads are a great way to add festive flair to any country meal...year round! Fresh Corn Salad has a tangy appealing flavor that tastes great with Pork Chops with Corn Dressing. For a change-of-pace side dish, serve Corn Balls. And round out the meal with the unique flavor of Corn and Sausage Chowder.

REFRESHING RECIPES. Clockwise from top left: **Fresh Corn Salad** (p. 19), **Pork Chops with Corn Dressing** (p. 49), **Corn and Sausage Chowder** (p. 17) and **Corn Balls** (p. 27).

Main-Dish & Side Salads

CRANBERRY SALAD
Nell Bass, Macon, Georgia

1 cup sugar
1 cup water
1 package (6 ounces) lemon-flavored gelatin
4 cups fresh cranberries, ground
2 large unpeeled apples, cored and ground
1 unpeeled orange, seeded and ground
1/2 cup chopped pecans
Lettuce leaves, optional
Mayonnaise, optional

In a saucepan, bring sugar and water to a boil, stirring constantly. Remove from the heat; immediately stir in gelatin until dissolved. Chill until mixture is the consistency of unbeaten egg whites. Fold in the cranberries, apples, orange and pecans. Spoon into oiled individual salad molds, a 6-1/2-cup ring mold or an 11-in. x 7-in. x 2-in. dish. Chill until firm. If desired, serve on lettuce leaves and top with a dollop of mayonnaise. **Yield:** 12-15 servings.

FRESH CORN SALAD
Carol Shaffer, Cape Girardeau, Missouri
(PICTURED ON OPPOSITE PAGE)

 This tasty dish uses less sugar, salt and fat. Recipe includes *Diabetic Exchanges*.

8 ears fresh corn, husked and cleaned
1/2 cup vegetable oil
1/4 cup cider vinegar
1-1/2 teaspoons lemon juice
1/4 cup minced fresh parsley
2 teaspoons sugar
1 teaspoon salt, optional
1/2 teaspoon dried basil
1/8 to 1/4 teaspoon cayenne pepper
2 large tomatoes, seeded and coarsely chopped
1/2 cup chopped onion
1/3 cup chopped green pepper
1/3 cup chopped sweet red pepper

In a large saucepan, cook corn in enough boiling water to cover for 5-7 minutes or until tender. Drain, cool and set aside. In a large bowl, mix the oil, vinegar, lemon juice, parsley, sugar, salt if desired, basil and cayenne pepper. Cut cooled corn off the cob (should measure 4 cups). Add corn, tomatoes, onion and peppers to the oil mixture. Mix well. Cover and chill for several hours or overnight. **Yield:** 10 servings. **Diabetic Exchanges:** One serving (without added salt) equals 1 starch, 1/2 vegetable, 1/2 fat; also, 102 calories, 251 mg sodium, 0 cholesterol, 21 gm carbohydrate, 3 gm protein, 2 gm fat.

CHICKEN SALAD ON BUNS
Mary Jo Vander West, Grant, Michigan

2 cups diced leftover cooked chicken
1/4 pound process American cheese, diced
1 to 2 tablespoons pickle relish
1/4 cup salad dressing *or* mayonnaise
2 tablespoons chopped onion
2 tablespoons chopped green pepper
Kaiser rolls

In a bowl, combine first six ingredients; mix well. Spoon about 1/3 cup onto each roll. Wrap each tightly in foil. Bake at 300° for 20-30 minutes or until heated through. **Yield:** 6-8 servings.

TANGY POTATO SALAD
Monika Grotegeer, Elmendorf AFB, Alaska

12 medium red potatoes (about 4 pounds)
1 medium onion, finely chopped
3 hard-cooked eggs, chopped
2 dill pickles, finely chopped
2 tablespoons snipped fresh parsley
3/4 cup chicken broth
3/4 cup salad dressing *or* mayonnaise
1-1/2 teaspoons salt
1/2 teaspoon pepper
1/4 teaspoon garlic powder
2 tomatoes, cubed
6 bacon strips, cooked and crumbled

Cook potatoes in boiling salted water until tender. Drain; cool slightly. Peel and slice potatoes; combine with onion, eggs, pickles and parsley in a large salad bowl. Set aside. Heat chicken broth until warm; remove from the heat. Add salad dressing, salt, pepper and garlic powder; mix until smooth. Pour over potato mixture and mix lightly. Cover and chill. Just before serving, gently stir in tomatoes and bacon. **Yield:** 10-12 servings.

TURKEY ALMOND SALAD
Donna Rear, Olds, Alberta

3 cups cubed leftover cooked turkey
2 cups shredded cabbage
3/4 cup diced celery
1/4 cup sliced green onions
1-1/2 cups chow mein noodles
1/2 cup slivered almonds, toasted
2 tablespoons sesame seeds, toasted
DRESSING:
2/3 cup salad dressing *or* mayonnaise
1 tablespoon milk
2 teaspoons prepared mustard
1-1/2 teaspoons sugar
1/2 teaspoon salt
1/4 teaspoon pepper

In a large bowl, toss together turkey, cabbage, celery and green onions. In another bowl, combine dressing ingredients. Pour over the turkey mixture. Chill for several hours. Just before serving, add the chow mein noodles, almonds and sesame seeds; toss to mix. **Yield:** 6 servings.

EASY AND CHEESY

To make hot cheesy-potato salad, add 1 cup mayonnaise, 1 lb. process cheese and 1/2 cup chopped onion to 8 sliced cooked potatoes. Top with 5-6 slices of bacon; bake at 325° for 1 hour.

GALA CRAB SALAD

Betty Follas, Morgan Hill, California

3 cups cooked rice
1-1/2 cups cracked crabmeat *or*
coarsely chopped imitation
crab
1 cup salad dressing *or*
mayonnaise
1/2 cup finely chopped green
pepper
1/2 cup finely chopped onion
1/2 cup finely chopped celery
Leaf lettuce
Fresh parsley, optional
Lemon slices *or* wedges, optional

In a bowl, combine rice, crab, salad dressing, green pepper, onion and celery. Pack into an oiled 6-cup mold. Chill at least 6 hours or overnight. Unmold onto a bed of leaf lettuce. Garnish with parsley and lemon if desired. **Yield:** 4-6 main-dish or 12-14 side-dish servings.

QUICK & EASY

RED GRAPE SALAD

Lorraine Black, Barnum, Iowa

1 can (20 ounces) pineapple
tidbits
2 packages (3 ounces *each*)
cream cheese, softened
2 tablespoons mayonnaise
3 cups miniature marshmallows
2 cups seedless red grapes,
halved
1 cup heavy cream, whipped

Drain the pineapple, reserving 2 tablespoons juice; set pineapple aside. In a mixing bowl, beat juice, cream cheese and mayonnaise until fluffy. Stir in pineapple, marshmallows and grapes. Fold in whipped cream. Serve immediately or refrigerate. **Yield:** 10-12 servings.

CALICO POTATO SALAD

Christine Hartry, Emo, Ontario
(PICTURED ON PAGE 44)

 This tasty dish uses less sugar, salt and fat. Recipe includes *Diabetic Exchanges*.

DRESSING:
1/2 cup olive oil
1/4 cup vinegar
1 tablespoon sugar
1-1/2 teaspoons chili powder
1 teaspoon salt, optional
Dash hot pepper sauce
SALAD:
4 large red potatoes (about 2
pounds), peeled and cooked

1-1/2 cups cooked whole kernel corn
1 cup shredded carrot
1/2 cup chopped red onion
1/2 cup diced green pepper
1/2 cup diced sweet red pepper
1/2 cup sliced pitted ripe olives

In a small bowl or jar, combine all dressing ingredients; cover and chill. Cube potatoes; combine with corn, carrot, onion, peppers and olives in a salad bowl. Pour dressing over; toss lightly. Cover and chill. **Yield:** 14 servings. **Diabetic Exchanges:** One serving (without added salt) equals 1-1/2 fat, 1 starch; also, 146 calories, 212 mg sodium, 0 cholesterol, 17 gm carbohydrate, 2 gm protein, 9 gm fat.

FLUFFY CRANBERRY DELIGHT

Ruth Bolduc, Conway, New Hampshire
(PICTURED ON PAGE 36)

4 cups cranberries
1-1/2 cups sugar
3/4 cup water
1 envelope plain gelatin
1/4 cup lemon juice
2 tablespoons orange juice
1-1/2 cups whipping cream
3 tablespoons confectioners'
sugar
1 teaspoon vanilla extract

In a saucepan, bring cranberries, sugar and water to a boil. Reduce heat and cook until berries burst. Strain through a food mill or sieve into a large bowl. Add gelatin, lemon juice and orange juice. Cool until mixture coats the back of a spoon. In a small bowl, whip cream until soft peaks form. Add confectioners' sugar and vanilla; whip until stiff peaks form. Fold into cranberry mixture. Chill until set. **Yield:** 8-10 servings.

QUICK & EASY

FRESH BROCCOLI SALAD

Jewel McRae, Hamlet, North Carolina

1 bunch broccoli (about 1
pound), cut into florets
1/2 small red onion, chopped
1 cup (4 ounces) shredded
mozzarella cheese
8 bacon strips, cooked and
crumbled
1/4 cup sugar
1/2 cup mayonnaise
1 tablespoon white wine vinegar

Place broccoli, onion, cheese and bacon in a salad bowl; set aside. In a small bowl, combine sugar, mayonnaise and vinegar; mix until the sugar dissolves and mixture is smooth. Just before serv-

ing, pour dressing over salad and toss. **Yield:** 6 servings.

ICEBOX VEGETABLE SALAD

Mary Anger, St. Clair Shores, Michigan

1 can (16 ounces) cut green
beans, drained
1 can (17 ounces) tiny peas,
drained
1 can (16 ounces) whole kernel
corn *or* shoe peg corn, drained
1 jar (4 ounces) chopped
pimientos, drained
1 cup finely chopped celery
1 medium onion, finely chopped
1 medium green pepper, finely
chopped
1 cup sugar
1/2 cup vinegar
1/2 cup vegetable oil
1 teaspoon salt
1/2 teaspoon pepper

Combine all vegetables in a large glass bowl; set aside. In a saucepan, combine sugar, vinegar, oil, salt and pepper; bring to a boil. Cool slightly and pour over vegetables. Cover and refrigerate overnight. **Yield:** 6-8 servings. **If Cooking for Two:** Salad may be stored in a plastic bag or covered container in the refrigerator for up to 1 week.

SPICY COLESLAW

Valerie Jones, Portland, Maine
(PICTURED ON OPPOSITE PAGE)

 This tasty dish uses less sugar, salt and fat. Recipe includes *Diabetic Exchanges*.

6 cups shredded cabbage
1 cup chopped unpeeled
cucumber
1 cup chopped tomato
1 cup chopped green pepper
1 cup sliced green onions
2/3 cup spicy vegetable juice
1/4 cup red wine vinegar
2 teaspoons sugar
1 teaspoon celery seed
1/2 teaspoon pepper
1/4 teaspoon salt, optional

In a large bowl, combine cabbage, cucumber, tomato, green pepper and green onions; set aside. In a small bowl, combine remaining ingredients; mix well. Pour over cabbage mixture and toss gently. Cover and chill for 2 hours; stir before serving. **Yield:** 12 servings. **Diabetic Exchanges:** One 3/4-cup serving (prepared without added salt) equals 1 vegetable; also, 26 calories, 105 mg sodium, 0 cholesterol, 5 gm carbohydrate, 1 gm protein, trace fat.

Coming up with original salad recipes for family picnics, barbecues and potlucks can be a challenge. Next time, add some variety (and flavor!) to your menu by making Spicy Coleslaw with crunchy Parmesan Chicken! Please the crowd by serving warm Caramel Apple Bars topped with a dollop of whipped cream.

SUPER 'SLAW. Clockwise from top: **Parmesan Chicken** (p. 47), **Spicy Coleslaw** (p. 22) and **Caramel Apple Bars** (p. 64).

FRUITED CHICKEN SALAD
Marilyn Hamilton, Kearsarge, New Hampshire

3 tablespoons vegetable oil
3 tablespoons red wine vinegar
2 tablespoons sugar
3 tablespoons orange juice
1 teaspoon dry mustard
1 tablespoon poppy seeds
10 cups torn fresh spinach
2 cans (11 ounces *each*)
　　mandarin oranges, drained
2 cups fresh strawberries,
　　hulled and halved
1-1/2 cups cubed cooked chicken

Combine first six ingredients in a jar with a tight-fitting lid; shake well. Chill for at least 2 hours. Just before serving, combine spinach, mandarin oranges, strawberries and chicken in a large salad bowl. Pour dressing over and toss lightly. **Yield:** 4 servings.

QUICK & EASY

WILTED LETTUCE
Doris Natvig, Jesup, Iowa

4 bacon strips, cut up
1/4 cup vinegar
2 tablespoons water
2 green onions with tops, sliced
2 teaspoons sugar
1/4 teaspoon salt
1/4 teaspoon pepper
8 to 10 cups torn leaf lettuce
1 hard-cooked egg, chopped

In a skillet, cook bacon until crisp. Remove from the heat. Stir in vinegar, water, onions, sugar, salt and pepper; stir until sugar is dissolved. Place lettuce in a salad bowl; immediately pour dressing over and toss lightly. Garnish with eggs. Serve immediately. **Yield:** 6 servings.

SWISS CHEESE SALAD
Laverne Branomeyer, San Antonio, Texas

1 cup sliced green onions
1 cup sliced celery
1 cup diced green pepper
1 cup sliced stuffed green olives
1/3 cup vegetable oil
2 tablespoons red wine vinegar
1 tablespoon Dijon mustard
Salt and pepper to taste
6 cups shredded lettuce
2 cups (8 ounces) shredded
　　Swiss cheese

In a small bowl, combine onions, celery, green pepper and olives. In another bowl, whisk together oil, vinegar, mustard, salt and pepper. Pour over vegetables and refrigerate several hours or overnight. Just before serving, place let-

tuce in a large salad bowl; add the cheese and dressing with vegetables. Toss lightly. **Yield:** 6-8 servings.

QUICK & EASY

BROCCOLI BACON SALAD
Joyce Blakley, Windsor Locks, Connecticut
(PICTURED ON PAGE 31)

1 large bunch broccoli,
　　separated into florets
1 small red onion,
　　coarsely chopped
1 cup raisins
10 to 12 bacon strips, cooked
　　and crumbled
DRESSING:
3 tablespoons vinegar
1/3 cup mayonnaise
1/3 cup sugar

In a large serving bowl, combine the broccoli, onion, raisins and bacon; set aside. In a mixing bowl, combine dressing ingredients. Just before serving, pour dressing over broccoli mixture; toss to coat. **Yield:** 6-8 servings.

ZESTY POTATO SALAD
Edward Toner Jr., Howell, New Jersey

4 medium unpeeled red potatoes
1 bunch green onions with
　　tops, chopped
Salt and pepper to taste
DRESSING:
2 tablespoons mayonnaise
2 tablespoons sour cream
2 tablespoons bottled ranch
　　dressing
1 to 2 tablespoons Dijon mustard
1 teaspoon tarragon vinegar
Hot paprika, optional

Place potatoes in a saucepan; cover with water. Bring to a boil and boil for 20-25 minutes. Drain and cool. Cut potatoes into cubes and place in a salad bowl. Add green onions, salt and pepper. For dressing, combine mayonnaise, sour cream, ranch dressing, mustard and vinegar; pour over potato mixture and toss well. Chill 1 hour before serving. Sprinkle with paprika if desired. **Yield:** 4 servings.

QUICK & EASY

PINEAPPLE COLESLAW
Betty Follas, Morgan Hill, California

3/4 cup mayonnaise
2 tablespoons vinegar
2 tablespoons sugar
1 to 2 tablespoons milk
4 cups shredded cabbage

1 can (8 ounces) pineapple
　　tidbits, well drained
Paprika, optional

In a mixing bowl, combine mayonnaise, vinegar, sugar and milk. Place cabbage and pineapple in a large salad bowl; add dressing and toss. Chill. Sprinkle with paprika before serving if desired. **Yield:** 8 servings.

AUTUMN APPLE SALAD
Melissa Bowers, Sidney, Ohio
(PICTURED ON PAGE 31)

1 can (20 ounces) crushed
　　pineapple, undrained
2/3 cup sugar
1 package (3 ounces)
　　lemon-flavored gelatin
1 package (8 ounces) cream
　　cheese, softened
1 cup diced unpeeled apples
1/2 to 1 cup chopped nuts
1 cup chopped celery
1 cup whipped topping
Lettuce leaves

In a saucepan, combine pineapple and sugar; bring to a boil and boil for 3 minutes. Add gelatin; stir until dissolved. Add cream cheese; stir until mixture is thoroughly combined. Cool. Fold in apples, nuts, celery and whipped topping. Pour into a 9-in. square baking pan. Chill until firm. Cut into squares and serve on lettuce leaves. **Yield:** 9-12 servings.

SEAFOOD MACARONI SALAD
Frances Harris, Coeur d'Alene, Idaho

3 cups (about 10 ounces)
　　uncooked elbow macaroni
6 ounces peeled and deveined
　　cooked shrimp, rinsed and
　　drained
1 can (6 ounces) crabmeat,
　　drained and flaked
2 cups sliced celery
1/2 small onion, finely chopped
3 to 4 hard-cooked eggs,
　　coarsely chopped
1 cup mayonnaise
3 tablespoons sweet pickle
　　relish *or* finely chopped
　　sweet pickles
1 tablespoon prepared mustard
1 tablespoon vinegar
1 teaspoon paprika
Salt and pepper to taste

Cook macaroni in boiling salted water until tender; drain and cool. In a large bowl, combine macaroni, shrimp, crabmeat, celery, onion and eggs; set aside. In a small bowl, mix the mayonnaise, pickle relish, mustard, vinegar and paprika. Add to macaroni mixture; toss lightly. Season with salt and pepper. Cover and chill. **Yield:** 8 servings.

OVERNIGHT VEGETABLE SALAD

Jackie Carlile, Bakersfield, California

    1 can (16 ounces) tiny green
        peas, drained
    1 can (16 ounces) French-style
        green beans, drained
    1 can (11 ounces) shoe peg
        white corn, drained
    1 medium onion, finely chopped
  3/4 cup finely chopped celery
    2 tablespoons chopped
        pimientos, optional
  3/4 cup sugar
  1/2 cup vegetable oil
  1/2 cup white wine vinegar
  1/2 teaspoon salt
  1/2 teaspoon pepper

In a large bowl, combine peas, beans, corn, onion, celery and pimientos if desired. In a saucepan, combine remaining ingredients; heat and stir until sugar dissolves. Pour over the vegetables. Cover and refrigerate overnight. **Yield:** 10-12 servings. **If Cooking for Two:** Salad will keep for several days stored in a covered container in the refrigerator.

BEET SALAD

Lani Hasbrouck, Cascade, Idaho

    1 can (16 ounces) diced *or*
        julienned beets
    1 package (6 ounces) lemon-
        flavored gelatin
1-1/2 cups cold water
    2 tablespoons finely chopped
        onion
    1 to 2 tablespoons prepared
        horseradish
    4 teaspoons vinegar
  1/4 teaspoon salt
1-1/2 cups chopped celery
  1/4 cup sliced stuffed green olives
Lettuce leaves, mayonnaise and
    whole stuffed olives for garnish,
    optional

Drain beets, reserving liquid; add water to reserved liquid to equal 2 cups. In a saucepan, bring liquid to a boil. Remove from the heat; stir in gelatin until dissolved. Add cold water, onion, horseradish, vinegar and salt. Chill until partially set. Stir in the beets, celery and olives. Pour into an 8-in. square dish. Chill until firm, about 3 hours. Cut salad into squares. If desired, serve on a lettuce-lined plate and top with a dollop of mayonnaise and an olive. **Yield:** 9-12 servings.

CRANBERRY WALDORF SALAD

Faye Huff, Longview, Washington
(PICTURED ON PAGE 65)

  1/2 pound fresh *or* frozen
        cranberries, halved
  3/4 cup sugar
    3 cups miniature marshmallows
    2 cups chopped apples
  1/2 cup chopped nuts
    1 can (8 ounces) pineapple
        tidbits, drained
    1 cup halved seedless grapes
    1 cup whipping cream, stiffly
        beaten

In a large mixing bowl, combine cranberries and sugar; let stand 30 minutes. Add next five ingredients and mix well. Gently fold in the whipped cream; chill before serving. **Yield:** 10-12 servings.

SAUERKRAUT SALAD

Evelyn Clarke, Hackensack, New Jersey

    1 can (27 ounces) sauerkraut,
        undrained
    1 large green pepper, finely
        chopped
    1 medium onion, finely chopped
    1 cup finely chopped celery
    1 jar (2 ounces) sliced
        pimientos, drained
1-1/2 cups sugar
  1/2 cup white wine vinegar
  1/4 cup vegetable oil
  1/2 teaspoon salt

In a large bowl, combine all ingredients. Cover and chill overnight. Drain before serving. Serve as a side dish or use as a relish on hot dogs or sandwiches. **Yield:** 10-12 servings. **If Cooking for Two:** Salad will keep up to a week stored tightly covered in the refrigerator.

CHILLED RICE SALAD

JoAnn Hall, Waverly, Iowa

    1 package (6.9 ounces)
        chicken-flavored rice mix
        with vermicelli
    1 teaspoon vegetable oil
   12 stuffed green olives, sliced
    4 green onions, thinly sliced
  1/2 green pepper, chopped
    2 jars (6-1/2 ounces *each*)
        marinated artichoke hearts,
        marinade drained and
        reserved
  1/3 cup mayonnaise
  1/2 to 3/4 teaspoon curry powder

Prepare rice mix according to package

directions, except substitute 1 teaspoon oil for butter called for. Cool. Add olives, green onions and green pepper; toss to mix. Cut the artichokes into quarters and add to rice mixture; set aside. In small bowl, combine mayonnaise, curry powder and reserved marinade; blend well. Pour over rice mixture; toss to mix. Cover and chill for at least 2 hours. **Yield:** 6-8 servings.

CROWD-PLEASING POTATO SALAD

Marcille Meyer, Battle Creek, Nebraska

    1 gallon potatoes (about 16
        large), cooked, peeled and
        sliced
   10 hard-cooked eggs
    1 cup chopped onion
    2 cups salad dressing *or*
        mayonnaise
    1 cup light cream
  1/3 cup vinegar
  1/3 cup sugar
    3 tablespoons prepared
        mustard
  1/2 teaspoon salt

Place potatoes in a large salad bowl. Separate eggs. Chop whites and add to potatoes with onion. Toss gently. In another bowl, mash yolks with salad dressing, cream, vinegar, sugar, mustard and salt. Pour over potatoes and stir to coat. Cover and chill. **Yield:** 16-20 servings.

COLESLAW WITH MUSTARD DRESSING

Eleanore Hill, Fresno, California

    2 eggs
  1/2 cup light cream
    2 tablespoons sugar
  1/2 teaspoon dry mustard
  1/2 teaspoon paprika
  1/2 teaspoon salt
  1/3 cup cider vinegar
    2 tablespoons vegetable oil
    2 tablespoons water
Shredded cabbage
Salted peanuts

In a small mixing bowl, beat eggs and cream; set aside. In a small saucepan, bring sugar, mustard, paprika, salt, vinegar, oil and water to a boil, stirring constantly. Remove from the heat; very slowly add to egg mixture, stirring constantly. Return all to saucepan. Cook and stir over low heat until mixture thickens enough to coat a spoon. Cool. Just before serving, pour dressing over cabbage and toss. Sprinkle with peanuts. **Yield:** 1-1/3 cups dressing. **If Cooking for Two:** Toss some dressing over enough cabbage for two. Refrigerate remaining dressing; use within a week.

S ide dishes are the perfect "filler" for any meal. Whether you use fresh produce, potatoes, pasta or rice, the possibilities are endless! A delicious dish like Fresh Vegetable Casserole works well with any main dish, like flavorful Chili Verde, Spicy Stuffed Green Peppers and Wild Rice Quiche.

DELICIOUS DISH. Clockwise from the top: **Fresh Vegetable Casserole** (p. 27), **Chili Verde** (p. 13), **Wild Rice Quiche** (p. 46) and **Spicy Stuffed Peppers** (p. 42).

Vegetables & Side Dishes

FRESH VEGETABLE CASSEROLE
Audrey Thibodeau, Lancaster, New Hampshire
(PICTURED ON COVER AND OPPOSITE PAGE)

2 cups broccoli florets
1-1/2 cups sliced carrots
1 cup mayonnaise
1 cup (4 ounces) shredded cheddar cheese
3 to 4 drops hot pepper sauce
1/4 teaspoon pepper
1/4 cup cooking sherry *or* dry white wine, optional
1-1/2 cups sliced zucchini
1 cup sliced celery
1/2 cup diced green pepper
1/2 cup diced onion
1 tablespoon minced fresh parsley
1 tablespoon minced fresh basil
3 tablespoons butter *or* margarine
12 saltines, crushed
1/3 cup grated Parmesan cheese

Steam broccoli and carrots until crisp-tender; drain and set aside. In a large bowl, mix together mayonnaise, cheddar cheese, hot pepper sauce, pepper, and sherry if desired. Add broccoli, carrots, remaining vegetables, parsley and basil; stir gently to mix. Spoon into a greased 2-qt. baking dish. Melt butter in a small saucepan. Add crushed saltines; stir until browned. Remove from the heat and stir in Parmesan cheese; sprinkle over vegetables. Bake, uncovered, at 350° for 30-40 minutes. **Yield:** 6-8 servings.

INSTANT PARTY POTATOES
Kathy Roosma, Zeeland, Michigan

3 cups water
4 tablespoons butter *or* margarine
1 teaspoon salt
3/4 cup milk
1 package (8 ounces) cream cheese, softened
1 cup (8 ounces) sour cream
1 teaspoon garlic powder
1 teaspoon dried minced onion
2-2/3 cups instant potato flakes
Paprika, optional

In a saucepan, bring water, butter and salt to a boil. Add milk, cream cheese, sour cream, garlic powder and minced onion; stir in potato flakes. Spoon into a greased 2-qt. baking dish. Sprinkle with paprika if desired. Bake, uncovered, at 350° for 30 minutes. **Yield:** 8-10 servings.

BROCCOLI-STUFFED ONIONS
Lori Gilbertoni, Fairbanks, Alaska

3 large sweet Spanish onions (3 to 4 inches)
1 package (10 ounces) frozen chopped broccoli, thawed
1/2 cup grated Parmesan cheese
1/3 cup mayonnaise
2 tablespoons lemon juice
2 tablespoons butter *or* margarine
2 tablespoons all-purpose flour
1/4 teaspoon salt
2/3 cup milk
1 package (3 ounces) cream cheese, cubed
Chopped fresh parsley
Additional Parmesan cheese

Peel and halve onions horizontally. Parboil in salted water for 10-12 minutes; drain. Leaving 3/4-in. edges, remove centers. Place onion shells in a greased 1-1/2-qt. shallow baking dish. Chop centers of onions to equal 1 cup. Combine chopped onion, broccoli, Parmesan cheese, mayonnaise and lemon juice; spoon into onion shells. In a saucepan, melt butter; stir in flour and salt. Gradually add milk; cook until thick, stirring constantly. Remove from the heat and blend in cream cheese. Spoon sauce over onions. Bake at 375° for 20 minutes. Sprinkle with parsley and additional Parmesan cheese. **Yield:** 6 servings.

MAKE-AHEAD CREAM CORN

Combine 8-10 cups corn cut from the cobs, 1 lb. butter or margarine and 1 pint of cream in a roaster. Cook for 1 hour at 350°, stirring every 15 minutes. Ladle into containers and freeze.

CORN BALLS
Sharon Knicely, Harrisonburg, Virginia
(PICTURED ON PAGE 18)

1/2 cup chopped onion
1 cup chopped celery
1/2 cup butter *or* margarine
3-1/2 cups herb-seasoned stuffing croutons
3 cups cooked whole kernel corn
3 eggs, beaten
1/2 cup water
1/2 teaspoon salt
1/4 teaspoon pepper

In a saucepan, cook onion and celery in butter until tender; set aside to cool. In a bowl, combine croutons, corn, eggs, water, salt, pepper and onion mixture; mix well. Shape into eight to 10 balls. Place in an ungreased shallow baking dish. Bake, uncovered, at 375° for 25-30 minutes. **Yield:** 8-10 servings.

CAULIFLOWER AU GRATIN
Jacki Ricci, Ely, Nevada

6 tablespoons butter *or* margarine
1 to 2 garlic cloves, minced
4 ounces cooked ham, chopped
1 head cauliflower, broken into florets
2 tablespoons all-purpose flour
1-1/2 cups whipping cream
1/4 teaspoon salt
Pepper to taste
Pinch cayenne pepper
1-1/2 cups (4 to 6 ounces) shredded Swiss cheese
2 to 3 tablespoons chopped fresh parsley

Melt butter in a large skillet. Saute garlic and ham for 2 minutes. Add cauliflower and cook just until crisp-tender. Combine flour and cream; stir into skillet and blend well. Add salt, pepper and cayenne pepper. Cook and stir until thickened and bubbly; cook and stir 1 minute more. Pour into a 2-qt. baking dish. Sprinkle with cheese. Place under a preheated broiler until lightly browned, about 2-4 minutes. Sprinkle with parsley. Serve immediately. **Yield:** 6-8 servings.

syrup if desired. **Yield:** 12 (2-inch) pancakes. **Diabetic Exchanges:** One pancake (with no added salt) equals 1 starch; also, 77 calories, 21 mg sodium, 36 mg cholesterol, 15 gm carbohydrate, 3 gm protein, 1 gm fat.

BARBECUE BEANS
Betty Follas, Morgan Hill, California

1/2 **pound ground beef**
1/2 **large onion, chopped**
1/4 **medium green pepper, chopped**
2 **celery ribs, chopped**
1/2 **cup packed brown sugar**
1/2 **cup ketchup**
1/2 **teaspoon ground ginger**
Dash ground cloves
2 **cans (31 ounces** *each***) pork and beans**

In a large skillet, brown beef with onion, green pepper and celery until meat is browned and vegetables are tender. Drain fat. Stir in brown sugar, ketchup, ginger and cloves. Add beans and mix well. Spoon into a 2-1/2-qt. casserole. Bake, uncovered, at 350° for 1 to 1-1/2 hours or until beans are as thick as desired. **Yield:** 8-10 servings.

IOWA CORN CASSEROLE
Dorothy Morgan, Cedar Falls, Iowa

1 **pound bacon, diced**
2 **cups soft bread crumbs**
1/4 **cup minced onion**
1/2 **cup chopped green pepper**
2 **cans (16.5 ounces** *each***) cream-style corn**

In a skillet, fry the bacon until lightly browned. Remove and set aside. Pour 1/8 to 1/4 cup of bacon drippings over bread crumbs; set aside. Discard all but 2 tablespoons of remaining drippings; saute onion and green pepper in drippings until tender. Stir in corn, bacon and half of the bread crumbs. Spoon into a 1-qt. baking dish; sprinkle with remaining crumbs. Bake at 350° for 20-25 minutes or until bubbly and heated through. **Yield:** 6-8 servings.

TEXAS-STYLE SPANISH RICE
Melissa Pride, Plano, Texas

1/4 **cup chopped onion**
1/4 **cup chopped green pepper**
2 **tablespoons cooking oil**
1 **cup uncooked long grain rice**
1/2 **cup tomatoes with green chilies**

1/4 **teaspoon ground turmeric**
1 **teaspoon ground cumin**
1/2 **teaspoon salt**
1/4 **teaspoon garlic powder**
2 **cups water**
2 to 3 **tablespoons chopped fresh cilantro, optional**

In a skillet, saute onion and green pepper in oil for about 2 minutes. Add rice and stir until coated with oil. Add tomatoes, turmeric, cumin, salt, garlic powder and water; bring to a boil. Reduce heat and simmer, covered, about 20 minutes or until liquid is absorbed. Add cilantro if desired. **Yield:** 6 servings.

APRICOT-GLAZED SWEET POTATOES
Joan Huggins, Waynesboro, Mississippi
(PICTURED ON PAGE 65)

3 **pounds sweet potatoes, cooked, peeled and cut up**
1 **cup packed brown sugar**
5 **teaspoons cornstarch**
1/4 **teaspoon salt**
1/8 **teaspoon ground cinnamon**
1 **cup apricot nectar**
1/2 **cup hot water**
2 **teaspoons grated orange peel**
2 **teaspoons butter** *or* **margarine**
1/2 **cup chopped pecans**

Place sweet potatoes in a 13-in. x 9-in. x 2-in. baking dish; set aside. In a saucepan, combine sugar, cornstarch, salt and cinnamon; stir in apricot nectar, water and orange peel. Bring to a boil, stirring constantly. Cook and stir 2 minutes more. Remove from heat, stir in butter and pecans. Pour over sweet potatoes. Bake, uncovered, at 350° for 20-25 minutes or until heated through. **Yield:** 8-10 servings.

CREAMED CUCUMBERS
Diane Maughan, Cedar City, Utah

5 **cucumbers, peeled and thinly sliced**
1 **bunch green onions with tops, chopped**
1 **cup mayonnaise**
1/4 **cup evaporated milk**
1/4 **cup vinegar**
1/4 **cup sugar**
2 **drops hot pepper sauce**
1 **teaspoon dried parsley flakes**
1 **teaspoon salt**
1/4 **teaspoon pepper**
1/4 **teaspoon garlic salt**
1/4 **teaspoon onion salt**

Combine cucumbers and green onions in a large bowl. Cover and let stand for

GOLDEN PINEAPPLE CASSEROLE
Beth Koehler, Mansfield, Pennsylvania
(PICTURED ABOVE)

2 **cans (20 ounces** *each***) crushed pineapple**
1/2 **cup sugar**
2 **tablespoons all-purpose flour**
3 **eggs, beaten**
4 **slices bread (crusts removed), buttered and cubed**

Drain pineapple, reserving 1 cup juice. In a mixing bowl, combine pineapple and juice with sugar, flour and eggs; mix well. Spoon into a 2-qt. baking dish; top with bread cubes. Bake at 350°, uncovered, for 45-50 minutes or until set and browned. Serve as a side dish with ham or poultry. **Yield:** 8 servings.

QUICK & EASY

POTATO PANCAKES
Roseanna Budell, Dunnellon, Florida

 This tasty dish uses less sugar, salt and fat. Recipe includes *Diabetic Exchanges*.

3 **cups finely shredded peeled potatoes, well drained**
2 **eggs, well beaten**
1-1/2 **tablespoons all-purpose flour**
1/8 **teaspoon baking powder**
1/2 to 1 **teaspoon salt**
1/2 **teaspoon grated onion**
Applesauce *or* **maple syrup, optional**

In a mixing bowl, gently combine potatoes and eggs. Combine dry ingredients and onion; stir into potato mixture. Drop by tablespoonfuls onto a preheated greased skillet. Brown lightly on both sides. Serve with applesauce or

1 hour. Combine all remaining ingredients; pour over cucumber mixture and mix well. Refrigerate for several hours. **Yield:** 10-12 servings.

CHEDDAR PARMESAN POTATOES

Nellie Webb, Athens, Tennessee
(PICTURED ON PAGE 31)

1/4 cup butter *or* margarine
1/4 cup all-purpose flour
2 cups milk
1/2 teaspoon salt
1 cup (4 ounces) shredded cheddar cheese
1/2 cup grated Parmesan cheese
5 cups sliced cooked peeled potatoes (about 5 medium)
1/4 cup buttered bread crumbs

In a saucepan, melt butter over low heat. Stir in flour until smooth. Gradually add milk; cook and stir over medium heat until mixture thickens. Remove from the heat. Add the salt, cheddar cheese and Parmesan cheese; stir until cheeses melt. Add potatoes; stir gently to mix. Place in a greased 2-qt. baking dish. Sprinkle bread crumbs on top. Bake, uncovered, at 350° for 30-35 minutes. **Yield:** 6-8 servings.

QUICK & EASY

EASY BAKED CORN

Kim McLaughlin, New Concord, Ohio

1 egg, beaten
1 cup (8 ounces) sour cream
1 package (8-1/2 ounces) corn bread mix
1/2 teaspoon salt
1/4 teaspoon pepper
2 cans (16 ounces *each*) whole kernel corn, drained

In a mixing bowl, combine egg and sour cream; stir in corn bread mix, salt and pepper. Add corn; mix well. Pour into a greased 11-in. x 7-in. x 1-1/2-in. baking pan. Bake, uncovered, at 400° for 25-30 minutes or till golden. **Yield:** 8 servings.

CORN BREAD DRESSING WITH OYSTERS

Nell Bass, Macon, Georgia

8 to 10 cups coarsely crumbled corn bread
2 slices white bread, toasted and torn into small pieces

2 hard-cooked eggs, chopped
2 cups chopped celery
1 cup chopped onion
1 pint shucked oysters, drained and chopped *or* 2 cans (8 ounces *each*) whole oysters, drained and chopped
2 eggs, beaten
1 teaspoon poultry seasoning
5 to 6 cups turkey *or* chicken broth

Combine the first eight ingredients in a large bowl. Stir in enough broth until the mixture is very wet. Pour into a greased 13-in. x 9-in. x 2-in. baking dish or shallow 3-qt. baking dish. Bake, uncovered, at 400° for 45 minutes or until lightly browned. **Yield:** 12-15 servings.

TORTELLINI BAKE

Donald Roberts, Amherst, New Hampshire

1 package (10 ounces) refrigerated cheese tortellini
1 tablespoon olive oil
1 small zucchini, diced
1 yellow squash, diced
1 onion, diced
1 sweet red pepper, diced
1 teaspoon dried basil
1/2 teaspoon pepper
1/2 teaspoon salt
1 cup (4 ounces) shredded mozzarella cheese
1 cup light cream

Cook tortellini according to package directions. Meanwhile, heat oil in a skillet; cook zucchini, squash, onion, red pepper and spices until vegetables are crisp-tender. Drain tortellini and rinse in hot water; combine with vegetable mixture, mozzarella and cream in a 1-1/2-qt. baking dish. Bake, uncovered, at 375° for 20 minutes or until heated through. **Yield:** 6-8 servings.

CALICO RICE

Deborah Hill, Coffeyville, Kansas

1 medium green pepper, diced
1 medium yellow pepper, diced
1 medium sweet red pepper, diced
1 medium onion, diced
2 tablespoons butter *or* margarine
1-1/2 cups uncooked long grain rice
1 envelope dry onion soup mix
2 tablespoons picante sauce *or* salsa
1 tablespoon ground cumin
4 garlic cloves, minced
1/2 teaspoon salt
3 cups water
Sour cream, optional

In a skillet or saucepan, saute peppers and onion in butter for 3 minutes. Stir in the rice, soup mix, picante or salsa, cumin, garlic, salt and water. Bring to a boil. Reduce heat; cover and simmer for 20-25 minutes or until rice is tender. Garnish with sour cream if desired. **Yield:** 6-8 servings.

CREAMY CARROT CASSEROLE

Laurie Heward, Fillmore, Utah
(PICTURED ON PAGE 31)

1-1/2 pounds carrots, peeled and sliced *or* 1 bag (20 ounces) frozen sliced carrots, thawed
1 cup mayonnaise
1 tablespoon grated onion
1 tablespoon prepared horseradish
1/4 cup shredded cheddar cheese
2 tablespoons buttered bread crumbs

In a saucepan, cook carrots just until crisp-tender; drain, reserving 1/4 cup cooking liquid. Place carrots in a 1-1/2-qt. baking dish. Combine mayonnaise, onion, horseradish and reserved cooking liquid; spread evenly over carrots. Sprinkle with cheese; top with bread crumbs. Bake, uncovered, at 350° for 30 minutes. **Yield:** 8-10 servings.

POTATO STUFFING CASSEROLE

Elsa Kerschner, Kunkletown, Pennsylvania

1/4 cup chopped celery
1 onion, chopped
4 tablespoons butter *or* margarine, *divided*
3 slices bread, cubed
4 to 5 large potatoes, peeled, cooked and mashed
1/4 cup chopped fresh parsley
1/2 teaspoon salt
1/4 teaspoon pepper
1 cup hot milk
1 egg, beaten
Additional parsley

In a medium skillet, saute celery and onion in 2 tablespoons of butter until tender. Add bread cubes and stir until lightly browned. Stir in potatoes, parsley, salt, pepper, milk and egg; mix well. Spoon into a greased 1-1/2-qt. baking dish. Dot with remaining butter. Bake at 350°, uncovered, for 30-40 minutes or until lightly browned. Garnish with additional parsley. **Yield:** 6-8 servings.

When the clan comes for dinner, you can bet they'll be hungry! So it pays to have extra side dishes on hand. No one will be able to resist the unique flavor of Creamy Carrot Casserole. And Cheddar Parmesan Potatoes are superb with any main meal, like One-Dish Pork Chop Dinner and Sour Cream 'n' Dill Chicken.

COME AND GET IT! Clockwise from lower left: **Blackberry Dumplings** (p. 71), **Sour Cream 'n' Dill Chicken** (p. 39), **Pecan-Chocolate Chip Pound Cake** (p. 60), **Creamy Carrot Casserole** (p. 29), **Broccoli Bacon Salad** (p. 24), **Cheddar Parmesan Potatoes** (p. 29), **Autumn Apple Salad** (p. 24) and **One-Dish Pork Chop Dinner** (p. 47).

CRUNCHY POTATO BALLS

Nancy Eash, Gambier, Ohio

        2 cups very stiff mashed
            potatoes
        2 cups finely chopped fully
            cooked ham
        1 cup (4 ounces) shredded
            cheddar *or* Swiss cheese
      1/3 cup mayonnaise
        1 egg, beaten
        1 teaspoon prepared mustard
      1/4 teaspoon pepper
        2 to 4 tablespoons all-purpose
            flour
    1-3/4 cups crushed cornflakes

In a bowl, combine the potatoes, ham, cheese, mayonnaise, egg, mustard and pepper; mix well. Add enough of the flour to make a stiff mixture. Chill. Shape into 1-in. balls; roll in cornflakes. Place on a greased baking sheet. Bake at 350° for 25 to 30 minutes. Serve hot. **Yield:** about 6 dozen.

CREAMED ONIONS

Peggy Ratliff, North Tazewell, Virginia

      24 boiling onions, peeled
        2 tablespoons butter *or*
            margarine
        2 tablespoons all-purpose flour
      1/2 teaspoon salt
        1 cup milk
    Dash ground cloves
      1/4 cup chopped fresh parsley

In a large saucepan, cook onions in boiling salted water until tender. Drain; set aside. In the same saucepan, melt butter. Blend in flour and salt until smooth. Add milk all at once; cook and stir over medium heat until thickened and bubbly. Cook and stir 1 minute more. Stir in the cloves and parsley. Add onions; stir gently until heated through. **Yield:** 6 servings.

CREAMED POTATOES

Mary Lewis, Memphis, Tennessee

    3-1/2 to 4 pounds potatoes, peeled
            and quartered
      1/4 cup butter *or* margarine
        1 ounce cream cheese, softened
      1/3 to 2/3 cup evaporated milk *or*
            heavy cream
    Salt and pepper to taste

Cook potatoes in boiling salted water until tender; drain. Add butter, cream cheese and 1/3 cup milk or cream. Whip with electric mixer on low speed or mash with potato masher, adding remaining milk or cream as needed to make pota-toes light and fluffy. Season with salt and pepper. **Yield:** 8-10 servings.

COMPANY VEGETABLE CASSEROLE

Leora Clark, Lincoln, Nebraska
(PICTURED ON PAGE 45)

        1 can (15 ounces) cut green
            beans, drained *or* 2 cups
            frozen cut green beans,
            thawed
        1 can (15 ounces) whole kernel
            corn, drained *or* 2 cups
            cooked fresh *or* frozen
            whole kernel corn
        1 can (10-3/4 ounces)
            condensed cream of celery
            soup, undiluted
      1/2 cup sour cream
      1/2 cup shredded cheddar cheese
      1/2 cup chopped onion
      1/4 cup butter *or* margarine,
            melted
      3/4 cup saltine crumbs
      1/4 cup sliced almonds, toasted

In a bowl, combine beans, corn, soup, sour cream, cheese and onion. Pour in-to an ungreased 2-qt. baking dish. Com-bine butter, crumbs and almonds; sprin-kle over vegetables. Bake, uncovered, at 350° for 35-40 minutes or until bubbly. **Yield:** 6-8 servings.

OVEN-BAKED BEANS

Eleanore Hill, Fresno, California

        2 cups dry navy beans
        8 cups cold water
        1 teaspoon salt, *divided*
      2/3 cup packed brown sugar
        1 teaspoon dry mustard
      1/2 cup dark molasses
      1/4 teaspoon pepper
      1/4 pound salt pork, cut up
      1/2 cup finely chopped onion
      1/2 cup finely chopped celery
      1/2 cup finely chopped green
            pepper

Rinse beans; place in a Dutch oven with cold water. Bring to a boil; reduce heat and simmer for 2 minutes. Remove from the heat; cover and let stand for 1 hour. (Or, omit boiling and soak beans in wa-ter overnight.) Add 1/2 teaspoon salt to beans and soaking water. Bring to a boil. Reduce heat; simmer, covered for 1 hour. Drain, reserving cooking liquid. Combine brown sugar, mustard, mo-lasses, pepper and remaining salt. Stir in 2 cups reserved cooking liquid; add to beans with salt pork, onion, celery and green pepper. Spoon into a 2-1/2-qt. baking dish. Cover and bake at 300° for 2-1/2 hours, stirring occasionally, or until beans are as thick as desired. Add more cooking liquid if necessary. **Yield:** 8-10 servings.

FRUITED RICE MIX

Lillian Justis, Belleplain, New Jersey

        3 cups uncooked long grain rice
        1 cup chopped dried apples
      1/3 cup golden raisins
      1/3 cup slivered almonds
      1/4 cup instant chicken bouillon
            granules
        3 tablespoons dried minced
            onion
    4-1/2 teaspoons curry powder

Combine all ingredients and store in an airtight container. To prepare, combine 1 cup mix with 2 cups water and 2 table-spoons butter or margarine in a sauce-pan. Bring to a boil. Reduce heat; cover and simmer for 25-30 minutes or until water is absorbed. **Yield:** about 5 cups dry mix (each cup makes 4-6 servings).

COPPER PENNIES

Agnes Circello, Belle Rose, Louisiana

        2 pounds carrots, peeled and
            sliced into 1/4-inch coins
      1/2 cup vegetable oil
        1 cup sugar
        1 large onion, diced
        1 large green pepper, diced
        1 can (5-1/2 ounces) tomato
            juice
      3/4 cup red wine vinegar
        1 teaspoon prepared mustard
        1 teaspoon Worcestershire
            sauce
        1 teaspoon salt
      1/4 teaspoon pepper

Cook the carrots just until crisp-tender; drain. Combine all remaining ingredi-ents in a large bowl; mix well. Add car-rots and stir until well mixed. Cover and refrigerate at least 3-4 hours. Serve cold as a salad, or warm it and use as a side dish. Store in the refrigerator for up to 2 weeks. **Yield:** 8 cups.

MERRY CHRISTMAS RICE

Karen Hoylo, Duluth, Minnesota

        2 cups water, *divided*
    1-1/3 cups sugar, *divided*
        2 cups (1/2 pound) fresh *or*
            frozen cranberries
    1-1/3 cups quick-cooking rice

1/4 teaspoon ground cinnamon
1/8 teaspoon salt
1 apple, peeled and sliced

In a saucepan, combine 1/2 cup water and 1 cup sugar; bring to a boil. Add the cranberries; return to boiling. Reduce heat; simmer for 10 minutes or until most of the berries pop, stirring occasionally. Add rice, remaining water, remaining sugar, cinnamon and salt. Bring to a boil. Reduce heat; cover and simmer for 10 minutes. Remove from the heat and stir in apple. Cover and let stand for 10 minutes. **Yield:** 6 servings.

BAKED CORN CASSEROLE

Jackie Willingham, Pasadena, Texas

1/4 cup butter *or* margarine
2 packages (3 ounces *each*) cream cheese, softened
1 can (17 ounces) whole kernel corn, drained
1 can (16-1/2 ounces) cream-style corn
1 can (4 ounces) chopped green chilies
1/2 cup chopped onion
1 can (2.8 ounces) french-fried onions, *divided*

In a large bowl, beat together butter and cream cheese. Stir in the kernel corn, cream-style corn, chilies and onion; mix well. Pour into a greased 8-in. square baking dish. Bake, uncovered, at 350° for 15 minutes. Remove from oven; stir in half of the fried onions. Sprinkle remaining fried onions on top. Bake 15 minutes longer. **Yield:** 8-10 servings.

CALICO BEANS

Betty Claycomb, Alverton, Pennsylvania

4 ounces bacon, diced
1 pound lean ground beef
1/2 cup chopped onion
1 can (16 ounces) kidney beans, rinsed and drained
1 can (21 ounces) pork and beans
1 can (15 ounces) butter beans, rinsed and drained
1/2 cup ketchup
1/2 cup packed brown sugar
1 tablespoon vinegar
1 teaspoon prepared mustard
1 teaspoon salt

In a skillet, cook bacon until crisp. Remove to paper towels to drain. Discard drippings. In the same skillet, cook beef and onion until the beef is browned and the onion is tender. Drain fat. Combine ground beef and bacon with all remaining ingredients. Spoon into a 2-qt.

casserole. Bake, uncovered, at 300° for 1 hour or until the beans are as thick as desired. Recipe can be easily doubled for a larger group. **Yield:** 8-10 servings.

POTATO PUFFS

June Mullins, Livonia, Missouri
(PICTURED ON PAGE 72)

2 eggs, *separated*
2 cups leftover mashed potatoes
2 tablespoons grated Parmesan cheese
1 tablespoon minced fresh parsley *or* chives
1 teaspoon dried minced onion
1/8 teaspoon garlic powder
2 to 3 tablespoons butter *or* margarine, melted

In a mixing bowl, beat egg yolks. Add potatoes, Parmesan cheese, parsley, onion and garlic powder; mix well. Beat egg whites until stiff; fold into the potato mixture. Brush eight muffin cups or small ramekins generously with melted butter. Divide potato mixture into cups. Brush remaining butter over potatoes. Bake at 375° for 30-35 minutes or until lightly browned. Serve immediately. **Yield:** 8 puffs.

GREEN BEANS WITH BACON

Mary Lewis, Memphis, Tennessee

1-1/2 pounds green beans, cut into 1-inch pieces
6 bacon strips
Pepper and seasoned salt to taste

In a covered saucepan, cook beans in a small amount of water for 20-25 minutes or until tender. Drain. Meanwhile, in a skillet, cook bacon until crisp. Remove bacon, reserving drippings. Crumble bacon and set aside. Add beans to drippings; sprinkle with pepper and seasoned salt. Heat through. Add crumbled bacon and toss. **Yield:** 8 servings.

SCALLOPED CABBAGE

Freda Willoughby, Medical Lake, Washington

1/2 medium head cabbage, chopped (about 4 cups)
3 tablespoons cooking oil
3 tablespoons all-purpose flour
1/2 teaspoon salt
Dash pepper
1 cup milk
1 cup (4 ounces) shredded cheddar cheese

3/4 cup bread crumbs
2 tablespoons butter *or* margarine, melted

Place cabbage in a greased 2-qt. casserole; set aside. In a saucepan, heat oil over medium. Stir in flour, salt and pepper; cook until bubbly. Gradually stir in milk; cook and stir until thickened. Fold in cheese. Pour over cabbage. Combine bread crumbs and butter; sprinkle on top. Bake, uncovered, at 350° for 20-30 minutes or until bubbly. Serve immediately. **Yield:** 4-6 servings.

CAJUN CABBAGE

Florence Davis, Amesbury, Massachusetts

1 pound ground beef
2 small onions, chopped
1 green pepper, chopped
6 cups chopped cabbage
1-1/4 cups uncooked long grain rice
1 can (14-1/2 ounces) stewed tomatoes
1 can (8 ounces) tomato sauce
1 cup water
1 teaspoon sugar
1 teaspoon Cajun seasoning
1 teaspoon salt
1/2 teaspoon pepper

In a large Dutch oven, brown ground beef. Add onions and green pepper; cook until the onions are transparent. Add the cabbage, rice, tomatoes, tomato sauce, water, sugar and seasonings. Cover and bake at 375° for 50-60 minutes or until the cabbage is tender. **Yield:** 10-12 servings.

SQUASH BAKE

Thelma Mefford, Wetumka, Oklahoma

8 cups sliced yellow squash (about 2 pounds)
1/2 cup chopped onion
3/4 cup shredded carrots
1/4 cup butter *or* margarine
1 can (10-3/4 ounces) condensed cream of chicken soup, undiluted
1/2 cup sour cream
2 cups herb stuffing croutons, *divided*

Cook squash in lightly salted boiling water for 3 to 4 minutes or until crisp-tender; drain well. In a skillet, saute onion and carrots in butter until tender. Combine onion and carrots with soup, sour cream and 1-1/2 cups croutons. Add squash and mix lightly. Spoon into a lightly greased 12-in. x 8-in. x 2-in. baking dish or a 2-qt. casserole. Sprinkle with the remaining croutons. Bake, uncovered, at 350° for 25 minutes or until heated through. **Yield:** 8-10 servings.

CHEESE POTATOES
Karen Hoylo, Duluth, Minnesota

6 tablespoons butter *or* margarine
6 tablespoons all-purpose flour
3/4 teaspoon salt
1/4 teaspoon pepper
3 cups milk
12 ounces process American cheese, cubed
8 cups (about 4 pounds) potatoes, peeled, cooked and thinly sliced
Paprika

Melt butter in a saucepan; add flour, salt and pepper. Cook over low heat, stirring until mixture is smooth and bubbly. Add milk all at once; cook and stir over medium heat until thickened and bubbly. Cook and stir 1 minute more. Remove from the heat. Add cheese and stir until melted. Place potatoes in a large bowl; gently stir in cheese sauce. Transfer to a greased 2-1/2-qt. baking dish. Sprinkle with paprika. Bake, uncovered, at 350° for 30 minutes or until heated through. **Yield:** 6-8 servings.

BREADED TOMATOES
Marion Stanley, Gilroy, California

8 to 10 small to medium firm fresh tomatoes
1/2 cup butter *or* margarine, melted
1 cup crushed saltines
1 tablespoon grated Parmesan cheese
CHEESE SAUCE:
2 tablespoons butter *or* margarine
2 tablespoons all-purpose flour
1/4 teaspoon salt
Dash white pepper
1-1/2 cups milk
3 tablespoons grated Parmesan cheese

Peel and core tomatoes but leave them whole. Dip each whole tomato in melted butter. In a small bowl, combine saltine crumbs and Parmesan cheese. Roll tomatoes in crumb mixture, gently pressing crumbs onto tomato. Place tomatoes in a single layer in a greased shallow baking dish. If there are any crumbs or butter left, combine them and sprinkle over the tomatoes. Bake at 475° for 15 minutes or until tomatoes begin to brown and are heated through. Watch closely; they burn easily. Meanwhile, for cheese sauce, melt butter in a medium saucepan. Stir in flour, salt and pepper. Add milk all at once; cook and stir over medium heat until thickened and

bubbly. Remove from the heat; stir in Parmesan cheese. Serve over tomatoes. **Yield:** 8-10 servings.

SWEET POTATO CASSEROLE
Marlene Sale, Naples, Florida

2 eggs
3 cups mashed sweet potatoes
1 cup sugar
1/2 cup butter *or* margarine, melted
1/3 cup milk
1 teaspoon vanilla extract
TOPPING:
3 cups cornflakes
2/3 cup butter *or* margarine, melted
1 cup packed brown sugar
1/2 cup chopped nuts
1/2 cup raisins

In large bowl, beat eggs. Add next five ingredients; mix well. Spoon into ungreased 13-in. x 9-in. x 2-in. baking dish. Combine topping ingredients; sprinkle over potatoes. Bake at 350° for 30-40 minutes. **Yield:** 6-8 servings.

HUSH PUPPIES
Karyl Goodhart, Geraldine, Montana
(PICTURED ON PAGE 45)

2 cups yellow cornmeal
1/2 cup all-purpose flour
2 tablespoons sugar
2 teaspoons baking powder
1 teaspoon salt
1/2 teaspoon baking soda
1 egg, beaten
3/4 cup milk
3/4 cup cream-style corn
Cooking oil for frying
Confectioners' sugar, optional

In a bowl, combine cornmeal, flour, sugar, baking powder, salt and baking soda. Add egg, milk and corn; stir just until mixed. In a deep-fat fryer, heat oil to 375°. Drop batter by teaspoonfuls into oil. Fry until golden brown. Allow to cool slightly and roll in confectioners' sugar if desired. Serve immediately with fried chicken, ham or sausage. **Yield:** 12-15 servings.

SUPER SPUDS

To make easy scalloped potatoes, slice leftover boiled potatoes into a casserole dish. Add white sauce and bake uncovered at 350° until heated through.

EGGPLANT WITH TOMATO SAUCE
Theresa Grassi, St. Louis, Missouri

2 pounds eggplant, unpeeled
1 teaspoon salt
1 tablespoon olive oil
1 can (28 ounces) crushed tomatoes in puree
2 garlic cloves, minced
1 teaspoon dried basil
1 to 2 teaspoons sugar
Salt and pepper to taste
Olive oil *or* vegetable oil for frying
1/4 cup shredded Parmesan cheese

Cut eggplant into 1/2-in.-thick slices. Sprinkle with salt. Place in a deep dish; cover and let stand for 30 minutes. Rinse with cold water; drain and dry on paper towels. In a 2-qt. saucepan, heat olive oil over medium heat. Add tomatoes, garlic, basil and sugar; bring to a boil. Reduce heat and simmer, uncovered, about 45 minutes or until thickened, stirring occasionally. Season with salt and pepper. Keep warm while preparing eggplant. In a large skillet, heat about 1/4 cup oil; brown eggplant, a quarter at a time, adding more oil as needed. Place on a serving platter one row at a time. Cover with sauce and sprinkle with cheese. Serve warm. **Yield:** 8 servings.

QUICK & EASY

SWEET CORN AND TOMATO SAUTE
Kim L'Hote, Neillsville, Wisconsin

1/4 cup butter *or* margarine
2 cups cooked whole kernel corn
1/4 cup chopped onion
1/4 cup chopped green pepper
2 tablespoons brown sugar
1/2 teaspoon salt
1 large tomato, diced

In a saucepan, melt butter. Add corn, onion, green pepper, brown sugar and salt. Cover and simmer 10 minutes. Stir in the tomato; simmer 5 minutes longer. **Yield:** 4 servings.

SWEET POTATO BAKE
Nell Bass, Macon, Georgia

2 to 2-1/2 pounds sweet potatoes
1/4 cup butter *or* margarine, melted
1/4 to 1/2 cup sugar
1/4 cup raisins
1/3 cup chopped nuts

1/3 cup miniature marshmallows

Place sweet potatoes and enough water to cover in a large saucepan or Dutch oven. Cover and cook over medium-low heat for 25-35 minutes or just until tender. Drain; cool slightly and peel. In a large bowl, mash potatoes. Stir in butter, sugar and raisins. Place in a 2-qt. baking dish; sprinkle with nuts and marshmallows. Bake, uncovered, at 350° for 30 minutes or until heated through and marshmallows begin to brown. **Yield:** 8-10 servings.

POTATO STUFFING
Betty McCloskey, Pennsauken, New Jersey

- 1 large onion, finely chopped
- 2 to 3 celery ribs, finely chopped
- 6 tablespoons butter *or* margarine
- 2 slices white bread, torn
- 3 cups mashed potatoes
- 2 tablespoons minced fresh parsley

In a large saucepan, saute the onion and celery in butter until tender. Remove from the heat. Add bread, potatoes and parsley; mix well. Spoon into a greased 1-qt. casserole. Bake, uncovered, at 350° for 45 minutes or until top is lightly browned. **Yield:** 6 servings.

FAVORITE DEVILED EGGS
Sue Crabtree, Bentonville, Arkansas

- 6 hard-cooked eggs, finely chopped
- 1 teaspoon minced onion
- 3 bacon strips, fried and crumbled
- 1/2 teaspoon salt, optional
- 1/2 teaspoon pepper
- 1/4 teaspoon prepared mustard
- 1/4 cup mayonnaise
- 1 cup (4 ounces) shredded cheddar cheese

In a bowl, mix together first seven ingredients until creamy. Form into 1-in. balls. Roll in cheese. Cover and refrigerate until serving. **Yield:** about 2 dozen.

SKILLET VEGETABLE SIDE DISH
Ada Gendell, Claremont, New Hampshire

- 2 tablespoons olive oil
- 3 carrots, thinly sliced
- 1 large onion, chopped
- 1/2 medium head cabbage, chopped
- 1/2 medium green pepper, chopped
- 2 garlic cloves, minced
- 2 tablespoons Worcestershire sauce
- 1 tablespoon minced fresh parsley
- 1 teaspoon caraway seed
- 1 teaspoon dried Italian seasoning
- 1/2 teaspoon celery salt

In a large skillet, heat oil over medium-high. Cook and stir the carrots, onion, cabbage and green pepper for 5 minutes. Add remaining ingredients; cook and stir about 5 minutes longer or until the vegetables are cooked to desired doneness. **Yield:** 8 servings.

TOMATO VINAIGRETTE
Donna Aho, Fargo, North Dakota

 This tasty dish uses less sugar, salt and fat. Recipe includes *Diabetic Exchanges*.

- 12 thick tomato slices
- 1/2 cup olive oil
- 2 to 3 tablespoons red wine vinegar
- 1 garlic clove, minced
- 1 teaspoon snipped fresh oregano
- 1/2 teaspoon salt
- 1/4 teaspoon pepper
- 1/4 teaspoon dry mustard
- 6 large lettuce leaves

Minced green onions
Minced fresh parsley

Arrange tomato slices in an 8-in. square dish; set aside. In a small bowl, whisk together oil, vinegar, garlic, oregano, salt, pepper and mustard. Pour over tomatoes. Cover and chill for 1-2 hours. To serve, place each lettuce leaf on an individual plate and top with two tomato slices. Drizzle with dressing. Sprinkle with onions and parsley. **Yield:** 6 servings. **Diabetic Exchanges:** One serving equals 3 fat, 1 vegetable; also, 174 calories, 197 mg sodium, 0 cholesterol, 3 gm carbohydrate, 1 gm protein, 18 gm fat.

SCALLOPED POTATOES
Eleanore Hill, Fresno, California

- 2 tablespoons butter *or* margarine
- 1 tablespoon all-purpose flour
- 1-1/2 cups milk
- 1 teaspoon salt
- 1/4 teaspoon pepper
- 4 cups thinly sliced peeled potatoes (about 2 pounds)
- 1 medium onion, finely chopped
- 1 small green pepper, finely chopped

Buttered bread crumbs
Shredded cheddar cheese

In a saucepan, melt butter; stir in flour. Add milk all at once, stirring constantly. Cook and stir over low heat until thickened and bubbly. Season with salt and pepper. In a greased 1-1/2-qt. baking dish, arrange half the potatoes, onion and green pepper in layers; cover with half of the sauce. Repeat layers. Cover and bake at 350° for 35 minutes. Sprinkle with buttered bread crumbs. Bake, uncovered, about 40 minutes longer or until potatoes are tender. Sprinkle with cheddar cheese. Let stand for 5 minutes before serving. **Yield:** 4-6 servings.

HOMINY CASSEROLE
Lila Thurman, Crossett, Arkansas
(PICTURED BELOW)

- 1 medium onion, chopped
- 1 garlic clove, minced
- 1 tablespoon cooking oil
- 1 cup (8 ounces) sour cream
- 3/4 cup shredded cheddar cheese, *divided*
- 1/4 cup milk
- 1 can (4 ounces) chopped green chilies
- 1/4 teaspoon ground cumin
- 3 cans (15 ounces *each*) golden hominy, drained

In a small skillet, cook onion and garlic in oil until tender. Remove from heat. In a bowl, combine onion mixture, sour cream, half of the cheese, milk, chilies and cumin. Add hominy; mix well. Pour into a greased 2-qt. baking dish. Bake, uncovered, at 350° for 30 minutes or until heated through. Sprinkle with remaining cheese. Serve immediately. **Yield:** 8-10 servings.

Mmmain dishes! Whether they're made with pork, beef, poultry, seafood or eggs, main dishes are the backbone of country cooking. Dazzle family and friends with elegant Stuffed Crown Roast of Pork and fruity, Fluffy Cranberry Delight. Then savor the rich, chocolaty flavor of Fudge Truffle Cheesecake!

A TOAST TO ROASTS. Clockwise from lower left: **Stuffed Crown Roast of Pork** (p. 37), **Fudge Truffle Cheesecake** (p. 61) and **Fluffy Cranberry Delight** (p. 22).

Meats & Main Dishes

HAM LOAF WITH GOLDEN SAUCE
Donna Smith, Palisade, Colorado

- 1 pound ground fully cooked ham
- 1 pound ground pork
- 2 cups soft bread crumbs
- 1/3 cup pineapple juice
- 2 eggs, lightly beaten
- 1/2 cup chopped onion
- 1/4 cup packed brown sugar
- 2 tablespoons chopped fresh parsley
- 2 tablespoons cider vinegar
- 1/4 teaspoon ground cloves

SAUCE:
- 2 cups pineapple juice
- 3 tablespoons cornstarch
- 1 to 2 tablespoons brown sugar
- 2 teaspoons lemon juice
- 1/4 to 1/2 teaspoon ground ginger

In a large bowl, combine first 10 ingredients. Pack into a 9-in. x 5-in. x 3-in. loaf pan. Bake at 350° for 1-1/2 hours. Meanwhile, combine all sauce ingredients in a saucepan. Slowly bring to a boil, stirring constantly until thickened and translucent. Allow loaf to stand for 5 minutes. Remove loaf from pan and serve sauce over it. **Yield:** 6-8 servings.

STUFFED CROWN ROAST OF PORK
Marianne Severson, West Allis, Wisconsin
(PICTURED ON OPPOSITE PAGE)

- 1 crown roast of pork (about 8 pounds)
- 1 pound ground pork
- 1/2 pound bulk pork sausage
- 3/4 cup finely chopped onion
- 3 tablespoons butter *or* margarine
- 1/2 cup diced peeled apple
- 1/4 cup finely chopped celery
- 1-1/2 cups soft bread crumbs
- 1/2 cup minced fresh parsley
- 1-1/2 teaspoons salt
- 1/2 teaspoon pepper
- 1/2 teaspoon dried sage
- Spiced crab apples, optional

Tie roast and place on a rack in a large roasting pan. Cover the bone ends with foil. Insert meat thermometer. Roast at 350° for 2 hours. Meanwhile, in a large skillet, cook the pork and sausage until browned; drain and set aside. In the same skillet, saute onion in butter until tender. Add apple and celery; cook for 5 minutes. Remove from the heat. Add the cooked pork and sausage, crumbs, parsley, salt, pepper and sage; mix well. Remove roast from oven. Carefully press a double layer of foil down through open center of roast to form a base for stuffing. Spoon stuffing lightly into crown. Return to oven and bake for 1 hour more or until thermometer reads 160°. Transfer roast to serving platter. Garnish with spiced crab apples if desired. Cut between ribs to serve. **Yield:** 16-20 servings.

NOODLES WITH CREAMY MEAT SAUCE
May Nevenschwander, Dalton, Ohio

- 2 pounds lean ground beef
- 1 can (10-3/4 ounces) condensed cream of onion soup, undiluted
- 1 can (10-3/4 ounces) condensed cream of mushroom soup, undiluted
- 1 can (10-3/4 ounces) condensed golden mushroom soup, undiluted
- Cooked egg noodles

Crumble uncooked ground beef into a large Dutch oven or casserole. Combine soups; pour over beef. Cover and bake at 350° for 1 to 1-1/4 hours or until the beef is no longer pink. Serve over noodles. **Yield:** 6-8 servings.

FLORIDA SEAFOOD CASSEROLE
Lucille Pennington, Ormond Beach, Florida

- 1/3 cup minced onion
- 1/4 cup butter *or* margarine
- 1/4 cup all-purpose flour
- 1 cup milk
- 1 cup light cream
- 1/2 teaspoon salt
- 1/2 teaspoon pepper
- 1 tablespoon chopped pimientos
- 1 can (8 ounces) sliced water chestnuts, drained
- 2 tablespoons lemon juice
- 1 tablespoon snipped fresh parsley
- 1 cup flaked cooked crabmeat
- 1 cup peeled cooked shrimp
- 3 cups cooked rice
- 1 cup (4 ounces) shredded cheddar cheese, *divided*

In a saucepan, saute onion in butter; blend in flour. Add milk and cream; cook and stir until thick and bubbly. Remove from the heat; stir in salt, pepper, pimientos, water chestnuts, lemon juice, parsley, crabmeat, shrimp, rice and half of the cheese. Spoon into a 2-1/2-qt. casserole. Bake at 350° for 25 minutes or until heated through. Sprinkle with remaining cheese just before serving. **Yield:** 6 servings.

RHUBARB PORK CHOP CASSEROLE
Jeanie Castor, Decatur, Illinois
(PICTURED ON PAGE 75)

- 4 pork loin chops (3/4 inch thick)
- 1 tablespoon cooking oil
- Salt and pepper to taste
- 2-1/2 to 3 cups soft bread crumbs
- 3 cups sliced fresh *or* frozen rhubarb (1-inch pieces)
- 1/2 cup packed brown sugar
- 1/4 cup all-purpose flour
- 1 teaspoon ground cinnamon

In a large skillet, brown pork chops in oil and season with salt and pepper. Remove to a warm platter. Mix 1/4 cup pan drippings with bread crumbs. Reserve 1/2 cup; sprinkle remaining crumbs into a 13-in. x 9-in. x 2-in. baking dish. Combine rhubarb, sugar, flour and cinnamon; spoon half over the bread crumbs. Arrange pork chops on top. Spoon remaining rhubarb mixture over chops. Cover with foil and bake at 350° for 30-45 minutes. Remove foil. Sprinkle with reserved bread crumbs. Bake 10-15 minutes longer or until chops test done. **Yield:** 4 servings.

CAMPFIRE HASH
Janet Danilow, Winkelman, Arizona

2 tablespoons cooking oil
1 large onion, chopped
2 garlic cloves, minced
4 large potatoes, peeled and cubed (about 2 pounds)
1 pound fully cooked smoked kielbasa, cubed
1 can (4 ounces) chopped green chilies
1 can (15 to 16 ounces) whole kernel corn, drained

In a Dutch oven, heat oil. Saute onion and garlic until tender. Add potatoes. Cook, uncovered, over medium heat for 20 minutes, stirring occasionally. Add kielbasa; cook and stir until potatoes are tender and well browned, about 10 minutes more. Stir in chilies and corn; cook until heated through. **Yield:** 6 servings.

OVERNIGHT EGG CASSEROLE
La Vonne Propst, Sweet Home, Oregon

8 slices bread, cubed
3/4 pound cheddar cheese, shredded
1-1/2 pounds bulk pork sausage *or* Italian sausage
4 eggs
2-1/2 cups milk
1 tablespoon prepared mustard
1 can (10-3/4 ounces) condensed cream of mushroom soup, undiluted
1/4 cup chicken broth

Place bread cubes in a greased 13-in. x 9-in. x 2-in. baking dish. Sprinkle with cheese; set aside. In a skillet; brown sausage over medium heat; drain. Crumble sausage over cheese and bread. Beat eggs, milk, mustard, soup and broth; pour over sausage. Cover and refrigerate overnight or at least 2-3 hours before baking. Bake at 350° for 50-60 minutes or just until set. **Yield:** 6-8 servings.

STEAK AND ONION PIE
Ardis Wirtz, Newburgh, Indiana
(PICTURED ON PAGE 55)

1 large onion, sliced
1/3 cup shortening
1/3 cup all-purpose flour
1 teaspoon salt
1 teaspoon pepper
1/2 teaspoon ground ginger

1-1/2 teaspoons ground allspice
1-1/2 pounds boneless round steak, cut into 1-inch cubes
2 cups boiling water
1-1/2 cups diced peeled potatoes
1 cup diced carrots
1 cup frozen peas
Pie pastry (9 to 10 inches)

In a Dutch oven, lightly brown onion in shortening. Meanwhile, combine flour, salt, pepper, ginger and allspice in a plastic bag. Place meat cubes in the bag, a few pieces at a time, and shake well to coat. Remove onion and set aside. Brown beef on all sides. Add water; cover and simmer for 1 hour or until meat is tender, stirring occasionally. Add potatoes, carrots and reserved onions; cover and cook for 10 minutes. Stir in peas and continue cooking until all vegetables are tender, about 10 minutes. Spoon meat mixture into a 9-in. square baking pan. Roll pastry out to a 10-in. square; place over meat mixture and seal edges to pan. Cut several small steam vents in crust. Bake at 450° for 25-30 minutes or until pastry is browned. **Yield:** 6-8 servings.

QUICK & EASY

CHICKEN FEED
Jill Kinder, Richlands, Virginia

1 small onion, sliced
2 cups fresh mushrooms, sliced
1 garlic clove, minced
1/2 teaspoon dried thyme, *divided*
1 tablespoon butter *or* margarine
4 cups cubed leftover cooked chicken
4 cups leftover gravy
1 chicken bouillon cube, crushed
Dash pepper
3 cups mashed potatoes

In a skillet, saute the onion, mushrooms, garlic and 1/4 teaspoon thyme in butter. Stir in the chicken, gravy, bouillon and pepper; spoon into a greased 3-qt. casserole. Combine potatoes and remaining thyme; spoon over mixture. Bake, uncovered, at 350° for 45 minutes. **Yield:** 6-8 servings.

ORANGE TURKEY STIR-FRY
Anne Frederick, New Hartford, New York

3/4 cup orange juice
1/4 cup orange marmalade
2 tablespoons soy sauce
2 tablespoons cornstarch
1/8 teaspoon ground ginger

1/8 teaspoon hot pepper sauce
1/4 cup all-purpose flour
1 pound turkey cutlets, cut into 1-inch strips
2 tablespoons cooking oil, *divided*
4 green onions, cut into 1-inch pieces
1/2 cup coarsely chopped green pepper
1 seedless orange, peeled, sliced and halved
Cooked rice

In a small bowl, stir together first six ingredients; set aside. Place flour on a sheet of waxed paper; coat turkey strips, then shake off excess. In a 10-in. skillet, heat 1 tablespoon oil over medium-high heat. Cook turkey in three batches until strips are tender and lightly browned on all sides. Remove turkey and keep warm. Add remaining oil to skillet; cook and stir green onions and green pepper for 1 minute. Stir in orange juice mixture. Bring to a boil; reduce heat and simmer for 3 minutes. Add turkey and orange slices; heat through. Serve over rice. **Yield:** 4 servings.

NEW ENGLAND LAMB BAKE
Frank Grady, Fort Kent, Maine
(PICTURED ON PAGE 11)

1 tablespoon cooking oil
2 pounds boneless lean lamb, cubed
1 large onion, chopped
1/4 cup all-purpose flour
5 cups chicken broth
2 large carrots, sliced
2 large leeks, cut into 2-inch pieces
2 tablespoons minced fresh parsley, *divided*
1 bay leaf
1/2 teaspoon dried rosemary
1/4 teaspoon dried thyme
1/2 teaspoon salt
1/4 teaspoon pepper
3 large potatoes, peeled and sliced
1/4 cup butter *or* margarine

In a large Dutch oven, heat oil. Brown lamb and onion. Stir in flour; mix well. Gradually add broth. Bring to a boil, stirring to remove browned bits from pan. Add carrots, leeks, 1 tablespoon parsley, bay leaf, rosemary, thyme, salt and pepper. Spoon into a greased 3-qt. casserole. Cover with potatoes and dot with butter. Bake at 375° for 1-1/2 to 2 hours or until the meat is tender and the potatoes are golden brown. Garnish with remaining parsley. **Yield:** 6-8 servings.

SOUR CREAM 'N' DILL CHICKEN

Rebekah Brown, Three Hills, Alberta
(PICTURED ON PAGE 30)

8 to 10 chicken pieces, skinned
Pepper to taste
1 can (10-3/4 ounces) condensed cream of mushroom soup, undiluted
1 envelope dry onion soup mix
1 cup (8 ounces) sour cream
1 tablespoon lemon juice
1 tablespoon fresh dill, chopped *or* 1 teaspoon dill weed
1 can (4 ounces) sliced mushrooms, drained
Paprika
Cooked wide egg noodles, optional

Place chicken in a single layer in a 13-in. x 9-in. x 2-in. baking pan. Sprinkle with pepper. Combine soup, soup mix, sour cream, lemon juice, dill and mushrooms; pour over chicken. Sprinkle with paprika. Bake, uncovered, at 350° for 1 hour or until chicken is tender. Serve over egg noodles if desired. **Yield:** 4-6 servings.

QUICK & EASY

TACOED EGGS

Mary Smith, Huntington, Indiana

8 eggs, beaten
1/2 cup shredded cheddar cheese
2 tablespoons finely chopped onion
2 tablespoons finely chopped green pepper
1 to 4 drops hot pepper sauce
1/2 cup leftover cooked taco-seasoned ground beef
Flour tortillas, warmed, optional
Salsa, optional

In a bowl, combine eggs, cheese, onion, green pepper and hot pepper sauce. Cook and stir in a nonstick skillet until eggs begin to set. Add taco meat; cook until eggs are completely set. If desired, spoon onto a warmed tortilla and roll up; top with salsa. **Yield:** 4 servings.

REUBEN LOAF

Armetta Keeney, Carlisle, Iowa

3-1/4 to 3-3/4 cups all-purpose flour
1 package (1/4 ounce) active dry yeast
1 tablespoon sugar
1 tablespoon butter *or* margarine, softened
1 teaspoon salt
1 cup warm water (120° to 130°)

1/4 cup Thousand Island salad dressing
6 ounces thinly sliced corned beef
4 ounces sliced Swiss cheese
1 can (8 ounces) sauerkraut, drained
1 egg white, beaten
Poppy seeds

In a mixing bowl, combine 2-1/4 cups flour, yeast, sugar, butter and salt. Stir in warm water and mix until a soft dough forms. Add remaining flour if necessary. Turn out onto a lightly floured surface; knead until smooth, about 4 minutes. On a lightly greased baking sheet, roll dough to a 14-in. x 10-in. rectangle. Spread dressing down the middle of one half of dough, leaving a 3/4-in. space along edges. Top with layers of beef, cheese and sauerkraut. Fold the remaining half of dough over the meat mixture. Pinch edges together to seal. Cut small slits in the dough to vent steam. Cover and let rise in a warm place for 15 minutes. Brush with egg white and sprinkle with poppy seeds. Bake at 400° for 25 minutes or until lightly browned. Serve immediately; refrigerate leftovers. **Yield:** 6-8 servings.

COUNTRY CHICKEN CASSEROLE

Frances Gleichmann, Baltimore, Maryland

1/2 pound fresh mushrooms, quartered
2 medium onions, chopped
5 tablespoons butter *or* margarine, *divided*
2 cups cubed cooked chicken
2 cups diced cooked peeled potatoes
1 jar (2 ounces) pimientos, drained
1/4 cup chopped fresh parsley
1 cup light cream
1 teaspoon instant chicken bouillon granules
1 teaspoon salt
1/2 teaspoon dried rosemary, crushed
1/8 teaspoon pepper
1 cup soft bread crumbs
Additional parsley, optional

In a skillet, saute the mushrooms and onions in 3 tablespoons butter until tender. Add chicken, potatoes, pimientos, parsley, cream, bouillon, salt, rosemary and pepper; heat through. Spoon into a greased 2-qt. casserole. Melt remaining butter; combine with the bread crumbs and sprinkle over casserole. Bake, uncovered, at 350° for 20-25 minutes or until crumbs are toasted. Garnish with parsley if desired. **Yield:** 6 servings.

ITALIAN SAUSAGE AND SPINACH PIE

Teresa Johnson, Peru, Illinois
(PICTURED ON PAGE 58)

1 pound bulk Italian sausage
1 medium onion, chopped
6 eggs, beaten
2 packages (10 ounces *each*) frozen chopped spinach, thawed and well drained
4 cups (16 ounces) shredded mozzarella cheese
1 cup ricotta cheese
1/2 teaspoon garlic powder
1/4 teaspoon pepper
Pastry for a two-crust pie (10 inches)
1 tablespoon water

In a skillet, brown sausage and onion until the sausage is done and onion is tender. Drain. Separate 1 egg and set aside the yolk. In a mixing bowl, beat the remaining egg white and whole eggs. Stir in the sausage and onion, spinach, mozzarella, ricotta, garlic powder and pepper. Line a 10-in. pie plate with bottom pastry. Add filling. Top with upper crust; seal and flute edges. Cut slits in top crust. Combine water with reserved egg yolk; brush over top crust. Bake at 375° for 50 minutes or until golden brown. Let stand 10 minutes before serving. **Yield:** 8 servings.

BAVARIAN POT ROAST

Susan Robertson, Hamilton, Ohio
(PICTURED ON PAGE 62)

1 boneless beef chuck pot roast (about 3 pounds)
2 tablespoons cooking oil
1-1/4 cups water
3/4 cup beer *or* beef broth
1 can (8 ounces) tomato sauce
1/2 cup chopped onion
2 tablespoons sugar
1 tablespoon vinegar
2 teaspoons salt
1 teaspoon ground cinnamon
1 bay leaf
1/2 teaspoon pepper
1/2 teaspoon ground ginger
Cornstarch and water, optional

In a Dutch oven, brown roast in hot oil. Combine water, beer or broth, tomato sauce, onion, sugar, vinegar, salt, cinnamon, bay leaf, pepper and ginger. Pour over meat and bring to a boil. Reduce heat; cover and simmer until meat is tender, for 2-1/2 to 3 hours. Remove meat. Discard bay leaf. If desired, thicken juices with cornstarch and water. **Yield:** 8-10 servings.

*S*unday meals are a time for your family's favorite dishes. You're sure to satisfy your hungry brood when you serve Perfect Pot Roast or Golden Ham Croquettes with fresh-from-the-oven Freeze-and-Bake Rolls. And for dessert, get ready to dish out second helpings of deliciously sweet Apple Roly-Poly.

SUNDAY SPREAD. Clockwise from the top: **Freeze-and-Bake Rolls** (p. 52), **Perfect Pot Roast** (p. 41), **Golden Ham Croquettes** (p. 41) and **Apple Roly-Poly** (p. 76).

PERFECT POT ROAST
Melody Sroufe, Wichita, Kansas
(PICTURED ON OPPOSITE PAGE)

1 teaspoon seasoned salt
1/2 teaspoon onion powder
1/4 teaspoon pepper
1/8 teaspoon garlic powder
1 beef chuck pot roast
(3 to 4 pounds)
1 tablespoon olive oil
3/4 cup water
1 large onion, chopped
1/4 cup chopped green pepper
2 garlic cloves, minced
2 bay leaves
2 teaspoons dried parsley
flakes
1/4 teaspoon dried thyme
All-purpose flour

Combine first four ingredients; rub on-to roast. In a skillet, brown roast in oil. Place in a roasting pan. Add water, onion, green pepper and seasonings. Cover and bake at 325° for 2-1/2 to 3 hours or until roast is tender. Remove and keep warm. Discard bay leaves. Skim fat from pan juices. Measure juices and return to pan. For each cup of juices, combine 1 tablespoon flour with 2 tablespoons water; mix well. Stir flour mixture into pan; cook over medium heat, stirring constantly, until thickened and bubbly. Serve gravy with roast. **Yield:** 8-10 servings.

GREEN PEPPER STEAK
Emmalee Thomas, Laddonia, Missouri

1 pound boneless beef sirloin
steak
1/4 cup soy sauce
1/4 cup water
1 tablespoon cornstarch
2 to 3 tablespoons cooking oil,
divided
2 small onions, thinly sliced
and separated into rings
1 green pepper, cut into 1-inch
pieces
2 celery ribs, sliced diagonally
2 tomatoes, cut into wedges
Cooked rice

Partially freeze beef. Thinly slice across the grain into bite-size strips; set aside. For sauce, combine soy sauce, water and cornstarch; set aside. Heat 1 tablespoon oil in a large skillet or wok over high heat. Stir-fry half of the beef until browned. Remove and repeat with remaining beef, adding additional oil as needed. Remove meat and keep warm. Add onions, green pepper and celery to pan; stir-fry until crisp-tender, about 3-4 minutes. Return beef to pan. Stir the sauce; add to pan. Cook and stir until thickened and bubbly. Cook and stir 2 minutes more. Add tomatoes; cook just until heated through. Serve over rice. **Yield:** 4 servings.

CHICKEN CANNELLONI
Barbara Nowakowski, N. Tonawanda, New York

1 small onion, sliced
1 garlic clove, minced
3/4 cup thinly sliced carrots
1/2 cup thinly sliced celery
1/2 cup sliced mushrooms
1 tablespoon cooking oil
1 can (6 ounces) tomato paste
1 can (8 ounces) tomatoes with
liquid, cut up
1-1/2 teaspoons Italian seasoning,
divided
1 teaspoon sugar
6 boneless skinless chicken
breast halves
1/2 cup ricotta cheese
1/4 cup sliced green onions
3 tablespoons grated Parmesan
cheese
Dash pepper
1/2 cup mozzarella cheese
Cooked pasta, optional

In a large saucepan, saute onion, garlic, carrots, celery and mushrooms in oil until onion is tender. Add tomato paste, tomatoes, 1 teaspoon Italian seasoning and sugar; bring to a boil. Reduce heat and simmer, uncovered, for 10 minutes. Meanwhile, pound chicken breasts to 1/4-in. thickness. Combine ricotta cheese, green onions, Parmesan, pepper and remaining Italian seasoning; divide evenly and spoon on top of chicken breasts. Roll up; place seam side down in an 8-in. square baking dish. Spoon sauce over chicken. Bake, uncovered, at 375° for 25-30 minutes or until the chicken is tender. Sprinkle with mozzarella cheese; let stand for 5 minutes. Serve with pasta if desired. **Yield:** 4-6 servings.

QUICK & EASY

MEXICAN CORN SCRAMBLE
Brenda Spann, Granger, Indiana

1 small onion, chopped
3 tablespoons butter or
margarine
1 can (11 ounces) whole kernel
corn with peppers, drained
1 can (2-1/4 ounces) sliced ripe
olives, drained
8 eggs, lightly beaten
1 cup cubed fully cooked
smoked ham or sausage
3/4 cup shredded cheddar
cheese
Tortilla chips
Picante sauce

In a medium skillet, saute onion in butter until tender. Stir in corn and olives. Add eggs; cook and stir over medium heat until eggs just begin to set. Add ham or sausage and cheese. Cook until eggs are fully cooked and cheese is melted. Serve with tortilla chips and picante sauce. **Yield:** 6 servings.

GOLDEN HAM CROQUETTES
Peggy Anderjaska, Haigler, Nebraska
(PICTURED ON OPPOSITE PAGE)

3 tablespoons butter or
margarine
1/4 to 1/2 teaspoon curry powder
1/4 cup all-purpose flour
3/4 cup milk
2 to 3 teaspoons prepared
mustard
1 teaspoon grated onion
2 cups coarsely ground fully
cooked ham
2/3 cup dry bread crumbs
1 egg, beaten
2 tablespoons water
Cooking oil for deep-fat frying
CHEESE SAUCE:
2 tablespoons butter or
margarine
2 tablespoons all-purpose flour
1/4 teaspoon salt
Dash pepper
1-1/4 cups milk
1/2 cup shredded cheddar cheese
1/2 cup shredded Swiss cheese

In a saucepan, melt butter; stir in curry powder and flour. Gradually add milk; cook and stir until bubbly. Cook and stir 2 minutes more. Remove from the heat. Stir in mustard and onion; add ham and mix well. Cover and chill thoroughly. With wet hands, shape mixture into 10 balls. Roll balls in bread crumbs; shape each into a cone. Whisk together egg and water. Dip cones into egg mixture; roll again in crumbs. Heat oil in a deep-fat fryer to 365°. Fry croquettes, a few at a time, for 2 to 2-1/2 minutes or until golden brown. Drain on paper towels; keep warm. For the cheese sauce, melt butter in a saucepan; stir in flour, salt and pepper. Gradually add milk; cook and stir until thickened and bubbly. Cook and stir 2 minutes more. Add cheeses; heat and stir until melted. Spoon over croquettes. **Yield:** 5 servings.

PORK STUFFED WITH CORN BREAD DRESSING

Fern Kleeman, Tell City, Indiana
(PICTURED ON PAGE 65)

1/4 cup boiling water
1/4 cup raisins
2 slices bacon, cut up
1/2 cup diced celery
2 tablespoons diced onion
1 egg, beaten
1 teaspoon salt
1/4 teaspoon pepper
2-1/2 cups corn bread crumbs
6 center cut pork chops (1-1/4 inches thick) or 1 pork blade roast (3 to 4 pounds), boned for stuffing

Pour water over raisins; set aside. In a saucepan, cook bacon until crisp; add celery and onion. Cook and stir for 2 minutes; remove from the heat. In a medium bowl, combine egg, salt, pepper and bacon and raisin mixtures. Stir in crumbs; toss lightly. If stuffing pork chops, cut a pocket in each chop by slicing from the fat side almost to the bone. Spoon about 1/3 cup stuffing into each chop; place on a rack in a shallow roasting pan. Bake at 375° for 40-50 minutes or until the meat is no longer pink. If stuffing a roast, fill pocket in roast with stuffing. Tie roast with string and place on a rack in a shallow roasting pan. Insert meat thermometer into center of meat. Roast at 325° for 1-3/4 to 2-1/4 hours or until the thermometer registers 160° for medium-well or 170° for well-done. Cover and let stand 10 minutes before carving. **Yield:** 6 servings (chops) or 8-10 servings (roast).

SPICY STUFFED PEPPERS

Adele Bernard, Clinton, Missouri
(PICTURED ON COVER AND PAGE 26)

4 green peppers, tops and seeds removed
1 pound lean ground beef
1 cup finely chopped onion
1/2 cup cooked rice
1 teaspoon celery salt
1/2 teaspoon salt
1/4 teaspoon pepper
Dash cayenne pepper
1 jar (8 ounces) picante sauce

Cook peppers in boiling salted water for 3 minutes. Drain and rinse with cold water. Combine ground beef, onion, rice and seasonings; spoon into peppers. Place in a greased baking dish; top with picante sauce. Bake, uncovered, at

375° for 35-40 minutes or until meat is no longer pink. **Yield:** 4 servings.

HAM AND CHEESE SOUFFLE

Airy Murray, Williamsport, Maryland

16 slices white bread (crusts removed), cubed
16 slices (about 1 pound) ham, cut into bite-size pieces
2 cups (8 ounces) shredded cheddar cheese
2 cups (8 ounces) shredded Swiss cheese
5 eggs, beaten
3 cups milk
1 teaspoon dry mustard
1/2 teaspoon onion salt
2-1/2 cups crushed cornflakes
1/3 cup butter or margarine, melted

In a greased 13-in. x 9-in. x 2-in. baking dish, layer half of the bread, ham, cheddar cheese and Swiss cheese. Repeat. Combine eggs, milk, mustard and onion salt; pour over layered mixture. Cover and refrigerate overnight. Combine cornflakes and butter; sprinkle on top. Bake at 375° for 40 minutes or until hot and bubbly. **Yield:** 8-10 servings.

COUNTRY BEEF BRISKET

Beth Blair, Kansas City, Missouri

1 beef brisket (2-1/2 to 3 pounds), trimmed
MARINADE:
1/2 cup soy sauce
1 can (10-1/2 ounces) condensed beef broth
2-1/2 tablespoons lemon juice
1/2 teaspoon garlic powder
Paprika
SEASONED BROTH:
1/4 cup vinegar
1/4 cup Worcestershire sauce
1/4 cup packed brown sugar
1/2 to 1 teaspoon liquid smoke

Place brisket in a shallow pan. Combine all marinade ingredients except paprika; pour over meat. Cover and refrigerate overnight. Drain meat, reserving 1 cup marinade. Refrigerate reserved marinade. Place meat in a shallow baking pan; sprinkle with paprika. Cover tightly with foil. Bake at 325° for 3 hours or until meat is tender. Cool and refrigerate meat; discard cooking juices. When thoroughly chilled, slice meat and return to the baking pan. Combine seasoned broth ingredients and reserved marinade in a saucepan. Simmer for 10 minutes; pour over meat. Cover and bake at 300° for 1 hour. **Yield:** 10-12 servings.

COLOSSAL CORNBURGER

Lesley Colgan, London, Ontario
(PICTURED ON PAGE 44)

1 egg, beaten
1 cup cooked whole kernel corn
1/2 cup coarsely crushed cheese crackers
1/4 cup sliced green onions
1/4 cup chopped fresh parsley
1 teaspoon Worcestershire sauce
2 pounds ground beef
1 teaspoon salt
1/2 teaspoon pepper
1/2 teaspoon ground sage

In a medium bowl, combine egg, corn, crackers, green onions, parsley and Worcestershire sauce; set aside. In a large bowl, combine ground beef and seasonings. On sheets of waxed paper, pat half of the beef mixture at a time into an 8-1/2-in. circle. Spoon corn mixture onto one circle of meat to within 1 in. of the edge. Top with second circle of meat; remove top sheet of waxed paper and seal edges. Invert onto a well-greased wire grill basket; peel off waxed paper. Grill over medium coals, turning once, for 25-30 minutes or until burger reaches desired doneness. For oven method, place burger on a baking pan. Bake at 350° for 40-45 minutes or until burger reaches desired doneness. Cut into wedges to serve. **Yield:** 6 servings.

LEFTOVER MEAT LOAF PARMESAN

Laddie Nichols, Lakeside, Arizona

1 cup crushed saltines
1/4 cup grated Parmesan cheese
1 egg
3 tablespoons water
4 leftover meat loaf slices (each about 3/8 inch thick)
Shortening for pan-frying
Ketchup, optional

Combine the saltine crumbs and Parmesan cheese in a shallow dish; set aside. Beat egg with water. Dip meat loaf slices in egg mixture, then in crumb mixture. Heat shortening in a skillet. Brown meat loaf slices on both sides. Serve with ketchup if desired. **Yield:** 2-4 servings.

MOIST MEAT LOAF

For tender, juicy meat loaf, first mix all ingredients except beef. Then add meat and mix lightly. When shaping loaf, handle only as much as necessary.

FRESH CORN CAKES
Gaynelle Fritsch, Welches, Oregon
(PICTURED ON PAGE 45)

1 cup all-purpose flour
1/2 cup yellow *or* blue cornmeal
1 tablespoon sugar
1 tablespoon baking powder
1/2 teaspoon salt
2 eggs, *separated*
1 cup milk
1/4 cup butter *or* margarine, melted
1 cup cooked whole kernel corn
4 green onions, thinly sliced
1/2 medium sweet red pepper, finely chopped
1 can (4 ounces) chopped green chilies
Butter, margarine *or* cooking oil for frying
Maple syrup, optional

In a medium bowl, combine flour, cornmeal, sugar, baking powder and salt. In a small bowl, beat egg yolks; blend in milk and butter. Add to dry ingredients; stir until just mixed. (Batter may be slightly lumpy). Stir in the corn, green onions, red pepper and green chilies; set aside. In a small mixing bowl, beat egg whites until stiff peaks form. Gently fold into batter. For each pancake, pour about 1/4 cup batter onto a lightly greased hot griddle; turn when bubbles form on tops of cakes. Cook second side until golden brown. Serve immediately with syrup if desired. **Yield:** 20 pancakes.

WILD RICE HOT DISH
Sandra McWithey, South St. Paul, Minnesota

3 cups boiling water
1 cup uncooked wild rice
1-1/2 pounds ground beef
1 medium onion, chopped
2 cans (10-3/4 ounces *each*) condensed cream of chicken soup, undiluted
2 cans (4 ounces *each*) sliced mushrooms, undrained
1 can (28 ounces) bean sprouts, drained
1 can (10-1/2 ounces) condensed beef broth
1-1/3 cups water
1/4 cup soy sauce
1 bay leaf, crushed
1 tablespoon dried parsley flakes
1/4 teaspoon *each* celery salt, onion salt, poultry seasoning, garlic powder, paprika and pepper
1/8 teaspoon dried thyme
1/2 cup sliced almonds

In a large bowl, pour water over rice; let stand for 15 minutes. Drain and set aside. In a skillet, brown ground beef and onion. Drain; add to rice with remaining ingredients except almonds. Transfer to a 13-in. x 9-in. x 2-in. baking dish. Cover and bake at 350° for 2 hours. Sprinkle almonds on top; bake, uncovered, 30 minutes longer. **Yield:** 8-12 servings.

BEEF PINWHEELS
Ruthmarie Hosler, Endwell, New York

3/4 cup vegetable oil
2/3 cup water
1/4 cup soy sauce
1 tablespoon lemon pepper
2 teaspoons Worcestershire sauce
4 drops hot pepper sauce
1 flank steak (2 to 2-1/2 pounds), trimmed

In a bowl, combine oil, water, soy sauce, lemon pepper, Worcestershire sauce and hot pepper sauce; set aside. Pound flank steak on each side. Cut into 1/2-in. strips on the diagonal; add to marinade. Cover and refrigerate for 4 hours or overnight. Divide meat strips into eight portions. Roll and shape strips, using larger strips around edges, into pinwheels. Secure each with a skewer. Grill over hot coals for 5-6 minutes per side or until done. **Yield:** 8 servings.

CORN AND CHICKEN DINNER
Doralee Pinkerton, Milford, Indiana
(PICTURED ON PAGE 45)

3 garlic cloves, minced, *divided*
1/2 cup butter *or* margarine, *divided*
3 pounds chicken legs and thighs (about 8 pieces)
3 ears fresh corn, husked, cleaned and cut into thirds
1/4 cup water
2 teaspoons dried tarragon, *divided*
1/2 teaspoon salt
1/4 teaspoon pepper
2 medium zucchini, sliced into 1/2-inch pieces
2 tomatoes, seeded and cut into chunks

In a Dutch oven or large skillet over medium-high heat, saute 2 of the garlic cloves in 2 tablespoons butter. Add the chicken and brown on both sides. Reduce heat. Add corn and water. Sprinkle with 1 teaspoon tarragon, salt and pepper. Cover and simmer for 20-25 min-

utes or until chicken is tender. Meanwhile, in a small saucepan, melt remaining butter. Add remaining garlic and tarragon; simmer for 3 minutes. Layer zucchini and tomatoes over the chicken mixture. Drizzle seasoned butter over all; cover and cook for 3-5 minutes. **Yield:** 6-8 servings.

PINEAPPLE HAM BALLS
Alice Whitlow, Didsbury, Alberta

3 cups ground fully cooked ham
1/2 pound ground pork
1 cup soft bread crumbs
2 eggs, beaten
1/4 teaspoon pepper
1 can (20 ounces) sliced pineapple
3/4 cup packed brown sugar
1/4 cup vinegar
1/2 teaspoon dry mustard

In a bowl, combine ham, pork, bread crumbs, eggs and pepper and mix well. Chill. Form into 10 balls; set aside. Drain pineapple, reserving 1/2 cup of juice. Place juice in a saucepan with sugar, vinegar and dry mustard; cook and stir over low heat until sugar is dissolved. Arrange pineapple slices in the bottom of an ungreased 13-in. x 9-in. x 2-in. baking dish. Place a ham ball on each pineapple slice. Pour sugar mixture over all. Cover and bake at 350° for 1 hour or until ham balls are thoroughly cooked. **Yield:** 4-5 servings.

STUFFED SPINACH LOAF
Anita Harmala, Howell, Michigan

1 pound bulk Italian sausage
1/2 teaspoon salt
1/2 teaspoon dried basil
1 loaf (1 pound) frozen bread dough, thawed
1 package (10 ounces) frozen spinach, thawed and well-drained
2 cups (8 ounces) shredded mozzarella cheese

In a skillet, brown sausage. Drain; sprinkle with salt and basil. Roll out bread dough to a 13-in. x 10-in. rectangle. Sprinkle meat on top of dough. Place spinach on top of meat; top with cheese. Roll up from one of the long sides; seal seams and ends. Using a spatula, carefully place loaf on a greased baking sheet or jelly roll pan. Bake at 350° for 25-30 minutes or until the crust is golden brown. Serve warm. Refrigerate leftovers. **Yield:** 10 servings.

Variety is the best way to describe the use of sweet, golden corn, especially when it comes to main dishes. Next time you barbecue, switch from your typical hamburgers to the flavorful Colossal Corn Burger. Served with fresh fruit salad and ham, Fresh Corn Cakes make a nice change-of-pace main meal. The Corn and Chicken Dinner is a great meal-in-one dish for picnics or reunions.

CORNUCOPIA! Clockwise from lower left: **Colossal Cornburger** (p. 42), **Calico Potato Salad** (p. 22), **Corn Relish** (p. 7), **Corn Muffins with Honey Butter** (p. 54), **Company Vegetable Casserole** (p. 32), **Corn and Chicken Dinner** (p. 43), **Hush Puppies** (p. 34) and **Fresh Corn Cakes** (p. 43).

SWEET-AND-SOUR PORK CHOPS
Ophelia Williams, Otterville, Missouri
(PICTURED ON PAGE 11)

        6 pork loin chops (about 3/4
          inch thick)
    1/2 cup pineapple juice
    1/2 cup ketchup
        2 tablespoons honey
        2 tablespoons white wine
          vinegar
    1-1/2 teaspoons Dijon mustard
    1/4 teaspoon salt
        4 teaspoons cornstarch
        2 tablespoons water

Place pork chops in a 13-in. x 9-in. x 2-in. baking dish. In a bowl, combine pineapple juice, ketchup, honey, vinegar, mustard and salt. Pour over the chops. Cover and bake at 350° for 30 minutes. Uncover and bake about 30 minutes longer or until the meat is tender. Remove chops to a serving platter and keep warm. Strain pan juices into a saucepan. Combine cornstarch and water; add to pan juices. Cook and stir until thickened and bubbly; cook and stir 2 minutes longer. Serve immediately over chops. **Yield:** 6 servings.

CHICKEN ENCHILADAS
Mary Anne McWhirter, Pearland, Texas

        2 cups diced cooked chicken
        2 cups (8 ounces) shredded
          Monterey Jack cheese
        1 can (2-1/4 ounces) sliced ripe
          olives, drained
        2 teaspoons dried parsley flakes
    1/2 teaspoon garlic powder
    1/2 teaspoon salt
    1/8 teaspoon pepper
        6 to 8 flour tortillas (8 inches)
SAUCE:
        1 medium onion, diced
    1/2 green pepper, diced
        1 tablespoon cooking oil
        1 can (4 ounces) chopped
          green chilies
        1 can (15 ounces) tomato sauce
        2 teaspoons chili powder
        1 teaspoon sugar
    1/2 teaspoon garlic powder
        1 cup (4 ounces) shredded
          cheddar cheese

Combine first seven ingredients. Divide evenly among tortillas. Roll up and place, seam side down, in a 13-in. x 9-in. x 2-in. baking pan. For sauce, in a skillet, saute onion and green pepper in oil until tender. Add chilies, tomato sauce, chili powder, sugar and garlic powder; mix well. Pour over tortillas.

Cover with foil. Bake at 350° for 30 minutes. Sprinkle with cheddar cheese and return to the oven for 10 minutes. **Yield:** 6-8 servings.

TROPICAL CHICKEN
Becky Palac, Escondido, California

        1 can (8 ounces) crushed
          pineapple, undrained
    1/3 cup lime juice
    1/4 teaspoon ground cloves
        4 boneless skinless chicken
          breast halves
    1/3 cup all-purpose flour
        1 teaspoon salt
        2 to 4 tablespoons cooking oil
    1/3 cup slivered almonds
    1/3 cup flaked coconut

In a bowl, combine pineapple, lime juice and cloves. Pound chicken to 1/4-in. thickness; add to marinade. Cover and refrigerate for at least 45 minutes. Drain, reserving marinade. Combine flour and salt; dredge chicken. In a skillet, brown chicken on both sides in oil. Place in a shallow baking dish. Add reserved marinade to skillet; cook until hot and bubbly. Pour over chicken. Sprinkle with almonds and coconut. Bake, uncovered, at 400° for 20-25 minutes. **Yield:** 4 servings.

TURKEY DRESSING PIE
De De Boekelheide, Northville, South Dakota
(PICTURED ON PAGE 72)

    3-1/2 to 4 cups leftover cooked
          turkey dressing
    1/2 cup turkey or chicken broth
        2 tablespoons butter or
          margarine, melted
        1 egg, beaten
    1/2 cup chopped onion
        1 tablespoon cooking oil
        3 cups diced leftover cooked
          turkey
        1 cup leftover turkey gravy
        1 cup peas, optional
        2 tablespoons dried parsley
          flakes
        2 tablespoons diced pimientos
        1 teaspoon Worcestershire
          sauce
    1/2 teaspoon dried thyme
        4 slices process American
          cheese, optional

In a large bowl, combine dressing, broth, butter and egg; mix well. Press into the bottom and up the sides of an ungreased 10-in. pie plate; set aside. In a large skillet, saute onion in oil until ten-

der. Stir in turkey, gravy, peas if desired, parsley, pimientos, Worcestershire sauce and thyme; heat through. Pour over crust. Bake at 375° for 20 minutes or until golden. If desired, arrange cheese slices on top of pie and return to oven for 5 minutes or until cheese is melted. **Yield:** 6 servings.

WILD RICE QUICHE
Dotty Egge, Pelican Rapids, Minnesota
(PICTURED ON COVER AND PAGE 26)

        1 unbaked pastry shell
          (9 inches)
    1/3 cup chopped Canadian
          bacon or fully cooked ham
        1 small onion, finely chopped
        1 tablespoon butter or
          margarine
        1 cup (4 ounces) shredded
          Monterey Jack cheese
        1 cup cooked wild rice
        3 eggs
    1-1/2 cups light cream
    1/2 teaspoon salt
Snipped parsley, optional

Bake crust at 425° for 5 minutes. Remove from the oven and set aside. Reduce heat to 325°. In a skillet, saute Canadian bacon or ham and onion in butter until onion is tender. Spoon into the crust. Sprinkle with cheese and wild rice. In a small bowl, beat eggs, cream and salt. Pour over all. Bake at 325° for 35 minutes or until a knife inserted near the center comes out clean. Let stand 10 minutes before cutting. Garnish with parsley if desired. **Yield:** 6-8 servings.

MEXICAN PIZZA
Gail Reino, Franklinville, New York

        1 tube (8 ounces) refrigerated
          crescent rolls
        2 cups leftover thick chili
    1/2 cup sliced ripe olives
    1/4 cup chopped onion
    3/4 cup shredded cheddar
          cheese
    1/2 cup crushed corn chips
**Avocado slices, shredded lettuce,
     chopped tomatoes and/or sour
     cream, optional**

Unroll the crescent roll dough; pat into the bottom and up the sides of an ungreased 13-in. x 9-in. x 2-in. baking pan. Pinch edges together to seal. Bake at 400° for 10 minutes. In a bowl, combine the chili, olives and onion. Spread evenly over baked crust. Sprinkle with cheese and corn chips. Bake for 8-10 minutes or until bubbly. Top with avocado, lettuce, tomatoes and/or sour cream if desired. **Yield:** 6-8 servings.

PARMESAN CHICKEN
Wendy Masters, Grand Valley, Ontario
(PICTURED ON PAGE 23)

3/4 cup coarsely crushed saltines
1/3 cup grated Parmesan cheese
1/2 teaspoon salt
1/2 teaspoon celery salt
1/2 teaspoon paprika
1/4 teaspoon onion salt
3 tablespoons evaporated milk
3 tablespoons vegetable oil
1 broiler-fryer chicken (about
   3-1/2 pounds), cut up

Combine first six ingredients in a shallow dish. In another dish, combine milk and oil. Dip chicken pieces into milk mixture, then roll in the Parmesan mixture. Place chicken, skin side up, in a shallow baking pan. Bake, uncovered, at 375° for 1 hour or until chicken is tender and no longer pink. **Yield:** 4-6 servings.

BARBECUED BEEF SANDWICHES
Karen Ann Bland, Gove, Kansas

1 boneless beef brisket (2-1/2
   pounds)
1/2 cup vegetable oil
1/3 cup ketchup
1/4 cup red wine vinegar
1/4 cup minced onion
1 tablespoon Worcestershire
   sauce
1-1/2 teaspoons salt
1 teaspoon dried oregano
1/2 teaspoon dry mustard
1/4 teaspoon cayenne pepper
1/4 teaspoon pepper
1/2 cup water
1 bottle (18 ounces) barbecue
   sauce
Hamburger buns

Place brisket in a large Dutch oven or soup kettle. Combine next 10 ingredients; pour over brisket. Add water; bring to a boil. Reduce heat; cover and simmer for 4-1/2 to 5 hours or until meat is tender. Remove brisket and discard marinade. Shred meat; return to Dutch oven. Add barbecue sauce and cook until heated through, stirring frequently. To serve, spoon onto hamburger buns. **Yield:** 10-12 servings.

SUNDAY FRIED CHICKEN
Carolyn Burton, Evanston, Wyoming

3 cups all-purpose flour
2 to 3 teaspoons poultry
   seasoning
2 teaspoons paprika
2 to 3 teaspoons onion powder
1 to 2 teaspoons garlic powder
1/2 teaspoon salt
Dash pepper
2 eggs
1 tablespoon milk
2 broiler-fryer chickens
   (3 pounds *each*), cut up *or* 16
   of your favorite poultry pieces
Cooking oil

Combine dry ingredients in a plastic bag. In a bowl, lightly beat eggs and milk. Dip chicken pieces in egg mixture and shake off excess. Shake a few chicken pieces in the bag at a time, coating well. In an electric skillet, heat 1/4 in. of oil to 350°; brown chicken on all sides. Reduce heat to 275° and continue cooking for 30 minutes. **Yield:** 6-8 servings.

ONE-DISH PORK CHOP DINNER
Pat Waymire, Yellow Springs, Ohio
(PICTURED ON PAGE 31)

 This tasty dish uses less sugar, salt and fat. Recipe includes *Diabetic Exchanges.*

8 pork chops (1/2 inch thick)
1/3 cup all-purpose flour
1/4 cup butter *or* margarine
Salt and pepper to taste
2 cups apple juice, *divided*
2 pounds small red potatoes
1 pound *or* 1 jar (16 ounces)
   small whole onions, drained
1 pound carrots, peeled and
   cut into 3-inch pieces
6 to 8 cups shredded cabbage

Coat pork chops in flour; reserve excess flour. In a large Dutch oven, melt butter over medium-high heat. Brown chops on both sides. Season with salt and pepper if desired. Remove and set aside. Stir reserved flour into pan; cook and stir until a paste forms. Gradually whisk in 1-1/2 cups apple juice; blend until smooth. Return chops to Dutch oven; cover and bake at 350° for 30 minutes. Add potatoes, onions, carrots and remaining apple juice. Cover and bake 30 minutes longer. Top with cabbage; cover and bake for 1 to 1-1/2 hours or until the pork chops are tender, basting occasionally with juices. **Yield:** 8 servings. **Diabetic Exchanges:** One

serving (prepared with margarine and without additional salt) equals 2 meat, 2 starch, 2 vegetable, 2-1/2 fat; also, 464 calories, 333 mg sodium, 56 mg cholesterol, 43 gm carbohydrate, 19 gm protein, 24 gm fat.

MY MOTHER'S MAC AND CHEESE
Phyllis Burkland, Portland, Oregon

2 cups elbow macaroni, cooked
   and drained
1 can (28 ounces) tomatoes with
   liquid, cut up
1/2 teaspoon onion salt, optional
1/4 teaspoon pepper
2 cups (8 ounces) shredded
   cheddar cheese, *divided*
2 tablespoons butter *or*
   margarine

In a bowl, combine macaroni, tomatoes, onion salt, pepper and 1-1/2 cups cheddar cheese. Pour into a greased 2-qt. baking dish. Dot with butter. Bake, uncovered, at 350° for 45 minutes. Sprinkle with remaining cheese; bake 15 minutes longer. **Yield:** 4 servings.

CHICKEN AND OYSTER PIE
Mrs. Vernon Gergley, Lititz, Pennsylvania

1/4 cup all-purpose flour
3 cups chicken broth, *divided*
4 cups cubed cooked peeled
   potatoes
3 cups chopped cooked chicken
1 pint shucked oysters, drained
   and chopped *or* 2 cans
   (8 ounces *each*) whole oysters,
   drained and chopped
1 package (16 ounces) frozen
   peas, thawed
1/2 cup chopped celery
2 hard-cooked eggs, chopped
1 tablespoon snipped fresh
   parsley
Butter *or* margarine
Pastry for double-crust pie

In a large saucepan, stir flour and 1/2 cup chicken broth until smooth. Add remaining broth; cook and stir until thickened and bubbly. Cook and stir 1 minute more. Remove from the heat. Add the potatoes, chicken, oysters, peas, celery, eggs and parsley; mix gently. Pour into a greased 13-in. x 9-in. x 2-in. baking dish. Dot with butter. Roll pastry into a 14-in. x 10-in. rectangle; place over chicken mixture. Seal pastry edges to sides of baking dish. Cut steam vents in top of pastry. Bake at 425° for 35 minutes or until golden brown. **Yield:** 8-10 servings.

Barbecuing is a perfectly fun way to enjoy the outdoors, especially when the recipes are easy-to-make and delicious! Enjoy tangy Picante-Dijon Grilled Chicken with cool, refreshing Macaroni Salad with Basil Dressing. Rich, moist Fudgy Brownies are irresistible!

THE GREAT OUTDOORS. Clockwise from the bottom: **Picante-Dijon Grilled Chicken** (p. 49), **Fudgy Brownies** (p. 67) and **Macaroni Salad with Basil Dressing** (p. 20).

POT ROAST WITH SPAGHETTI

Ellen Cote, Sealy, Texas

2 tablespoons cooking oil
2 tablespoons butter *or* margarine
1 chuck roast (2 to 3 pounds)
1 garlic clove, minced
1 small onion, chopped
2 teaspoons dried oregano
1 teaspoon dried thyme
1/2 teaspoon dried basil
1/8 teaspoon ground cinnamon
1-1/2 to 2 teaspoons salt
1/2 teaspoon pepper
3 cups hot water
3 cans (6 ounces *each*) tomato paste
1 pound spaghetti, cooked and drained
Grated Parmesan cheese, optional

Heat oil and butter in a Dutch oven; brown roast evenly on all sides. Remove and set aside. Add garlic, onion and seasonings. Cook slowly for about 5 minutes, stirring constantly. Stir in water and tomato paste; blend well. Return roast to Dutch oven and spoon sauce over it. Cover and simmer for 2-1/2 to 3 hours or until the meat is tender. Remove roast; cut into slices. Serve with spaghetti and sauce. Sprinkle with Parmesan cheese if desired. **Yield:** 6-8 servings.

PICANTE-DIJON GRILLED CHICKEN

Karen Page, St. Louis, Missouri
(PICTURED ON OPPOSITE PAGE)

8 chicken breast halves, skinned and boned
1-1/2 cups picante sauce
2 tablespoons Dijon mustard
1/4 cup packed brown sugar

Pound chicken breasts to about 1/2-in. thickness; set aside. Combine picante sauce, mustard and sugar; mix well. Place chicken over medium-hot coals; brush generously with sauce. Grill about 6-8 minutes per side or until chicken is tender and no longer pink, brushing occasionally with remaining sauce. **Yield:** 8 servings.

BARBECUED BEEF ON BUNS

Carol Scharl, Oostburg, Wisconsin

1 boneless beef chuck roast (3 pounds)
1 medium onion, chopped

1/2 cup chopped celery
Water
1-1/2 cups ketchup
1/4 cup packed brown sugar
1/4 cup vinegar
2 tablespoons dry mustard
2 teaspoons salt
2 teaspoons Worcestershire sauce
1 teaspoon chili powder
1/2 teaspoon paprika
1/2 teaspoon garlic salt
Few drops hot pepper sauce
Hamburger buns

Place beef, onion and celery in a Dutch oven; add water to almost cover meat. Bring to a boil; reduce heat. Cover and simmer for 2-1/2 to 3 hours or until meat is tender. Remove meat; strain and reserve cooking liquid. Trim and shred meat; return to Dutch oven. Add 2 cups of strained cooking liquid (save remaining cooking liquid) and chill. Skim and discard fat. Add ketchup, brown sugar, vinegar and seasonings. Cover and simmer for 1 hour, stirring occasionally. If mixture becomes too thick, add additional reserved cooking liquid. Serve on hamburger buns. **Yield:** 15-20 servings.

PORK CHOPS WITH CORN DRESSING

June Hassler, Sultan, Washington
(PICTURED ON PAGE 18)

1 egg, beaten
2 cups soft bread crumbs
1 can (17 ounces) whole kernel corn, drained *or* 1-1/2 cups cooked whole kernel corn
1/4 cup water
1/2 cup chopped green pepper
1 small onion, chopped
1 teaspoon Worcestershire sauce
2 tablespoons cooking oil
6 butterfly (boneless) pork chops (about 1 inch thick)
Salt and pepper to taste
1 can (10-3/4 ounces) condensed cream of mushroom soup, undiluted
1/2 soup can milk

In a bowl, combine egg, bread crumbs, corn, water, green pepper, onion and Worcestershire sauce; set aside. In a large ovenproof skillet or a Dutch oven, heat oil over medium-high. Lightly brown pork chops on both sides. Season with salt and pepper. Top with corn dressing mixture. Add enough water to cover bottom of pan. Bake, uncovered, at 350° for about 1 hour or until pork is tender. Add additional water to pan if necessary. Remove pork chops and dressing to a

serving platter; keep warm. Add soup and milk to pan drippings. Cook and stir over medium heat until hot and bubbly. Serve with pork chops. **Yield:** 6 servings.

CHURCH SUPPER HOT DISH

Norma Turner, Haslett, Michigan

1 pound ground beef
2 cups sliced peeled potatoes
2 cups finely chopped celery
3/4 cup finely chopped carrots
1/4 cup finely chopped green pepper
1/4 cup finely chopped onion
2 tablespoons butter *or* margarine
1 cup water
2 cans (10-3/4 ounces *each*) condensed cream of mushroom soup, undiluted
1 can (5 ounces) chow mein noodles, *divided*
1 cup (4 ounces) shredded cheddar cheese

In a skillet, brown beef. Drain and set aside. In a large saucepan or another skillet, saute potatoes, celery, carrots, green pepper and onion in butter for 5 minutes. Add water; cover and simmer for 10 minutes. Add soup and cooked ground beef; mix well. Sprinkle half of the chow mein noodles into a greased shallow 2-qt. baking dish. Spoon meat mixture over noodles. Cover and bake at 350° for 20 minutes. Top with the cheese and remaining noodles. Bake, uncovered, 10 minutes longer or until heated through. **Yield:** 8 servings.

SAUSAGE AND SAUERKRAUT CASSEROLE

Deltie Tackette, Eubank, Kentucky

2 cups uncooked elbow macaroni
1 pound bulk pork sausage
1 can (16 ounces) tomatoes with liquid, cut up
1 cup sauerkraut
1 teaspoon sugar
4 to 5 tablespoons shredded cheddar cheese

Cook macaroni according to package directions. Meanwhile, brown sausage in a skillet; drain, reserving 1 tablespoon drippings. Add tomatoes, sauerkraut and sugar to sausage and cook for 2 minutes. Drain macaroni; stir into skillet along with cheese. Spoon into a greased 8-in. square baking dish. Bake, uncovered, at 350° for 20 minutes. **Yield:** 4-6 servings.

*B*reads, coffee cakes and muffins are guaranteed to bring a touch of spring to your table. Just look at the colorful and tasty Raspberry Cream Cheese Coffee Cake! Blueberry Buckle is sure to become a family favorite...both because of its sweet flavor and its ease to make.

SPRING SWEETS. Clockwise from the top: **Raspberry Cream Cheese Coffee Cake** (p. 51), **Blueberry Buckle** (p. 51) and **Strawberry Ice Cream** (p. 73).

Breads, Coffee Cakes & Muffins

RASPBERRY CREAM CHEESE COFFEE CAKE

Susan Litwiller, Medford, Oregon
(PICTURED ON OPPOSITE PAGE)

2-1/4 cups all-purpose flour
3/4 cup sugar
3/4 cup butter *or* margarine
1/2 teaspoon baking powder
1/2 teaspoon baking soda
1/2 teaspoon salt
3/4 cup sour cream
1 egg, beaten
1-1/2 teaspoons almond extract
FILLING:
1 package (8 ounces) cream cheese, softened
1/2 cup sugar
1 egg
1/2 cup raspberry jam
1/2 cup slivered almonds

In a large mixing bowl, combine flour and sugar. Cut in butter as for pastry. Remove 1 cup and set aside. To the remaining crumbs, add baking powder, baking soda, salt, sour cream, egg and almond extract; mix well. Spread in the bottom and 2 in. up the sides of a 9-in. springform pan. For the filling, beat cream cheese, sugar and egg in a small bowl; mix well. Pour over batter; spoon raspberry jam on top. Sprinkle with almonds and reserved crumbs. Bake at 350° for 55-60 minutes. Let stand 15 minutes before removing sides from pan. **Yield:** 9-12 servings.

HONEY-WHEAT SUNFLOWER BREAD

Lillian Wittler, Wayne, Nebraska

 This tasty dish uses less sugar, salt and fat. Recipe includes *Diabetic Exchanges*.

2 cups water (120° to 130°)
2-3/4 to 3-1/4 cups all-purpose *or* bread flour
2 packages (1/4 ounce *each*) active dry yeast
1 tablespoon sugar
2 cups whole wheat flour
1 cup old-fashioned oats
1/3 cup instant dry milk powder
1/4 cup butter *or* margarine,
melted and cooled
1/4 cup honey
2 teaspoons salt
1 cup unsalted sunflower seeds

In a mixing bowl, combine the water, 2 cups all-purpose or bread flour, yeast and sugar. Beat on low speed for 3 minutes. Cover and let rise in a warm place until doubled, about 30 minutes. (Mixture will be spongy.) Stir in whole wheat flour, oats, milk powder, butter, honey and salt; mix well. Stir in sunflower seeds and as much of the remaining all-purpose or bread flour as you can with a spoon. Turn out onto a lightly floured surface and knead until smooth and elastic, about 6-8 minutes. Shape into a ball. Place in a greased bowl; turn once. Cover and let rise until doubled, about 30-45 minutes. Punch down and divide in half. Cover and let rest 10 minutes. Shape into two loaves; place in two greased 8-in. x 4-in. x 2-in. loaf pans. Cover and let rise until doubled, about 30 minutes. Bake at 375° for 20 minutes. Cover with foil; bake 15 minutes longer. Remove from pans and cool on wire racks. **Yield:** 2 loaves (16 slices each). **Diabetic Exchanges:** One serving (one slice, prepared with margarine) equals 1 fat, 1 starch; also, 121 calories, 162 mg sodium, trace cholesterol, 18 gm carbohydrate, 4 gm protein, 4 gm fat.

BANANA BREAD

Irene Evans, Bradley, Illinois

2/3 cup sugar
1/3 cup shortening
2 cups all-purpose flour
2 teaspoons baking powder
1/4 teaspoon baking soda
1/4 teaspoon salt
1 cup mashed ripe bananas

Note: This recipe does NOT contain eggs or milk. In a large bowl, cream sugar and shortening for about 5 minutes (mixture does not get smooth). Combine flour, baking powder, baking soda and salt; add to creamed mixture alternately with bananas, beating after each addition (the batter will be thick). Spoon into a greased 9-in. x 5-in. x 3-in. loaf pan. Bake at 350° for 40-45 minutes or until bread tests done with a toothpick. Cool in pan for 10 minutes before removing to a wire rack. **Yield:** 1 loaf.

BLUEBERRY BUCKLE

Debbie Thackrah, Latrobe, Pennsylvania
(PICTURED ON OPPOSITE PAGE)

1/2 cup shortening
1 cup sugar, *divided*
1 egg, beaten
2-1/2 cups all-purpose flour, *divided*
2-1/2 teaspoons baking powder
1/2 teaspoon salt
1/2 cup milk
2 cups fresh *or* frozen blueberries
2 teaspoons lemon juice
1/2 teaspoon ground cinnamon
1/4 cup butter *or* margarine

In a mixing bowl, cream shortening and 1/2 cup sugar. Add egg and mix well. Combine 2 cups flour, baking powder and salt; add to creamed mixture alternately with the milk. Spread into a greased 9-in. square baking pan. Toss blueberries with lemon juice; sprinkle over batter. In a small bowl, combine cinnamon and remaining sugar and flour; cut in butter until mixture is the size of peas. Sprinkle over berries. Bake at 350° for 60-65 minutes. **Yield:** 9-12 servings.

BREAKFAST OATMEAL MUFFINS

Edna Bowyer, Simcoe, Ontario

1 cup all-purpose flour
1 cup packed brown sugar
1 teaspoon baking powder
1 teaspoon baking soda
1/2 cup vegetable oil
2 eggs, lightly beaten
1 cup leftover oatmeal
1 cup raisins
1 teaspoon vanilla extract

In a large bowl, combine flour, brown sugar, baking powder and baking soda. In another bowl, combine oil, eggs, oatmeal, raisins and vanilla; add to dry ingredients and stir just until moistened (the batter will be thin). Spoon into 12 greased muffin cups. Bake at 350° for 18 minutes or until the muffins test done. **Yield:** 1 dozen.

FREEZE-AND-BAKE ROLLS

Jayne Duce, Raymond, Alberta
(PICTURED ON PAGE 40)

 This tasty dish uses less sugar, salt and fat. Recipe includes *Diabetic Exchanges*.

2 packages (1/4 ounce *each***)**
active dry yeast
1-1/2 cups warm water (110° to 115°)
1/2 cup plus 2 teaspoons sugar,
divided
1-1/2 cups warm milk (110° to 115°)
1/4 cup vegetable oil
4 teaspoons salt
7-1/2 to 8-1/2 cups all-purpose flour
Butter *or* **margarine, melted**

In a large mixing bowl, dissolve yeast in water. Add 2 teaspoons sugar; let stand for 5 minutes. Add milk, oil, salt and remaining sugar. Add enough flour to form a stiff dough. Turn out onto a floured surface; knead until smooth and elastic, about 6-8 minutes. Place in a greased bowl, turning once to grease top. Cover and let rise in a warm place until doubled, about 1-1/2 hours. Punch dough down. Divide into four pieces. Cover three pieces with plastic wrap. Divide one piece into 12 balls. To form knots, roll each ball into a 10-in. rope; tie into a knot and pinch ends together. Repeat with remaining dough. Place rolls on greased baking sheets; brush with melted butter. Cover and let rise until doubled, about 20-30 minutes. To serve immediately, bake at 375° for 15-18 minutes. To freeze for later use, partially bake at 300° for 15 minutes. Allow to cool; freeze. Reheat frozen rolls at 375° for 12-15 minutes or until browned. **Yield:** 4 dozen. **Diabetic Exchanges:** One serving (one roll, prepared with skim milk) equals 1-1/2 starch; also, 120 calories, 197 mg sodium, trace cholesterol, 24 gm carbohydrate, 3 gm protein, 1 gm fat.

SOFT PRETZELS

Karen Stewart-Linkhart, Xenia, Ohio

2 packages (1/4 ounce *each***)**
active dry yeast
2 cups warm water (110° to 115°)
1/2 cup sugar
2 teaspoons salt
1/4 cup butter *or* **margarine,**
softened
1 egg
6-1/2 to 7-1/2 cups all-purpose flour
1 egg yolk
2 tablespoons water
Coarse salt, optional

In a large bowl, dissolve yeast in warm water. Add sugar, salt, butter and egg. Stir in 3 cups of flour; mix until smooth.

Add enough additional flour to make a stiff dough. Cover bowl tightly with foil; refrigerate for 2-24 hours. Punch dough down and divide in half. On a lightly floured surface, cut each half into 16 equal pieces. Roll each piece into a 20-in. rope. Shape into the traditional pretzel shape and place on a greased baking sheet. In a small bowl, combine egg yolk and water; brush over the pretzels. Sprinkle with salt if desired. Cover and let rise in a warm place until doubled, about 25 minutes. Bake at 400° for 15 minutes or until brown. **Yield:** 32 pretzels.

MAPLE-PECAN CORN BREAD

Shirley Brownell, Amsterdam, New York
(PICTURED ON BACK COVER)

1 cup all-purpose flour
1 cup yellow cornmeal
1 teaspoon baking powder
1 teaspoon baking soda
1 teaspoon salt
3 tablespoons butter *or*
margarine, softened
2 tablespoons brown sugar
2 eggs
1/3 cup pure maple syrup
3/4 cup buttermilk
1/2 cup chopped pecans
Additional maple syrup, optional

Combine flour, cornmeal, baking powder, baking soda and salt; set aside. In a mixing bowl, combine butter, sugar and eggs; mix well. Add syrup and buttermilk. Stir in dry ingredients just until moistened. Stir in pecans. Pour into a greased 8-1/2-in. x 4-1/2-in. x 2-1/2-in. loaf pan. Bake at 350° for 35-40 minutes or until bread tests done. Cool for 10 minutes in pan. Serve warm with syrup if desired or allow to cool. **Yield:** 1 loaf.

CHOCOLATE CHIP PUMPKIN BREAD

Vicki Raboine, Kansasville, Wisconsin

1 cup packed brown sugar
1 cup sugar
2/3 cup butter *or* **margarine,**
softened
3 eggs
2-1/3 cups all-purpose flour
1-1/2 cups canned pumpkin
1/2 cup water
2 teaspoons baking soda
1 teaspoon ground cinnamon
1 teaspoon salt
1/2 teaspoon ground cloves
2 cups (12 ounces)
semisweet chocolate chips

In a mixing bowl, cream sugars, butter and eggs. Add flour, pumpkin, water, baking soda, cinnamon, salt and cloves. Mix thoroughly. Fold in chocolate chips. Pour into four greased and floured 6-in. x 3-in. x 2-in. loaf pans. Bake at 350° for 45 minutes or until breads test done. **Yield:** 4 mini loaves.

CHRISTMAS WREATHS

Margaret Foreman, La Verne, California

FILLING:
9 ounces pitted prunes,
cooked, drained and mashed
(about 1-1/2 cups)
1-1/2 cups chopped peeled apples
3/4 cup finely chopped walnuts
3/4 cup packed brown sugar
1/3 cup sugar
1/2 teaspoon ground cinnamon
1/2 teaspoon salt
DOUGH:
1 cup warm milk (110° to 115°)
1/2 cup sugar
1 teaspoon salt
2 packages (1/4 ounce *each***)**
active dry yeast
2 eggs, lightly beaten
1/2 cup shortening
4-1/2 to 5 cups all-purpose flour
ICING:
2 cups confectioners' sugar
2 to 3 tablespoons milk
1 teaspoon vanilla extract
Candied cherries, optional

Combine all filling ingredients in a bowl; cover and refrigerate until ready to use. For dough, combine warm milk, sugar, salt and yeast in a mixing bowl. Let stand for 5 minutes. Add eggs, shortening and 3 cups flour; mix until smooth. Add enough of the remaining flour to form a soft dough. Turn out onto a floured surface; knead until smooth and elastic, about 6-8 minutes. Place in a greased bowl, turning once to grease top. Cover and let rise in a warm place until doubled, about 1 to 1-1/2 hours. Punch dough down; divide in half. Roll each half into an 18-in. x 9-in. rectangle. Spread each with half of the filling. Starting at the long end, roll up tightly and seal edges. Place on a greased baking sheet, sealing ends together and forming a ring. With a scissors, cut two-thirds of the way through the ring at 1-in. intervals. Carefully turn each section onto its side. Cover and let rise until nearly doubled, 30-45 minutes. Bake at 350° for 25-30 minutes or until golden. Cool for 20 minutes. Beat confectioners' sugar, milk and vanilla until smooth. Remove wreaths to a platter; drizzle with icing while warm. Decorate with candied cherries if desired. **Yield:** 2 loaves.

GOLDEN POTATO ROLLS

Noni Ruegner, Salt Lake City, Utah
(PICTURED ON PAGE 72)

 This tasty dish uses less sugar, salt and fat. Recipe includes *Diabetic Exchanges*.

- 1 package (1/4 ounce) active dry yeast
- 1/2 cup warm water (110° to 115°)
- 1 cup milk
- 3/4 cup shortening *or* margarine
- 1-1/4 cups leftover mashed potatoes
- 1/2 cup sugar
- 2 teaspoons salt
- 8 to 8-1/2 cups all-purpose flour, *divided*
- 2 eggs, beaten

Dissolve yeast in water; set aside. In a saucepan, combine milk, shortening and potatoes; cook and stir over low heat just until shortening is melted. Remove from the heat and place in a large bowl with sugar, salt, 2 cups of flour and the yeast mixture. Add eggs; mix well. Cover loosely and allow to stand for 2 hours (the dough will be like a sponge). Stir in enough of the remaining flour to make a soft dough. Turn out onto a floured surface and knead until smooth and elastic, about 6 minutes. Place in a greased bowl, turning once to grease top. Cover and let rise in a warm place until doubled, about 1 hour. Punch down and divide into thirds. On a floured surface, roll each portion into a 12-in. circle. Cut each circle into 12 pie-shaped wedges. Beginning at the wide end, roll up each wedge. Place rolls, point side down, 2 in. apart on greased baking sheets. Cover and let rise 30 minutes or until nearly doubled. Bake at 400° for 15 minutes or until golden. **Yield:** 3 dozen. **Diabetic Exchanges:** One roll (prepared with skim milk and margarine) equals 1-1/2 starch, 1 fat; also, 170 calories, 168 mg sodium, 12 mg cholesterol, 28 gm carbohydrate, 4 gm protein, 5 gm fat.

HONEY-NUT BREAKFAST TWISTS

Holly Baird, Zurich, Montana

- 1 package (1/4 ounce) active dry yeast
- 1/4 cup warm water (105° to 115°)
- 2 tablespoons sugar
- 1 teaspoon salt
- 2 tablespoons butter *or* margarine, melted
- 1 cup (8 ounces) sour cream
- 1 egg
- 2-1/2 to 3 cups all-purpose flour

GLAZE:
- 1/3 cup packed brown sugar
- 3 tablespoons butter *or* margarine, melted
- 3 tablespoons honey, warmed
- 3 tablespoons heavy cream

FILLING:
- 1/3 cup butter *or* margarine, softened
- 1/4 cup finely chopped nuts
- 1/4 cup honey

In a mixing bowl, combine yeast and water; let stand 5 minutes. Stir in sugar, salt and butter. Add sour cream and egg; beat until smooth. Add 1-1/2 cups flour; blend at low speed until moistened. Beat 3 minutes at medium speed, scraping bowl twice. By hand, stir in enough remaining flour to make a soft dough. Turn out onto a floured surface; knead until smooth and elastic, about 5 minutes. Place in a greased bowl, turning once to grease top. Cover and let rise in a warm place until doubled, about 1 hour. Combine glaze ingredients; spread evenly in a 13-in. x 9-in. x 2-in. baking dish; set aside. Punch dough down. Roll into a 24-in. x 9-in. rectangle. Combine filling ingredients; spread over dough. Fold dough lengthwise over filling, forming a 12-in. x 9-in. rectangle. Cut lengthwise into six 9-in. x 2-in. pieces. Twist each piece loosely and place over glaze in baking dish. Cover and let rise until doubled, about 1 hour. Bake at 350° for 25-30 minutes or until golden brown. Invert pan onto a large platter; let set 1 minute before removing. Serve warm or refrigerate overnight. **Yield:** 6 servings.

CRANBERRY MUFFINS

Ronni Dufour, Lebanon, Connecticut
(PICTURED ON PAGE 62)

- 2 cups all-purpose flour
- 1 cup sugar
- 1-1/2 teaspoons baking powder
- 1 teaspoon ground nutmeg
- 1 teaspoon ground cinnamon
- 1/2 teaspoon baking soda
- 1/2 teaspoon ground ginger
- 1/2 teaspoon salt
- 2 teaspoons grated orange peel
- 1/2 cup shortening
- 3/4 cup orange juice
- 2 eggs, beaten
- 1 tablespoon vanilla extract
- 1-1/2 cups coarsely chopped cranberries
- 1-1/2 cups chopped pecans

In a large bowl, combine flour, sugar, baking powder, nutmeg, cinnamon, baking soda, ginger, salt and orange peel. Cut in shortening until crumbly. Stir in orange juice, eggs, and vanilla just until moistened. Fold in cranberries and nuts. Fill 18 greased or paper-lined muffin cups

two-thirds full. Bake at 375° for 18-20 minutes or until golden. **Yield:** 1-1/2 dozen.

STRAWBERRY RHUBARB COFFEE CAKE

Dorothy Morehouse, Massena, New York
(PICTURED ON PAGE 68)

FILLING:
- 3 cups sliced fresh *or* frozen rhubarb (1-inch pieces)
- 1 quart fresh strawberries, mashed
- 2 tablespoons lemon juice
- 1 cup sugar
- 1/3 cup cornstarch

CAKE:
- 3 cups all-purpose flour
- 1 cup sugar
- 1 teaspoon baking powder
- 1 teaspoon baking soda
- 1/2 teaspoon salt
- 1 cup butter *or* margarine, cut into pieces
- 1-1/2 cups buttermilk
- 2 eggs
- 1 teaspoon vanilla extract

TOPPING:
- 1/4 cup butter *or* margarine
- 3/4 cup all-purpose flour
- 3/4 cup sugar

In a large saucepan, combine rhubarb, strawberries and lemon juice. Cover and cook over medium heat about 5 minutes. Combine sugar and cornstarch; stir into saucepan. Bring to a boil, stirring constantly until thickened; remove from heat and set aside. In a large bowl, combine flour, sugar, baking powder, baking soda and salt. Cut in butter until mixture resembles coarse crumbs. Beat buttermilk, eggs and vanilla; stir into crumb mixture. Spread half of the batter evenly into a greased 13-in. x 9-in. x 2-in. baking dish. Carefully spread filling on top. Drop remaining batter by tablespoonfuls over filling. For topping, melt butter in a saucepan over low heat. Remove from heat; stir in flour and sugar until mixture resembles coarse crumbs. Sprinkle over batter. Lay foil on lower rack to catch any juicy fruit spillovers. Place coffee cake on middle rack; bake at 350° for 40-45 minutes. Cool in pan. Cut into squares. **Yield:** 16-20 servings.

EASY EQUIVALENTS

A pound of rhubarb equals 3 to 4 cups sliced or 2 cups of cooked and pureed rhubarb.

APRICOT BREAD
Ruth Jones, Maitland, Florida

   1 cup snipped dried apricots
   2 cups warm water
   1 cup sugar
   2 tablespoons butter *or*
      margarine, softened
   1 egg
   3/4 cup orange juice
   2 cups all-purpose flour
   2 teaspoons baking powder
   1/4 teaspoon baking soda
   1 teaspoon salt
   3/4 cup chopped nuts

Soak apricots in warm water for 30 minutes. Meanwhile, in a mixing bowl, cream the sugar, butter and egg. Stir in orange juice. Combine flour, baking powder, baking soda and salt; stir into creamed mixture just until combined. Drain apricots well; add to batter with nuts. Pour into a greased 9-in. x 5-in. x 3-in. loaf pan. Bake at 350° for 55 minutes or until bread tests done. Cool 10 minutes in pan before removing to a wire rack. **Yield:** 1 loaf.

PUMPKIN CINNAMON ROLLS
Janet Wells, Hazel Green, Kentucky

   2-3/4 to 3-1/4 cups all-purpose
      flour, *divided*
   1 package (1/4 ounce) active dry
      yeast
   1/2 cup solid-pack pumpkin
   2/3 cup milk
   2 tablespoons sugar
   4 tablespoons butter *or*
      margarine, *divided*
   1/2 teaspoon salt
   1 egg, beaten
   1/2 cup packed brown sugar
   1 teaspoon ground cinnamon
CARAMEL FROSTING:
   2 tablespoons butter *or*
      margarine
   1/4 cup packed brown sugar
   1 tablespoon milk
   1/4 teaspoon vanilla extract
Dash salt
   1/4 to 1/3 cup confectioners'
      sugar

In a mixing bowl, combine 1-1/2 cups flour and yeast; set aside. In a saucepan, heat and stir pumpkin, milk, sugar, 2 tablespoons butter and salt until warm (120°-130°) and butter is almost melted. Add to flour/yeast mixture along with egg. Beat on low speed for 30 seconds. Beat on high speed for 3 minutes. Stir in enough remaining flour to make a moderately stiff dough. Knead on a lightly floured surface until smooth and elastic, about 6-8 minutes. Place in a greased bowl, turning once to grease top. Cover

and let rise until doubled, about 1 hour. Roll into a 12-in. x 10-in. rectangle. Melt remaining butter; brush on dough. Combine brown sugar and cinnamon; sprinkle over dough. Roll dough, jelly roll style, starting with the longer side. Cut into 12 slices, 1 in. each. Place rolls, cut side down, in a greased 13-in. x 9-in. x 2-in. baking pan. Cover and let rise until doubled, about 30 minutes. Bake at 375° for 20-25 minutes or until golden brown. Cool on a wire rack. For frosting, melt butter in a saucepan; stir in brown sugar and milk. Cook and stir over medium-low heat for 1 minute. Stir in vanilla, salt and 1/4 cup confectioners' sugar; beat until well blended. Add more sugar, if necessary, to achieve desired consistency. Drizzle over rolls. **Yield:** 1 dozen.

CORN MUFFINS WITH HONEY BUTTER
Marilyn Platner, Marion, Iowa
(PICTURED ON PAGE 45)

   2 cups all-purpose flour
   2 cups yellow cornmeal
   1 cup dry milk powder
   1/4 cup sugar
   2 tablespoons baking powder
   1 teaspoon salt
   1/2 teaspoon baking soda
   2-2/3 cups water
   1/2 cup butter *or* margarine,
      melted
   2 eggs, beaten
   1 tablespoon lemon juice
HONEY BUTTER:
   2 tablespoons honey
   1/2 cup butter, softened
      (no substitutes)

In a bowl, combine flour, cornmeal, milk powder, sugar, baking powder, salt and baking soda. Add water, butter, eggs and lemon juice; stir until dry ingredients are moistened. Spoon into 24 greased muffin cups. Bake at 425° for 13-15 minutes. In a small mixing bowl, beat together honey and softened butter. Serve with the muffins. **Yield:** 2 dozen.

IRISH BREAD
Martha Glenn, Enid, Oklahoma
(PICTURED ON OPPOSITE PAGE)

   2-3/4 cups all-purpose flour,
      divided
   3 tablespoons sugar
   1 package (1/4 ounce) active
      dry yeast

   1/2 teaspoon salt
   1/2 teaspoon baking soda
   1 cup warm buttermilk
      (120° to 130°)
   2 tablespoons butter *or*
      margarine, melted
   3/4 cup raisins

In a mixing bowl, combine 2 cups flour, sugar, yeast, salt and baking soda. Combine buttermilk and butter; gradually add to dry ingredients and beat well. Turn out onto a lightly floured surface; knead in raisins and enough remaining flour to make a soft dough, about 6-8 minutes. Place in a greased bowl, turning once to grease top. Cover and let rise in a warm place until doubled, about 1-1/2 hours. Punch dough down. Knead on a lightly floured surface about 15 times, forming a smooth round ball. Place on a greased baking sheet. Press dough down to form an 8-in. circle. Cover and let rise until doubled, about 30 minutes. Sprinkle dough lightly with flour; cut a 4-in. cross about 1/4 in. deep on the top. Bake at 350° for 30 minutes or until bread tests done. Remove to a wire rack. **Yield:** 1 loaf.

APPLE CREAM COFFEE CAKE
Oriana Churchill, Londonderry, New Hampshire

   1/2 cup chopped walnuts
   2 teaspoons ground cinnamon
   1-1/2 cups sugar, *divided*
   1/2 cup butter *or* margarine,
      softened
   2 eggs
   1 teaspoon vanilla extract
   2 cups all-purpose flour
   1 teaspoon baking powder
   1 teaspoon baking soda
   1/2 teaspoon salt
   1 cup (8 ounces) sour cream
   1 medium apple, peeled, cored
      and thinly sliced

Combine nuts, cinnamon and 1/2 cup sugar; set aside. In a large mixing bowl, cream butter; gradually add remaining sugar, beating until light and fluffy. Add eggs, one at a time, beating well after each addition. Blend in vanilla. Combine dry ingredients; add to creamed mixture alternately with sour cream, beating well after each addition. Spread half of the batter in a well-greased 10-in. tube pan with a removable bottom. Top with apple slices; sprinkle with half of the nut mixture. Top with remaining batter, then with remaining nut mixture. Bake at 375° for 40 minutes or until cake tests done. Remove from oven; let stand 30 minutes. Loosen sides of cake; lift cake with removable bottom from pan. Cool. Before serving, carefully lift cake from pan. **Yield:** 12-16 servings.

Nothing welcomes your family home like the aroma of bread baking in the oven. Your family will love to slather the fresh-from-the-oven Irish Bread with sweet, soft butter. Serve it with Potato Soup with Spinach Dumplings or Steak and Onion Pie for a tasty, hearty meal.

BAKED GOODNESS. Clockwise from left: **Irish Bread** (p. 54), **Potato Soup with Spinach Dumplings** (p. 10) and **Steak and Onion Pie** (p. 38).

MEXICAN CORN BREAD
Donna Hypes, Ramona, California

- 1 cup yellow cornmeal
- 1 cup all-purpose flour
- 1 tablespoon baking powder
- 1 teaspoon salt
- 2 tablespoons sugar
- 1 cup buttermilk
- 1 egg, beaten
- 1 can (8-3/4 ounces) cream-style corn
- Dash hot pepper sauce
- 1/4 cup bacon drippings, melted
- 1/4 cup minced green onions with tops
- 1/2 cup shredded cheddar cheese

Combine first five ingredients in a large mixing bowl; set aside. In another bowl, combine buttermilk and egg; add corn and remaining ingredients. Pour over dry ingredients and stir just until blended. *Do not overmix.* Pour batter into a greased 8-in. square baking pan. Bake at 400° for 35 minutes or until bread tests done. Cool 5 minutes before cutting into squares. Serve warm or cold. **Yield:** 9 servings.

APPLE DANISH
Sandy Lynch, Decatur, Illinois
(PICTURED ON BACK COVER)

PASTRY:
- 3 cups all-purpose flour
- 1/2 teaspoon salt
- 1 cup shortening
- 1 egg yolk
- 1/2 cup milk

FILLING:
- 6 cups sliced peeled apples
- 1-1/2 cups sugar
- 1/4 cup butter *or* margarine, melted
- 2 tablespoons all-purpose flour
- 1 teaspoon ground cinnamon

GLAZE:
- 1 egg white, lightly beaten
- 1/2 cup confectioners' sugar
- 2 to 3 teaspoons water

In a mixing bowl, combine flour and salt; cut in shortening until mixture resembles coarse crumbs. Combine egg yolk and milk; add to flour mixture. Stir just until dough clings together. Divide dough in half. On a lightly floured surface, roll half of dough into a 15-in. x 10-in. rectangle; transfer to a greased 15-in. x 10-in. x 1-in. baking pan. Set aside. In a bowl, toss together filling ingredients; spoon over pastry in pan. Roll out remaining dough to another 15-in. x 10-in. rectangle. Place over filling. Brush with egg white. Bake at 375° for 40 minutes or un-

til golden brown. Cool on a wire rack. Combine the confectioners' sugar and enough water to achieve a drizzling consistency. Drizzle over warm pastry. Cut into squares. Serve warm or cold. **Yield:** 20-24 servings.

CHEERY CHERRY LOAF
Mina Dyck, Boissevain, Manitoba
(PICTURED ON PAGE 4)

- 1 jar (6 ounces) red maraschino cherries
- 2-1/2 cups all-purpose flour
- 1 cup sugar
- 4 teaspoons baking powder
- 1/2 teaspoon salt
- 2 eggs
- 2/3 cup milk
- 1/3 cup butter *or* margarine, melted
- 1 jar (8 ounces) green maraschino cherries, drained and cut up
- 1/2 cup chopped pecans
- 1 tablespoon grated orange peel

Drain red cherries, reserving liquid; add water, if needed, to liquid to equal 1/3 cup. Cut up cherries; set cherries and liquid aside. In a large bowl, combine flour, sugar, baking powder and salt. In a small bowl, lightly beat eggs. Add milk, butter and cherry liquid; stir into dry ingredients just until combined. Fold in red and green cherries, pecans and orange peel. Pour into a greased 9-in. x 5-in. x 3-in. loaf pan. Bake at 350° for 1 hour or until bread tests done. **Yield:** 1 loaf.

APPLE ZUCCHINI BREAD
Patti Dillingham, Scranton, Arkansas

- 4 cups all-purpose flour
- 1 tablespoon baking soda
- 1-1/2 teaspoons ground cinnamon
- 1/2 teaspoon ground nutmeg
- 1/4 teaspoon salt
- 5 eggs
- 1-1/2 cups vegetable oil
- 2 cups sugar
- 1 cup packed brown sugar
- 1 tablespoon vanilla extract
- 2 cups shredded unpeeled zucchini
- 1 cup shredded peeled apples
- 1-1/2 cups chopped pecans

In a large bowl, combine flour, baking soda, cinnamon, nutmeg and salt. In another bowl, beat eggs. Add oil, sugars and vanilla. Pour over dry ingredients; mix well. Stir in zucchini, apples and pecans (batter will be stiff). Spoon into three greased 8-in. x 4-in. x 3-in. loaf

pans. Bake at 350° for 50-55 minutes or until done. Cool in pans for 10 minutes before removing to a wire rack to cool completely. **Yield:** 3 loaves.

CARAMEL APPLE COFFEE CAKE
Ruth Turner, Marinette, Wisconsin

- 3 eggs
- 2 cups sugar
- 1-1/2 cups vegetable oil
- 2 teaspoons vanilla extract
- 3 cups all-purpose flour
- 1 teaspoon salt
- 1 teaspoon baking soda
- 3 cups chopped peeled apples
- 1 cup coarsely chopped pecans

TOPPING:
- 1/2 cup butter *or* margarine
- 1/4 cup milk
- 1 cup packed brown sugar
- Pinch salt

In a mixing bowl, beat eggs until foamy; gradually add sugar. Blend in oil and vanilla. Combine flour, salt and baking soda; add to egg mixture. Stir in apples and pecans. Pour into a greased 10-in. tube pan; bake at 350° for 1 hour and 15 minutes or until cake tests done. Cool in pan on a wire rack for 10 minutes. Remove cake to a serving platter. For topping, combine all ingredients in a saucepan; boil 3 minutes, stirring constantly. Slowly pour over warm cake (some topping will run down onto the serving platter). **Yield:** 12-16 servings.

QUICK & EASY

NUTTY RHUBARB MUFFINS
Mary Kay Morris, Cokato, Minnesota

- 3/4 cup packed brown sugar
- 1/2 cup buttermilk *or* sour milk
- 1/3 cup vegetable oil
- 1 egg, beaten
- 1 teaspoon vanilla extract
- 2 cups all-purpose flour
- 1/2 teaspoon baking soda
- 1/2 teaspoon salt
- 1 cup diced rhubarb
- 1/2 cup chopped nuts

TOPPING:
- 1/4 cup packed brown sugar
- 1/4 cup chopped nuts
- 1/2 teaspoon ground cinnamon

In a small mixing bowl, combine brown sugar, buttermilk, oil, egg and vanilla; mix well. Set aside. In a medium mixing bowl, combine flour, baking soda and salt. Add egg mixture; stir just until combined. Fold in rhubarb and nuts. Spoon the batter into 12 greased muffin cups. Mix together topping ingredients; sprinkle over tops of muffins. Bake at 375° for 20 minutes or until muffins test done. **Yield:** 1 dozen.

WALNUT-RAISIN BREAD
Charles Stuller, Winter Haven, Florida

    2 cups all-purpose flour
    1 teaspoon baking powder
1/2 teaspoon baking soda
1/2 teaspoon salt
1/2 cup butter *or* margarine, softened
3/4 cup sugar
    1 egg
1/4 cup orange juice
    1 can (8 ounces) crushed pineapple, undrained
    1 cup raisins
    1 cup chopped walnuts

In a mixing bowl, combine flour, baking powder, baking soda and salt; set aside. In another bowl, cream butter and sugar. Add egg and orange juice; beat well. Add 1/3 cup of flour mixture; beat until smooth. Mix in remaining flour mixture and the pineapple. Stir in raisins and walnuts. Pour into a greased 9-in. x 5-in. x 3-in. loaf pan. Bake at 350° for 60-70 minutes. Let cool in pan for 10 minutes. Remove to a wire rack to cool completely. **Yield:** 1 loaf.

KRIS KRINGLE STAR BREAD
Marilyn Kidder, Fruitland, Idaho

FILLING:
    1 cup chopped walnuts *or* filberts
1/3 cup honey
1/4 cup sugar
1/2 cup chopped maraschino cherries, blotted dry
BREAD:
    1 cup warm water (110° to 115°)
1/2 cup sugar
    1 teaspoon salt
    2 packages (1/4 ounce *each*) active dry yeast
    2 eggs, beaten
1/2 cup butter *or* margarine, softened
4-1/2 to 5 cups all-purpose flour
Confectioners' sugar icing

In a small bowl, combine filling ingredients. Set aside. In a mixing bowl, combine water, sugar and salt. Add yeast, stirring until dissolved. Let stand for 5 minutes, then stir in eggs and butter. Gradually add enough flour to form a soft dough. Turn dough onto a floured surface; knead until smooth and elastic, about 6-8 minutes. Place in a greased bowl, turning once to grease top. Cover and let rise in a warm place

until doubled, about 1 hour. Punch down. Divide dough in half; roll each half into a 14-in. circle. Transfer to two greased baking sheets. Cut five slits about 4 in. long into each circle. Place a spoonful of filling in the middle of each section, then spread a thin layer of filling in the center of each star. Fold the two outer edges of each section over each other to form star points. Pinch edges together to seal. Cover and let rise in a warm place until doubled, about 30 minutes. Bake at 350° for 25 minutes or until golden brown. Frost while warm with a confectioners' sugar icing. **Yield:** 2 breads.

COCONUT BREAD
Virginia Doyle, Pinedale, Wyoming

    3 cups all-purpose flour
    2 teaspoons baking powder
1/2 teaspoon baking soda
1/2 teaspoon salt
    2 cups sugar
    1 cup vegetable oil
    4 eggs, lightly beaten
    2 teaspoons coconut extract
    1 cup buttermilk
    1 cup shredded coconut
    1 cup chopped walnuts

Combine flour, baking powder, baking soda and salt; set aside. In a large bowl, combine sugar, oil, eggs and coconut extract. Add dry ingredients alternately with buttermilk; stir just until moistened. Fold in coconut and nuts. Pour into two greased and floured 8-1/2-in. x 4-1/2-in. x 2-1/2-in. loaf pans. Bake at 325° for 1 hour or until breads test done. Cool 10 minutes in pans before removing to a wire rack to cool completely. **Yield:** 2 loaves.

KATE SMITH COFFEE CAKE
Ruth Nast, Waterford, Connecticut

    1 egg
1/4 cup butter *or* margarine, melted
1/3 cup milk
    1 cup all-purpose flour
1/4 cup sugar
    2 teaspoons baking powder
1/4 teaspoon salt
    1 cup bran flakes, crushed
TOPPING:
    2 teaspoons butter *or* margarine, softened
    2 tablespoons brown sugar
1/3 cup bran flakes, crushed

In a mixing bowl, combine egg, butter and milk. Combine flour, sugar, baking powder and salt; stir into batter. Add bran flakes. Spread into a greased 8-in. round

baking pan. Combine topping ingredients; sprinkle over batter. Bake at 375° for 18-22 minutes or until cake tests done. Serve warm. **Yield:** 6 servings.

FRUIT AND NUT MUFFINS
Dorothy Boltman, Shorewood, Minnesota

    4 cups diced peeled tart baking apples (1/4-inch pieces)
    1 cup sugar
1-1/2 cups raisins
1-1/2 cups chopped nuts
    2 eggs
1/2 cup vegetable oil
    2 teaspoons vanilla extract
    2 cups all-purpose flour
1-1/2 teaspoons baking soda
    2 teaspoons ground cinnamon
1/8 teaspoon salt

In a large mixing bowl, combine apples, sugar, raisins and nuts; set aside. In another bowl, beat eggs, oil and vanilla; stir into apple mixture. Combine dry ingredients; carefully fold into apple mixture. Do not overmix. Fill 18 greased muffin cups almost to the top. Bake at 375° for 18-20 minutes or until muffins test done. **Yield:** 1-1/2 dozen.

RHUBARB PECAN MUFFINS
Mary Kubik, Lethbridge, Alberta
(PICTURED ON PAGE 74)

    2 cups all-purpose flour
3/4 cup sugar
1-1/2 teaspoons baking powder
1/2 teaspoon baking soda
    1 teaspoon salt
3/4 cup chopped pecans
    1 egg
1/4 cup vegetable oil
    2 teaspoons grated orange peel
3/4 cup orange juice
1-1/4 cups finely chopped rhubarb

In a large mixing bowl, combine flour, sugar, baking powder, baking soda, salt and nuts. In another bowl, combine egg, oil, orange peel and orange juice. Add to dry ingredients all at once and stir just until moistened. Stir in rhubarb. Fill 12 lightly greased muffin cups almost to the top. Bake at 375° for 25-30 minutes. **Yield:** 1 dozen.

SHARP TIP

It's easier to cut rhubarb into pieces with the kitchen shears than with a knife.

Cakes, cookies and candy are always on hand in any country cook's kitchen. Your family will love to dig into moist Cream Pound Cake topped with fresh fruit and whipped cream! But first, start out with a quick Salmon Spread appetizer and a satisfying meal of delicious Asparagus Leek Soup or flavorful Italian Sausage and Spinach Pie.

MOUTH-WATERING MORSELS. Clockwise from the top: **Cream Pound Cake** (p. 59), **Italian Sausage and Spinach Pie** (p. 39), **Asparagus Leek Soup** (p. 10) and **Salmon Spread** (p. 6).

Cakes, Cookies & Candy

CARROT CAKE
Melanie Habener, Santa Maria, California

3 eggs, beaten
3/4 cup vegetable oil
3/4 cup buttermilk
2 cups sugar
2 teaspoons vanilla extract
2 cups all-purpose flour
2 teaspoons ground cinnamon
2 teaspoons baking soda
1/2 teaspoon salt
1 can (8 ounces) crushed pineapple, undrained
2 cups grated carrots
1 cup raisins
1 cup chopped nuts
1 cup flaked coconut

CREAM CHEESE FROSTING:
1/2 cup butter *or* margarine, softened
1 package (8 ounces) cream cheese, softened
1 teaspoon vanilla extract
1 box (16 ounces) confectioners' sugar
2 tablespoons heavy cream

In a mixing bowl, combine eggs, oil, buttermilk, sugar and vanilla; mix well. Combine flour, cinnamon, baking soda and salt; stir into egg mixture. Stir in pineapple, carrots, raisins, nuts and coconut. Pour into a greased and floured 13-in. x 9-in. x 2-in. baking pan. Bake at 350° for 50-55 minutes or until cake tests done. *Do not overbake.* Remove to a wire rack to cool. In another mixing bowl, combine all frosting ingredients; beat until creamy. Spread on cooled cake. **Yield:** 12-16 servings.

WATERMELON COOKIES
A. Ruth Witmer, Stevens, Pennsylvania

3/4 cup butter *or* margarine
3/4 cup sugar
1 egg
1/2 teaspoon almond extract
2-1/4 cups all-purpose flour
1/4 teaspoon salt
1/4 teaspoon baking powder
Red and green food coloring
Dried currants
Sesame seeds

In a mixing bowl, cream butter, sugar, egg and extract until light and fluffy. Combine flour, salt and baking powder; stir into creamed mixture and mix well. Remove 1 cup of dough; set aside. At low speed, beat in enough red food coloring to tint dough deep red. Roll into a 3-1/2-in.-long tube; wrap in plastic wrap and refrigerate until firm, about 2 hours. Divide 1 cup of reserved dough into two pieces. To one piece, add enough green food coloring to tint dough deep green. Do not tint remaining piece of dough. Wrap each piece separately in plastic wrap; chill until firm, about 1 hour. On a floured sheet of waxed paper, roll untinted dough into an 8-1/2-in. x 3-1/2-in. rectangle. Place red dough along short end of rectangle. Roll up and encircle red dough with untinted dough; set aside. On floured waxed paper, roll the green dough into a 10-in. x 3-1/2-in. rectangle. Place tube of red/untinted dough along the short end of green dough. Roll up and encircle tube with green dough. Cover tightly with plastic wrap; refrigerate at least 8 hours or overnight. Unwrap dough and cut into 1/8-in. slices. Place 1 in. apart on ungreased baking sheets. Lightly press dried currants and sesame seeds into each slice to resemble watermelon seeds. Bake at 375° for 6-8 minutes or until cookies are firm but not brown. While still warm, cut each cookie in half or into pie-shaped wedges. Remove to a wire rack to cool. **Yield:** 3 dozen.

QUICK & EASY

EASY RHUBARB DESSERT
Deb Jesse, Storm Lake, Iowa

1 package (18-1/2 ounces) yellow cake mix
5 cups diced fresh or frozen rhubarb
1 cup sugar
1 cup heavy cream

Mix cake as instructed on package. Pour batter into a greased 13-in. x 9-in. x 2-in. baking pan. Spread rhubarb over batter. Sprinkle with sugar; pour cream over top. Do not mix. Bake at 350° for 35-40 minutes or until cake tests done. **Yield:** 12-16 servings.

CREAM POUND CAKE
Marguerite Bubon, Charlton, Massachusetts
(PICTURED ON OPPOSITE PAGE)

6 eggs
2-3/4 cups sugar
1 teaspoon vanilla extract
3 cups all-purpose flour
1 tablespoon baking powder
1/4 teaspoon salt
1 pint heavy cream

In a mixing bowl, beat eggs at high speed for 5 minutes or until pale yellow. Gradually beat in sugar and vanilla, mixing until sugar is dissolved. Combine flour, baking powder and salt; add to batter alternately with cream. Pour into a greased 10-in. tube pan. Bake at 350° for 60-70 minutes or until cake tests done. Cool in pan 15 minutes before removing to a wire rack to cool completely. **Yield:** 12-16 servings.

ADAMS COUNTY APPLE CAKE
Gretchen Berendt, Carroll Valley, Pennsylvania

3 cups all-purpose flour
1 tablespoon baking powder
2 cups plus 5 tablespoons sugar, *divided*
1 cup vegetable oil
4 eggs
1/3 cup orange juice
1/2 teaspoon salt
2-1/2 teaspoons vanilla extract
4 medium baking apples, peeled and thinly sliced
2 teaspoons ground cinnamon
Confectioners' sugar, optional

In a mixing bowl, combine flour, baking powder, 2 cups of the sugar, oil, eggs, orange juice, salt and vanilla. Beat until thoroughly combined. In another bowl, toss apples with cinnamon and remaining sugar. Spread one-third of batter in a greased 10-in. tube pan. Cover with half of the apples. Repeat layers. Spoon remaining batter over top. Bake at 350° for 1 hour and 30 minutes or until cake tests done. Cool in pan for 20 minutes before removing to a wire rack to cool completely. Just before serving, dust with confectioners' sugar if desired. **Yield:** 12-16 servings.

AMAZING CORN CAKE
Sallie Volz, Ypsilanti, Michigan

1 can (17 ounces) cream-style
   corn
1/2 cup packed brown sugar
3/4 cup sugar
3 eggs
1 cup vegetable oil
1 tablespoon baking powder
2-1/4 cups all-purpose flour
1 teaspoon baking soda
1 teaspoon salt
1 teaspoon ground cinnamon
1/2 cup raisins
1/2 cup chopped nuts
CARAMEL FROSTING:
4 tablespoons butter *or*
   margarine
1/2 cup packed brown sugar
1/4 cup milk
2 to 3 cups sifted
   confectioners' sugar

In a mixing bowl, combine corn and sugars. Add eggs and oil; beat until well blended. Combine dry ingredients; add to batter and mix well. Stir in raisins and nuts. Pour into a greased 13-in. x 9-in. x 2-in. baking pan. Bake at 350° for 30-35 minutes or until cake tests done. Cool thoroughly. For frosting, bring butter and brown sugar to a boil over medium heat. Remove from the heat. Stir in milk. Stir in confectioners' sugar until frosting is desired consistency. Frost cooled cake. **Yield:** 12-15 servings.

PRUNE CAKE
Betty Satterfield, Robbinsville, North Carolina

2 cups all-purpose flour
1-1/2 cups sugar
1 teaspoon baking soda
1 teaspoon ground nutmeg
1 teaspoon ground allspice
1 teaspoon ground cinnamon
1/2 teaspoon salt
1 cup vegetable oil
1 cup buttermilk
2 eggs, beaten
1 cup chopped cooked prunes,
   drained
1 cup chopped nuts
BUTTERMILK GLAZE:
1 cup sugar
1/2 cup butter *or* margarine
1/2 cup buttermilk
1 tablespoon light corn syrup
1/2 teaspoon baking soda

In a large mixing bowl, combine first seven ingredients. Add oil, buttermilk and eggs; mix well. Fold in prunes and nuts. Pour into a greased 13-in. x 9-in. x 2-in. baking pan. Bake at 325° for 40-45 minutes or until cake tests done. Remove

from oven and punch holes in top of cake with a wooden skewer or pick. Immediately combine glaze ingredients in a saucepan. Bring to a boil and boil for 2 minutes, stirring constantly; pour hot glaze over warm cake. Cool in pan. **Yield:** 12-16 servings.

ANGEL FOOD CANDY
Shelly Matthys, New Richmond, Wisconsin

1 cup sugar
1 cup dark corn syrup
1 tablespoon vinegar
1 tablespoon baking soda
1 pound chocolate almond
   bark, melted

In a heavy saucepan, combine sugar, corn syrup and vinegar. Cook over medium heat, stirring constantly, until sugar dissolves. Cook without stirring until the temperature reaches 300° (hard crack stage) on a candy thermometer. Do not overcook. Remove from the heat and quickly stir in baking soda. Pour into a buttered 13-in. x 9-in. x 2-in. baking pan. Do not spread candy; mixture will not fill pan. When cool, break into bite-size pieces. Dip into melted chocolate; place on waxed paper until the chocolate is firm. Store candy tightly covered. **Yield:** 1-1/2 pounds.

EASY STRAWBERRY SHORTCAKE
Sue Gronholz, Columbus, Wisconsin

 This tasty dish uses less sugar, salt and fat. Recipe includes *Diabetic Exchanges.*

2 cups all-purpose flour
2 tablespoons sugar
4 teaspoons baking powder
1/2 teaspoon salt
1/2 teaspoon cream of tartar
1/2 cup butter *or* margarine,
   softened
1 egg, beaten
2/3 cup milk
2 pints strawberries, sliced
Whipped cream, optional

In a bowl, combine flour, sugar, baking powder, salt and cream of tartar. Cut in butter until mixture is the size of peas. Add the egg and milk; mix well. Spread into a greased 8-in. square baking pan. Bake at 375° for 20-25 minutes. Cut into squares and top with strawberries and whipped cream if desired. **Yield:** 9 servings. **Diabetic Exchanges:** One serving (prepared with margarine and skim milk and served without whipped cream) equals 2 fat, 1-

3/4 starch; also, 217 calories, 436 mg sodium, 24 mg cholesterol, 27 gm carbohydrate, 5 gm protein, 11 gm fat.

PECAN-CHOCOLATE CHIP POUND CAKE
Ruth Ann Vernon, Hobe Sound, Florida
(PICTURED ON PAGE 30)

2-3/4 cups sugar
1-1/4 cups butter, softened
   (no substitutes)
5 eggs
1 teaspoon almond extract
3 cups all-purpose flour
1 teaspoon baking powder
1/4 teaspoon salt
1 cup milk
1 cup mini semisweet
   chocolate chips
1 cup chopped pecans

In a large mixing bowl, beat sugar, butter *(must be very soft but not melted)*, eggs and almond extract on low just until mixed. Beat on high for 5 minutes, scraping bowl occasionally. In a separate bowl, combine flour, baking powder and salt. On low speed, add flour mixture alternately with milk, mixing just until blended. Fold in chocolate chips. Sprinkle pecans in the bottom of a greased and floured 10-in. tube pan. Carefully pour batter over pecans. Bake at 325° for 1 hour and 40 minutes or until cake tests done. Cool 20 minutes in pan before removing to a wire rack to cool completely. **Yield:** 16-20 servings.

FRESH PEAR CAKE
Frances Lanier, Metter, Georgia

3 eggs
2 cups sugar
1-1/2 cups vegetable oil
3 cups all-purpose flour
2 teaspoons ground cinnamon
1 teaspoon salt
1 teaspoon baking soda
1-1/2 cups finely chopped peeled
   pears (about 2 medium)
1 teaspoon vanilla extract
1-1/4 cups confectioners' sugar
2 tablespoons milk

In a mixing bowl, beat eggs on medium speed. Gradually add sugar and oil; beat thoroughly. Combine flour, cinnamon, salt and baking soda; add to egg mixture and mix well. Stir in pears and vanilla. (The batter will be stiff.) Spoon into a greased and floured 10-in. tube pan. Bake at 350° for 60-65 minutes or until cake tests done. Let cool in pan 10 minutes before inverting onto a serving plate. In a small bowl, combine the confectioners' sugar and milk; beat until smooth. Drizzle over warm cake. Cool completely. **Yield:** 14-16 servings.

FUDGE TRUFFLE CHEESECAKE
S.E. Sanborn, Perry, Michigan
(PICTURED ON PAGE 36)

CRUST:
- 1-1/2 cups vanilla wafer crumbs
- 1/2 cup confectioners' sugar
- 1/3 cup baking cocoa
- 1/3 cup butter *or* margarine, melted

FILLING:
- 3 packages (8 ounces *each*) cream cheese, softened
- 1 can (14 ounces) sweetened condensed milk
- 2 cups (12 ounces) semisweet chocolate chips, melted
- 4 eggs
- 2 teaspoons vanilla extract
- Whipped cream and additional chocolate chips, optional

Combine all crust ingredients and press onto the bottom and 2 in. up the sides of a 9-in. springform pan; chill. For filling, beat cream cheese in a large mixing bowl until fluffy. Gradually add milk; beat until smooth. Add melted chips, eggs and vanilla; mix well. Pour into crust. Bake at 300° for 1 hour and 5 minutes. (Center will still jiggle slightly.) Cool for 15 minutes. Carefully run a knife between crust and sides of pan. Cool for 3 hours at room temperature. Chill overnight. Just before serving, remove sides of pan. Garnish with whipped cream and chocolate chips if desired. **Yield:** 12-16 servings.

BUTTERMILK POUND CAKE
Gracie Hanchey, De Ridder, Louisiana

- 1 cup butter (no substitutes)
- 3 cups sugar
- 4 eggs
- 3 cups all-purpose flour
- 1/4 teaspoon baking soda
- 1 cup buttermilk
- 1 teaspoon vanilla extract
- Confectioners' sugar, optional

In a mixing bowl, cream butter and sugar. Add eggs, one at a time, beating well after each addition. Combine flour and baking soda; add alternately with the buttermilk and beat well. Stir in vanilla. Pour into a greased and floured 10-in. fluted tube pan. Bake at 325° for 1 hour and 10 minutes or until cake tests done.

Cool in pan for 15 minutes before removing to a wire rack to cool completely. If desired, dust with confectioners' sugar. **Yield:** 16-20 servings.

PUMPKIN BARS
Brenda Keller, Andalusia, Alabama

- 4 eggs
- 1-2/3 cups sugar
- 1 cup vegetable oil
- 1 can (16 ounces) pumpkin
- 2 cups all-purpose flour
- 2 teaspoons ground cinnamon
- 2 teaspoons baking powder
- 1 teaspoon baking soda
- 1 teaspoon salt

ICING:
- 1 package (3 ounces) cream cheese, softened
- 2 cups confectioners' sugar
- 1/4 cup butter *or* margarine, softened
- 1 teaspoon vanilla extract
- 1 to 2 tablespoons milk

In a mixing bowl, beat eggs, sugar, oil and pumpkin. Combine flour, cinnamon, baking powder, baking soda and salt; gradually add to pumpkin mixture and mix well. Pour into an ungreased 15-in. x 10-in. x 1-in. baking pan. Bake at 350° for 25-30 minutes. Cool completely. For icing, beat cream cheese, sugar, butter and vanilla in a small mixing bowl. Add enough of the milk to achieve desired spreading consistency. Spread over bars. **Yield:** 2 dozen.

FRUITCAKE COOKIES
Hazel Staley, Gaithersburg, Maryland
(PICTURED ON PAGE 4)

- 6 cups chopped pecans (about 1-1/2 pounds)
- 2 cups graham cracker crumbs
- 1-1/2 cups raisins
- 1-1/4 cups chopped candied cherries (about 1/2 pound)
- 1-1/4 cups chopped candied pineapple (about 1/2 pound)
- 4-1/2 cups miniature marshmallows
- 1/2 cup evaporated milk
- 1/4 cup butter *or* margarine
- 1-1/2 cups flaked coconut

In a large bowl, combine pecans, cracker crumbs, raisins, cherries and pineapple. In a large saucepan, combine marshmallows, milk and butter. Cook over low heat, stirring constantly, until melted. Pour over pecan mixture and mix well. Shape into 1-in. balls and roll in the coconut, washing your hands frequently. **Yield:** 7-8 dozen.

CINDY'S CHOCOLATE CHIP COOKIES
Cindy Utter, Jacksonville, Illinois

- 1 cup butter *or* margarine, softened
- 1 cup shortening
- 1 cup sugar
- 2 cups packed light brown sugar
- 2 teaspoons vanilla extract
- 4 eggs
- 4-1/2 cups all-purpose flour
- 2 teaspoons baking soda
- 2 teaspoons salt
- 2 cups (12 ounces) semisweet chocolate chips
- 1 cup chopped pecans

In a large mixing bowl, cream butter, shortening, sugars and vanilla. Beat in eggs. Combine dry ingredients; add to creamed mixture. Stir in chocolate chips and nuts. Drop by tablespoonfuls onto greased baking sheets. Bake at 350° for 10-12 minutes or until lightly browned. **Yield:** 9 dozen.

BANANA OATMEAL COOKIES
Yvonne Miller, Chenango Forks, New York

- 1 cup sugar
- 1 cup butter flavored shortening
- 2 eggs
- 1 teaspoon vanilla extract
- 2 cups all-purpose flour
- 1 teaspoon baking soda
- 1 teaspoon ground cloves
- 1 teaspoon ground cinnamon
- 3 medium bananas, mashed
- 2 cups quick-cooking oats
- 1 cup (6 ounces) semisweet chocolate chips

In a large bowl, cream sugar, shortening, eggs and vanilla. Combine flour, baking soda, cloves and cinnamon; add to creamed mixture. Stir in bananas, oats and chocolate chips. Drop by rounded teaspoonfuls onto greased cookie sheets. Bake at 375° for 10-12 minutes. Immediately remove cookies to wire racks to cool. **Yield:** about 4 dozen.

FROSTING FINALE

For easy frosting decorations, use the back of a spoon to swirl circles and wavy lines in the frosting. Pull up for peaks.

*W*hen the days get shorter and the winds get colder, enjoy the aroma of a simmering Bavarian Pot Roast, rich with spices and tomato. You'll gladly heat up the oven for nutty Cranberry Muffins. For dessert, tangy Cran-Orange Delight will delight your family. Or make Caramel Custard and surprise everyone with their own individual treat!

FALL FLAVOR. Clockwise from the top: **Cran-Orange Delight** (p. 63), **Cranberry Muffins** (p. 53), **Caramel Custard** (p. 71) and **Bavarian Pot Roast** (p. 39).

BLACK FOREST TORTE
Glatis McNiel, Constantine, Michigan

1-1/3 cups all-purpose flour
1-3/4 cups sugar
1-1/4 teaspoons baking soda
1/4 teaspoon baking powder
2/3 cup butter or margarine
4 squares (1 ounce each)
  unsweetened chocolate
1-1/4 cups water
1 teaspoon vanilla extract
3 eggs
CHOCOLATE FILLING:
2 bars (4 ounces each) German
  sweet chocolate, divided
3/4 cup butter or margarine
1/2 cup chopped pecans
CREAM FILLING:
2 cups heavy cream
1 tablespoon confectioners'
  sugar
1 teaspoon vanilla extract

In a mixing bowl, combine flour, sugar, baking soda and baking powder. In a saucepan, melt butter and chocolate; cool. Pour chocolate mixture, water and vanilla into flour mixture. Beat on low for 1 minute, then on medium for 2 minutes. Add eggs, one at a time, beating well after each. Divide batter among two 9-in. round pans that have been greased, floured and lined with waxed paper. Bake at 350° for 25-30 minutes or until cakes test done. Cool in pans 10 minutes. Remove to a wire rack. For chocolate filling, melt 1-1/2 bars of German chocolate over low heat. Stir in butter and nuts. Watching closely, cool filling just until it reaches spreading consistency. For cream filling, whip cream with sugar and vanilla until stiff peaks form. To assemble, slice cooled cake layers in half horizontally. Place one bottom layer on a serving platter; cover with half of the chocolate filling. Top with a second cake layer; spread on half of the cream filling. Repeat layers. Grate remaining German chocolate; sprinkle on the top. Refrigerate until serving. **Yield:** 12-16 servings.

CHOCOLATE CHEWS
Donna Rhodes, Huntingdon, Pennsylvania

1/4 cup butter or margarine
1/2 cup dark corn syrup
6 tablespoons baking cocoa
1/2 teaspoon vanilla extract
3-1/4 cups confectioners' sugar,
  divided
3/4 cup nonfat dry milk powder

In a saucepan, melt butter over medium heat. Stir in corn syrup and cocoa; bring to a boil. Remove from the heat;

stir in vanilla, 2 cups confectioners' sugar and milk powder. (Mixture will be stiff.) Turn out onto a surface lightly dusted with confectioners' sugar. Knead in remaining confectioners' sugar; knead 3-4 minutes longer or until stiff. Divide into four pieces and roll each into an 18-in. rope. Cut into 3/4-in. pieces. Wrap each candy in cellophane or waxed paper. Store in refrigerator. **Yield:** 8 dozen.

PEANUT BUTTER OATMEAL COOKIES
Linda Fox, Soldotna, Alaska

1-1/2 cups shortening
1-1/2 cups peanut butter
2 cups packed brown sugar
3 eggs
2 teaspoons vanilla extract
3 cups quick-cooking oats
2 cups whole wheat flour
2 teaspoons baking soda
1 teaspoon salt

In a mixing bowl, cream shortening and peanut butter. Add brown sugar, eggs and vanilla; mix well. Combine oats, flour, baking soda and salt; add to the creamed mixture and mix well. Drop by rounded teaspoonfuls onto ungreased baking sheets. Flatten with a fork. Bake at 350° for 12 minutes or until done. **Yield:** 6 dozen.

CRAN-ORANGE DELIGHT
Joyce Gee, Blytheville, Arkansas
(PICTURED ON OPPOSITE PAGE)

1 package (18-1/4 ounces)
  yellow cake mix
1-1/3 cups orange juice
1/3 cup vegetable oil
3 eggs
1 teaspoon rum flavoring,
  optional
FROSTING:
1 carton (12 ounces) cranberry-
  orange sauce
1 package (3.4 ounces) instant
  vanilla pudding mix
2/3 cup orange juice
1 carton (8 ounces) frozen
  whipped topping, thawed
Sliced almonds, optional

In a mixing bowl, beat the first five ingredients until smooth. Pour into two greased and floured 9-in. cake pans. Bake at 350° for 25-30 minutes or until the cakes test done. Cool in pans for 15 minutes before removing to a wire rack. For frosting, combine cranberry-orange sauce, pudding mix and orange

juice in a mixing bowl. Fold in whipped topping. Split cooled cakes in half horizontally. Spread frosting between layers and over the top and sides of cake. Garnish with almonds if desired. Store in the refrigerator. **Yield:** 10-14 servings.

WASHBOARD COOKIES
John Cas Roulston, Stephenville, Texas

1/2 cup butter or margarine,
  softened
1 cup packed dark brown sugar
1 egg
1/2 teaspoon baking soda
1 tablespoon hot water
1 teaspoon vanilla extract
1-3/4 cups all-purpose flour
Sugar

In a mixing bowl, cream butter, brown sugar and egg. Stir together baking soda and water; add to creamed mixture. Add vanilla and flour; mix well. Shape into walnut-sized balls. Place on greased cookie sheets; flatten with a fork that has been dipped in water. Sprinkle with sugar. Bake at 325° for 15-20 minutes or until edges begin to brown. Cool on waxed paper. **Yield:** 3-1/2 dozen.

PRALINE COOKIES
Melody Sroufe, Wichita, Kansas

1/2 cup butter or margarine,
  softened
1-1/2 cups packed brown sugar
1 egg
1 teaspoon vanilla extract
1-1/2 cups all-purpose flour
1-1/2 teaspoons baking powder
1/4 teaspoon salt
1 cup pecans, coarsely chopped
ICING:
1 cup packed brown sugar
1/2 cup heavy cream
1 cup confectioners' sugar

In a mixing bowl, cream the butter and brown sugar. Add egg and vanilla; mix well. Combine flour, baking powder and salt; add to creamed mixture. Mix well. Cover and chill until dough is easy to handle, about 1 hour. Form into 1-in. balls; place 2 in. apart on greased baking sheets. Flatten cookies slightly with fingers; sprinkle each with 1 teaspoon pecans. Bake at 350° for 10 minutes. Cool on wire racks. Meanwhile, for icing, combine the brown sugar and cream in a saucepan. Cook over medium-high heat until sugar dissolves and mixture comes to a boil, stirring constantly. Remove from the heat; blend in confectioners' sugar until smooth. Drizzle over cookies. **Yield:** 4 dozen.

CARAMEL APPLE BARS
Carol Stuber, Osawatomie, Kansas
(PICTURED ON PAGE 23)

CRUST:
  1/2 cup butter *or* margarine
  1/4 cup shortening
    1 cup packed brown sugar
1-3/4 cups all-purpose flour
    1 cup old-fashioned *or*
      quick-cooking oats
    1 teaspoon salt
  1/2 teaspoon baking soda
  1/2 cup chopped pecans,
      optional
FILLING:
4-1/2 cups coarsely chopped peeled
      baking apples
    3 tablespoons all-purpose flour
    1 package (14 ounces) caramels
    3 tablespoons butter *or*
      margarine

In a mixing bowl, cream butter, shortening and brown sugar until fluffy. Add flour, oats, salt and baking soda; mix well. Stir in pecans if desired. Set aside 2 cups. Press remaining oat mixture into the bottom of an ungreased 13-in. x 9-in. x 2-in. baking pan. For filling, toss apples with flour; spoon over the crust. In a saucepan, melt the caramels and butter over low heat; drizzle over apples. Top with the reserved oat mixture. Bake at 400° for 25-30 minutes or until lightly browned. Cool before cutting into bars. **Yield:** 15-20 servings.

SOUR CREAM APPLE SQUARES
Nancy Wit, Fremont, Nebraska

    2 cups all-purpose flour
    2 cups packed brown sugar
  1/2 cup butter *or* margarine,
      softened
    1 cup chopped nuts
    2 teaspoons ground cinnamon
    1 teaspoon baking soda
  1/2 teaspoon salt
    1 cup (8 ounces) sour cream
    1 teaspoon vanilla extract
    1 egg, beaten
    2 cups chopped peeled apples
Whipped cream, optional

In a mixing bowl, combine flour, brown sugar and butter; blend at low speed until crumbly. Stir in the nuts. Press about 2-3/4 cups into the bottom of an ungreased 13-in. x 9-in. x 2-in. baking pan. To the remaining crumb mixture, add cinnamon, baking soda, salt, sour cream, vanilla and egg. Beat until thoroughly combined. Stir in apples. Spoon evenly over bottom layer. Bake at 350°

for 35-40 minutes or until cake tests done. Cool on a wire rack. Cut into squares. Garnish with whipped cream if desired. **Yield:** 12-15 servings.

CLASSIC CHOCOLATE CAKE
Betty Follas, Morgan Hill, California

  2/3 cup butter *or* margarine,
      softened
1-2/3 cups sugar
    3 eggs
    2 cups all-purpose flour
  2/3 cup baking cocoa
1-1/4 teaspoons baking soda
    1 teaspoon salt
1-1/3 cups milk
Confectioners' sugar *or* favorite
frosting

In a mixing bowl, cream butter and sugar until fluffy. Add eggs, one at a time, beating well after each addition. Combine flour, cocoa, baking soda and salt; add to creamed mixture alternately with milk, beating until smooth after each addition. Pour batter into a greased and floured 13-in. x 9-in. x 2-in. baking pan. Bake at 350° for 35-40 minutes or until cake tests done. Cool on a wire rack. When cake is cool, dust with confectioners' sugar or frost with your favorite frosting. **Yield:** 12-15 servings.

CHRISTMAS SPECIAL FRUITCAKE
Violet Cooper, Port Allegany, Pennsylvania
(PICTURED ON OPPOSITE PAGE)

    3 cups coarsely chopped Brazil
      nuts *or* other nuts (walnuts,
      pecans or hazelnuts)
    1 pound pitted dates, coarsely
      chopped
    1 cup halved maraschino
      cherries
  3/4 cup all-purpose flour
  3/4 cup sugar
  1/2 teaspoon baking powder
  1/2 teaspoon salt
    3 eggs
    1 teaspoon vanilla extract

In a mixing bowl, combine nuts, dates and cherries. In another bowl, stir together flour, sugar, baking powder and salt; add to nut mixture, stirring until nuts and fruit are well-coated. Beat eggs until foamy. Stir in vanilla; fold into nut mixture. Mix well. Pour into a greased and waxed paper-lined 9-in. x 5-in. x 3-in. loaf pan. Bake at 300° for 1 hour and 45 minutes. Cool 10 minutes in pan before removing to a wire rack. **Yield:** 24 servings.

ICED BROWNIES
Goldie Hanke, Tomahawk, Wisconsin

    1 cup sugar
  1/2 cup butter *or* margarine,
      softened
    4 eggs
    1 can (16 ounces)
      chocolate-flavored syrup
    1 cup all-purpose flour
  1/2 cup chopped nuts
ICING:
1-1/4 cups sugar
    6 tablespoons butter *or*
      margarine
    6 tablespoons milk *or* light
      cream
    1 teaspoon vanilla extract
    1 cup (6 ounces) semisweet
      chocolate chips

In a mixing bowl, cream sugar and butter. Add eggs, one at a time, beating well after each addition. Add syrup and flour; mix well. Stir in nuts. Pour into a greased 13-in. x 9-in. x 2-in. baking pan. Bake at 350° for 30-35 minutes or until top springs back when lightly touched. Cool slightly. Meanwhile, for icing, combine sugar, butter and milk in a small saucepan. Cook and stir until mixture comes to a boil. Reduce heat to medium and cook for 3 minutes, stirring constantly. Remove from the heat; stir in vanilla and chocolate chips until chips are melted. (Mixture will be thin.) Immediately pour over brownies. Cool completely before cutting. **Yield:** about 3 dozen.

SPICED OATMEAL COOKIES
Loretta Pakulski, Indian River, Michigan

    1 cup shortening
    2 cups packed brown sugar
    2 eggs
    2 tablespoons milk
2-1/2 cups all-purpose flour
    2 cups old-fashioned oats
    1 teaspoon baking soda
    1 teaspoon salt
    1 teaspoon ground cinnamon

In a mixing bowl, cream shortening and brown sugar. Add eggs and milk; mix well. Combine flour, oats, baking soda, salt and cinnamon; add to the creamed mixture. Drop by rounded teaspoonfuls 2 in. apart onto lightly greased cookie sheets. Bake at 350° for 12-15 minutes or until done. **Yield:** 4 dozen.

APPLE ADVICE

To prevent any browning when working with a quantity of peeled apples, slice them into water with 1 tablespoon of fresh lemon juice added.

*F*amily favorites, like delicious Pork Stuffed with Corn-bread Dressing and aromatic Apricot-Glazed Sweet Potatoes, are sure-fire recipes for holiday meals. Cranberry Waldorf Salad will become your trademark salad. And the holidays wouldn't be the same without Christmas Special Fruitcake for dessert!

TRUE-BLUE MEAL. Clockwise from the top: **Christmas Special Fruitcake** (p. 64), **Cranberry Waldorf Salad** (p. 25), **Pork Stuffed with Corn Bread Dressing** (p. 42) and **Apricot-Glazed Sweet Potatoes** (p. 28).

TOASTED OATMEAL COOKIES
Marilyn Krueger, Milwaukee, Wisconsin

3/4 cup butter *or* margarine
2-1/2 cups rolled oats
3/4 cup all-purpose flour
1 teaspoon baking soda
1 cup packed brown sugar
2 eggs, beaten
1 teaspoon vanilla extract
1/2 cup salted peanuts, coarsely chopped

In a large skillet over medium heat, melt butter until lightly browned. Add oats, stirring constantly until golden, about 8-10 minutes. Remove from the heat; cool. Combine flour and baking soda; set aside. In a large mixing bowl, beat brown sugar, eggs and vanilla until light. Stir in dry ingredients, oats and peanuts until well blended. Let stand for 15 minutes. Drop by rounded teaspoonfuls onto greased cookie sheets. Bake at 375° for 10 minutes or until golden. Remove to wire rack to cool. **Yield:** 3-1/2 dozen.

Quick & Easy

HOLIDAY SHORTBREAD COOKIES
Erma Hiltpold, Kerrville, Texas

5 cups all-purpose flour
1 cup sugar
1/2 teaspoon salt
2 cups cold butter (no substitutes)

In a large mixing bowl, combine flour, sugar and salt. Cut in butter until mixture resembles fine crumbs. Pat into an ungreased 15-in. x 10-in. x 1-in. baking pan. Prick all over with a fork. Bake at 325° for 35 minutes or until center is set. Cool for 10-15 minutes. Cut into small squares. Continue to cool to room temperature. **Yield:** 5 dozen.

ZUCCHINI-RAISIN COOKIES
Margie Wampler, Butler, Pennsylvania

1/2 cup shortening
1 cup sugar
1 egg
1 cup shredded peeled zucchini
2 cups all-purpose flour
1 teaspoon baking soda
1 teaspoon ground cinnamon
1/2 teaspoon baking powder
1/2 teaspoon salt
1/2 teaspoon ground nutmeg
1/4 teaspoon ground cloves
1 cup raisins

In a mixing bowl, cream shortening and sugar. Add egg; beat well. Stir in zuc-

chini; set aside. Combine flour, baking soda, cinnamon, baking powder, salt, nutmeg and cloves. Add to zucchini mixture; stir until thoroughly combined. Stir in raisins. Drop by rounded teaspoonfuls 2 in. apart on greased baking sheets. Bake at 375° for 12-15 minutes or until golden brown. Cool on pans for 2 minutes before removing to a wire rack. Cookies are cake-like. **Yield:** 3 dozen.

SPICED ALMOND COOKIES
Wanda Daily, Milwaukie, Oregon
(PICTURED ON PAGE 14)

1 cup butter *or* margarine, softened
1/2 cup shortening
1 cup packed brown sugar
1 cup sugar
2 eggs
4 cups all-purpose flour
2 teaspoons ground cinnamon
1 teaspoon baking soda
1 teaspoon salt
1 teaspoon ground cloves
1 teaspoon ground allspice
1 cup slivered almonds

In a mixing bowl, cream butter and shortening; beat in sugars until light and fluffy. Add eggs and beat well. Combine dry ingredients; stir into creamed mixture along with nuts. Shape into three 9-in. x 1-1/2-in. rolls; wrap in waxed paper. Chill 2-3 days for spices to blend. Slice cookies 1/4 in. thick and place on ungreased baking sheets. Bake at 350° for 12-14 minutes or until set. Remove cookies to a wire rack to cool. **Yield:** 7 dozen.

GREAT-GRANDMA'S LEMON CAKE
Glenda Stokes, Florence, South Carolina

1 cup butter (no substitutes), softened
3 cups sugar
5 eggs, *separated*
1 tablespoon finely shredded lemon peel
3 tablespoons lemon juice
4 cups all-purpose flour
1/2 teaspoon baking soda
1 cup milk
Confectioners' sugar

In a mixing bowl, cream butter; gradually add sugar, beating well. In a small mixing bowl, beat egg yolks until thick and lemon-colored. Add to creamed mixture and mix well. Stir in lemon peel and juice. Combine flour and baking soda; add alternately with milk, stirring

well after each addition. Beat egg whites until stiff; fold into batter. Pour into two well-greased 9-in. x 5-in. x 3-in. loaf pans. Bake at 325° for 65-70 minutes or until cakes test done. Cool on wire rack for 10 minutes. Remove from pans to cool completely. Dust tops with confectioners' sugar. **Yield:** 2 cakes (24 servings).

PECAN PIE BARS
Carolyn Custer, Clifton Park, New York

2 cups all-purpose flour
1/2 cup confectioners' sugar
1 cup butter *or* margarine, softened
1 can (14 ounces) sweetened condensed milk
1 egg
1 teaspoon vanilla extract
Pinch salt
1 package (6 ounces) toffee-flavored chips
1 cup chopped pecans

In a mixing bowl, combine flour and sugar. Cut in butter until mixture resembles coarse meal. Press firmly into a greased 13-in. x 9-in. x 2-in. baking dish. Bake at 350° for 15 minutes. Meanwhile, in another bowl, beat milk, egg, vanilla and salt. Stir in toffee chips and pecans; spread evenly over baked crust. Bake for another 20-25 minutes or until lightly browned. Cool, then refrigerate. When thoroughly chilled, cut into bars. Store in the refrigerator. **Yield:** 4 dozen.

Quick & Easy

PEANUT BUTTER FUDGE
Frances Castor, Lapel, Indiana

1 cup packed brown sugar
1 cup sugar
1/2 cup milk
5 large marshmallows
1 jar (12 ounces) creamy peanut butter

In a heavy 2-qt. saucepan, combine the sugars, milk and marshmallows. Bring to a boil over medium heat, stirring until the sugar dissolves and marshmallows melt. Remove from the heat; stir in peanut butter. Pour into a buttered 8-in. square baking pan. Cool. When firm, cut into squares. **Yield:** 3 dozen pieces.

A REAL SOFTIE
If your stored cookies have gotten too crisp for your liking, put them in a plastic bag with a piece of bread. The next day you'll have soft cookies again!

OATMEAL COOKIES

Diane Maughan, Cedar City, Utah

1 cup packed brown sugar
2 eggs
1/2 cup milk
3/4 cup vegetable oil
1 teaspoon vanilla extract
2 cups all-purpose flour
1 teaspoon baking soda
1 teaspoon salt
1 teaspoon ground cinnamon
1 teaspoon ground nutmeg
2 cups old-fashioned oats
1/2 cup semisweet chocolate
    chips
1/2 cup raisins

In a mixing bowl, combine brown sugar, eggs, milk, oil and vanilla; mix well. Combine flour, baking soda, salt, cinnamon and nutmeg; stir into batter. Stir in oats, chocolate chips and raisins. Let stand for 5-10 minutes. Drop by teaspoonfuls onto greased baking sheets. Bake at 350° for 10-12 minutes or until lightly browned. Remove immediately to wire racks. **Yield:** 3-1/2 dozen.

FROSTED SPICE COOKIES

Debbie Hurlbert, Howard, Ohio

1 cup butter *or* margarine,
    softened
1 cup sugar
1 cup molasses
1 egg
1 cup sour milk*
6 cups all-purpose flour
1 tablespoon baking powder
1 teaspoon baking soda
1 teaspoon ground cinnamon
1 teaspoon ground ginger
1/2 teaspoon salt
1 cup chopped walnuts
1 cup golden raisins
1 cup chopped dates
FROSTING:
3-3/4 cups confectioners' sugar
1/3 cup orange juice
2 tablespoons butter *or*
    margarine, melted

In a large mixing bowl, cream butter and sugar. Add molasses, egg and milk; mix well. Combine the flour, baking powder, baking soda, cinnamon, ginger and salt; gradually add to creamed mixture. Stir in walnuts, raisins and dates. Chill for 30 minutes. Roll dough out on a lightly floured surface to 1/4-in. thickness. Cut with a 2-1/2-in. cutter. Place on greased baking sheets. Bake at 350° for 12-15 minutes. Cool completely. For frosting, beat all ingredients in a small bowl until smooth. Frost cookies. (*To sour milk, add 1 tablespoon vinegar

to milk and let stand for 5 minutes.)
Yield: 5-6 dozen.

COCONUT FRUITCAKE

Lorraine Groh, Ferryville, Wisconsin

2 cups all-purpose flour
1 teaspoon baking powder
1 teaspoon salt
1 pound chopped fruitcake mix
1-1/2 cups flaked coconut
1 cup golden raisins
1 cup chopped nuts
1/2 cup butter *or* margarine
1 cup sugar
3 eggs, beaten
1 teaspoon lemon extract
1/2 cup orange juice
**Additional candied fruit *or* nuts,
optional**

In a large bowl, combine flour, baking powder and salt. Add fruitcake mix, coconut, raisins and nuts; mix well. In a mixing bowl, cream butter and sugar. Add eggs and extract; mix well. Stir in the flour mixture alternately with orange juice. Pack into a greased 10-in. tube pan lined with waxed paper. Bake at 250° for 2 to 2-1/2 hours or until cake tests done. Cool for 10 minutes. Loosen edges with a sharp knife. Remove from pan to cool completely on a wire rack. Garnish with candied fruit or nuts if desired. **Yield:** 12-16 servings.

FUDGY BROWNIES

Laura Katucki, Eagleville, Pennsylvania
(PICTURED ON PAGE 48)

1 cup butter *or* margarine,
    melted
3/4 cup baking cocoa
2 cups sugar
1-1/2 cups all-purpose flour
4 eggs
COCOA FROSTING:
1/4 cup butter *or* margarine,
    softened
2-1/2 cups confectioners' sugar
2 teaspoons vanilla extract
3 tablespoons baking cocoa
1/3 cup milk

In a mixing bowl, combine melted butter and cocoa. Mix in sugar and flour. Add eggs; mix well. Pour into a greased and floured 13-in. x 9-in. x 2-in. baking pan. Bake at 350° for 20-25 minutes. Meanwhile, for frosting, beat together all ingredients in a mixing bowl until smooth. Cool the brownies for 15 minutes before frosting. Cool completely. Cover with foil; freeze until firm. Serve frozen or thawed. **Yield:** 3 dozen. **Editor's Note:** Brownies are dense and resemble fudge.

AUNT IONE'S ICEBOX COOKIES

Jenny Hill, Meridianville, Alabama

6 cups all-purpose flour
1-1/2 teaspoons baking powder
1 teaspoon baking soda
1 teaspoon ground nutmeg
1 teaspoon ground cinnamon
2 cups butter *or* margarine,
    softened
1 cup sugar
1 cup packed brown sugar
3 eggs
1 teaspoon vanilla extract
1 teaspoon lemon extract
2 cups chopped nuts

Sift together first five ingredients; set aside. In a mixing bowl, cream butter and sugars. Add eggs, vanilla and lemon extract; beat well. Add dry ingredients; mix well. Stir in nuts. Divide dough into four parts and shape into 1-1/2-in. x 11-in. rolls. Wrap in foil and chill overnight. Slice cookies 3/8 in. thick. Bake on greased cookie sheets at 350° for about 10 minutes. **Yield:** about 17 dozen.

QUICK & EASY

CRUMB CAKE

Verna Hofer, Mitchell, South Dakota

2 cups all-purpose flour
1-1/3 cups sugar
2/3 cup butter *or* margarine,
    softened
1/2 teaspoon salt
1 teaspoon baking soda
1 teaspoon ground cinnamon
1/2 teaspoon ground cloves
1 egg, beaten
1 cup buttermilk
1/2 cup semisweet chocolate
    chips
1/2 cup chopped nuts

In a mixing bowl, combine flour, sugar, butter and salt until crumbly. Set aside 1 cup. Stir baking soda, cinnamon and cloves into the remaining crumb mixture. Add egg and buttermilk; mix well. Pour into a greased 13-in. x 9-in. x 2-in. baking pan. Sprinkle with reserved crumb mixture; top with chocolate chips and nuts. Bake at 350° for 30 minutes or until the cake tests done. Cool on a wire rack. **Yield:** 12-16 servings.

OUT OF WHIPPING CREAM?

Add sliced bananas to the white of an egg. Then beat until stiff.

*P*ies and desserts are the perfect ending to your country meals—especially when they're made with sweet and tangy rhubarb! Get ready...your gang will gobble up tasty Rhubarb Crumble and Rhubarb Cherry Pie. And you may as well start copying the recipes for Rhubarb Dumplings and Strawberry Rhubarb Coffee Cake...you're bound to be asked for them!

SUPERB RHUBARB. Clockwise from the top: **Strawberry Rhubarb Coffee Cake** (p. 53), **Rhubarb Dumplings** (p. 69), **Rhubarb Crumble** (p. 69) and **Rhubarb Cherry Pie** (p. 69).

Pies & Desserts

RHUBARB CRUMBLE
Linda Enslen, Schuler, Alberta
(PICTURED ON OPPOSITE PAGE)

3 cups sliced fresh *or* frozen rhubarb (1/2-inch pieces)
1 cup cubed peeled apples
1/2 to 1 cup sliced strawberries
1/3 cup sugar
1/2 teaspoon ground cinnamon
1/2 cup all-purpose flour
1 teaspoon baking powder
1/4 teaspoon salt
4 tablespoons butter *or* margarine
2/3 cup packed brown sugar
2/3 cup quick-cooking oats
Vanilla ice cream, optional

Combine rhubarb, apples and strawberries; spoon into a greased 8-in. square baking dish. Combine sugar and cinnamon; sprinkle over rhubarb mixture. Set aside. In a bowl, combine flour, baking powder and salt. Cut in butter until mixture resembles coarse crumbs. Stir in brown sugar and oats. Sprinkle over rhubarb mixture. Bake at 350° for 40-50 minutes or until lightly browned. Serve warm or cold with a scoop of ice cream if desired. **Yield:** 6-8 servings.

QUICK & EASY

CHOCOLATE CHERRY DESSERT
Cherry Turner, Eunice, Louisiana

26 chocolate wafer cookies, crushed
1/4 cup butter *or* margarine, melted
1 cup (8 ounces) sour cream
1 package (3.9 ounces) instant chocolate pudding mix
3/4 cup milk
1 can (21 ounces) cherry pie filling

In a mixing bowl, combine wafer crumbs with butter. Press into the bottom of an 8-in. square baking pan. Place in freezer for 10 minutes. In another mixing bowl, combine sour cream, pudding and milk; beat on low for 1-1/2 minutes.

Spread over crust. Spoon pie filling on top. Cover and refrigerate until ready to serve. **Yield:** 9 servings.

RHUBARB DUMPLINGS
Elsie Shell, Topeka, Indiana
(PICTURED ON OPPOSITE PAGE)

SAUCE:
1-1/2 cups sugar
1 tablespoon all-purpose flour
1/2 teaspoon ground cinnamon
1/4 teaspoon salt
1-1/2 cups water
1/3 cup butter *or* margarine
1 teaspoon vanilla extract
Red food coloring, optional
DOUGH:
2 cups all-purpose flour
2 tablespoons sugar
2 teaspoons baking powder
1/4 teaspoon salt
2-1/2 tablespoons cold butter *or* margarine
3/4 cup milk
FILLING:
2 tablespoons butter *or* margarine, softened
2 cups finely chopped fresh *or* frozen rhubarb
1/2 cup sugar
1/2 teaspoon ground cinnamon

In a saucepan, combine sugar, flour, cinnamon and salt. Stir in water; add butter. Bring to a boil; cook and stir 1 minute. Remove from heat. Add vanilla and, if desired, enough food coloring to tint sauce a deep pink; set aside. For dough, in a medium bowl, combine flour, sugar, baking powder and salt. Cut in butter until mixture resembles coarse crumbs. Add milk and mix quickly. Do not overmix. Gather dough into a ball and roll out on a floured surface into a 12-in. x 9-in. rectangle. Spread with softened butter; arrange rhubarb on top. Combine sugar and cinnamon; sprinkle over rhubarb. Roll up from the long side and place on a cutting board, seam side down. Cut roll into 12 slices. Arrange slices, cut side up, in a greased 13-in. x 9-in. x 2-in. baking dish. Pour sauce over. Bake at 350° for 35-40 minutes or until golden brown. **Yield:** 12 servings.

OLD-FASHIONED COCONUT PIE
Barbara Smith, Franklin, Georgia

1/4 cup all-purpose flour
1 cup sugar
Dash salt
2 cups milk
3 egg yolks, beaten
1-1/2 teaspoons vanilla extract
1-1/4 cups flaked coconut, *divided*
1 pie shell (9 inches), baked
MERINGUE:
3 egg whites
6 tablespoons sugar

In a saucepan, combine flour and sugar; add salt, milk and egg yolks. Mix well. Cook over medium heat, stirring constantly, until mixture is thickened and bubbly. Reduce heat; cook and stir 2 minutes more. Remove from the heat; stir in vanilla and 1 cup coconut. Pour hot filling into pie shell. For meringue, beat egg whites in a mixing bowl until soft peaks form. Gradually beat in sugar until mixture forms stiff glossy peaks and sugar dissolves. Spread meringue over hot filling. Sprinkle with remaining coconut. Bake at 350° for 12-15 minutes or until golden. Cool. Store in the refrigerator. **Yield:** 6-8 servings.

RHUBARB CHERRY PIE
Eunice Hurt, Murfreesboro, Tennessee
(PICTURED ON OPPOSITE PAGE)

3 cups sliced fresh *or* frozen rhubarb (1/2-inch pieces)
1 can (16 ounces) pitted tart red cherries, drained
1-1/4 cups sugar
1/4 cup quick-cooking tapioca
4 to 5 drops red food coloring, optional
Pastry for double-crust pie (9 inches)

In a mixing bowl, combine first five ingredients; let stand for 15 minutes. Line a 9-in. pie plate with pastry; add filling. Top with a lattice crust; flute the edges. Bake at 400° for 40-50 minutes or until the crust is golden and filling is bubbling. **Yield:** 8 servings.

STRAWBERRY RHUBARB ICE CREAM PIE
Connie Fleck, Fort Atkinson, Wisconsin
(PICTURED ABOVE)

> 1 quart vanilla ice cream, softened
> 1 graham cracker crust (9 inches)
> 1-1/2 cups sliced fresh *or* frozen rhubarb (1/2-inch pieces)
> 1/2 cup sugar
> 1 tablespoon cornstarch
> 1 tablespoon water
> 1 pint fresh strawberries, sliced

Spoon ice cream into crust; freeze. Meanwhile, in a saucepan over medium heat, cook rhubarb and sugar, stirring occasionally, until sugar dissolves and mixture boils. Combine cornstarch and water; stir into saucepan. Cook until thickened, stirring constantly. Cook 2 more minutes. Cool. Fold in berries; chill. Spread over ice cream. Let stand 10 minutes at room temperature before cutting. **Yield:** 8 servings.

BLUSHING APPLE CREAM PIE
Marny Eulberg, Wheat Ridge, Colorado

> 3/4 cup heavy cream
> 2 tablespoons red cinnamon candies
> 1/2 teaspoon ground cinnamon
> 1 cup sugar
> 1/4 cup all-purpose flour
> 2 tablespoons vinegar
> 4-1/2 cups thinly sliced peeled baking apples
> Pastry for double-crust pie (9 inches)

In a mixing bowl, combine first six in-gredients; mix well. Add apples and stir gently to mix. Pour into a pastry-lined pie plate. Roll out remaining pastry to fit top of pie. Cut slits in top crust; place over apples. Seal and flute edges. Bake at 400° for 50 minutes or until pastry is golden and apples are tender. **Yield:** 8 servings.

RASPBERRY ALMOND TORTE
Dana Pratt, De Land, Illinois

> 1-1/3 cups all-purpose flour
> 1 teaspoon baking powder
> 1 cup sugar, *divided*
> 1 cup butter or margarine, *divided*
> 3 eggs, *divided*
> 1/2 cup raspberry jam, *divided*
> 1 cup ground almonds
> 1/2 teaspoon almond extract
> 1/2 cup confectioners' sugar
> 2 to 2-1/2 teaspoons lemon juice

In a mixing bowl, combine flour, baking powder and 1/3 cup sugar. Cut in 1/2 cup butter until fine crumbs form. Beat 1 egg; add to mixing bowl and stir until dry ingredients are moistened. Press dough evenly into bottom and up the sides of a 9-in. x 1-1/2-in. tart pan with remov-able bottom. Spread 1/4 cup of jam over dough. Cover with plastic wrap and chill. Meanwhile, cream together remaining sugar and butter; stir in almonds and ex-tract. Add remaining eggs, one at a time, beating well after each addition; spoon filling over jam. Bake at 350° for 50 minutes. Cool in pan, then carefully re-move sides from pan. Spread remaining jam on top. Combine confectioners' sug-ar and lemon juice; drizzle over the top. **Yield:** 10-12 servings.

CREAMY PEAR PIE
Kathryn Gross, Fontanelle, Iowa

> 4 cups sliced peeled pears
> 1/3 cup sugar
> 2 tablespoons all-purpose flour
> 1 cup (8 ounces) sour cream
> 1/2 teaspoon vanilla extract
> 1/2 teaspoon lemon extract
> 1/2 teaspoon almond extract
> 1 unbaked pie pastry (9 inches)
> **TOPPING:**
> 1/4 cup all-purpose flour
> 2 tablespoons butter *or* margarine, melted
> 2 tablespoons brown sugar

In a large bowl, toss pears with sugar and flour. Combine sour cream and ex-tracts; add to pear mixture and mix well. Pour into pie shell. In a small bowl, mix topping ingredients until crumbly. Sprin-kle over pears. Bake at 400° for 10 min-utes. Reduce heat to 350°; bake 45 min-utes more or until the pears are tender. **Yield:** 6-8 servings.

FROZEN CHOCOLATE PIE
Bonnie Scott, Mc Louth, Kansas

> 1 package (3 ounces) cream cheese, softened
> 1/2 cup sugar
> 1 teaspoon vanilla extract
> 1/3 cup baking cocoa
> 1/3 cup milk
> 1 carton (8 ounces) frozen whipped topping, thawed
> 1 pie pastry (9 inches), baked
> Chocolate curls *or* chips, optional

In a mixing bowl, beat cream cheese, sugar and vanilla until smooth. Add co-coa alternately with milk; mix well. Fold in whipped topping. Pour into pie shell. Freeze for 8 hours or overnight. If de-sired, garnish with chocolate curls or chips. Serve directly from the freezer (pie does not need to be thawed to cut). **Yield:** 6-8 servings.

BIRD'S NEST PIE
Jeannine Bates, Wauseon, Ohio

> 4 to 5 medium apples, peeled and sliced
> 2 cups all-purpose flour
> 1 cup sugar
> 1/2 teaspoon baking soda
> 1/2 teaspoon cream of tartar
> 1 cup sour milk*
> 1 egg
> **TOPPING:**
> 1/4 cup sugar
> 1/2 teaspoon ground cinnamon
> 1/4 teaspoon ground nutmeg

Divide apples evenly between two greased 9-in. pie plates; set aside. In a mixing bowl, combine flour, sugar, bak-ing soda, cream of tartar, sour milk and egg; mix well. Divide batter and pour over apples. Bake at 350° for 25-30 min-utes or until pies are lightly browned and test done. Invert onto serving plates (so apples are on the top). Combine all top-ping ingredients; sprinkle over apples. Serve warm. (*To sour milk, place 1 ta-blespoon white vinegar in a measuring cup; add enough milk to equal 1 cup. Let stand for 5 minutes.) **Yield:** 12 servings.

EASY-DOES-IT DESSERT

For an easy, delicious berry trifle, lay-er yellow or pound cake, fresh or froz-en berries, vanilla pudding and whipped cream. Serve fresh from refrigerator.

CARAMEL CUSTARD

Linda McBride, Austin, Texas
(PICTURED ON PAGE 62)

1-1/2 cups sugar, *divided*
6 eggs
2 teaspoons vanilla extract
3 cups milk

In a heavy saucepan over low heat, cook and stir 3/4 cup sugar until melted and golden. Pour into eight 6-oz. custard cups, tilting to coat bottom of cup; let stand for 10 minutes. In a large bowl, beat eggs, vanilla, milk and remaining sugar until combined but not foamy. Pour over caramelized sugar. Place the cups in two 8-in. square baking pans. Pour boiling water in pans to a depth of 1 in. Bake at 350° for 40-45 minutes or until a knife inserted near center comes out clean. Remove from pans to cool on wire racks. To unmold, run a knife around rim of cup and invert onto dessert plate. Serve warm or chilled. **Yield:** 8 servings.

CHOCOLATE ECLAIRS

Janet Davis, Murfreesboro, Tennessee

1/2 cup butter *or* margarine
1 cup water
1 cup all-purpose flour
1/4 teaspoon salt
4 eggs
FILLING:
1 package (5.1 ounces) instant vanilla pudding mix
2-1/2 cups cold milk
1 cup whipping cream
1/4 cup confectioners' sugar
1 teaspoon vanilla extract
CHOCOLATE ICING:
2 squares (1 ounce *each*) semisweet chocolate
2 tablespoons butter *or* margarine
1 cup confectioners' sugar
2 to 3 tablespoons hot water

In a saucepan, combine butter and water. Bring to a rapid boil, stirring until the butter melts. Reduce heat to low; add flour and salt. Stir vigorously until mixture leaves the sides of the pan and forms a stiff ball. Remove from heat. Add eggs, one at a time, beating well after each addition. With a tablespoon or a pastry tube fitted with a No. 10 or larger tip, spoon or pipe dough into 4-in.-long x 1-1/2-in.-wide strips on a greased cookie sheet. Bake at 450° for 15 minutes. Reduce heat to 325°; bake 20 minutes longer. Cool on a wire rack. For filling, combine pudding mix and milk; mix according to package directions. In another bowl, whip the cream until soft peaks form. Beat in sugar and vanilla; fold into pudding. Fill cooled shells. (Chill remaining pudding for another use.) For icing, melt chocolate and butter in a saucepan over low heat. Stir in sugar. Add hot water until icing is smooth and reaches desired consistency. Cool slightly. Spread over eclairs. Chill until serving. **Yield:** 8-9 servings.

RHUBARB CUSTARD PIE

Lucile Proctor, Panguitch, Utah

3 eggs
3 tablespoons milk
2 cups sugar
3 tablespoons quick-cooking tapioca
Pastry for double-crust pie (9 inches)
4 cups diced rhubarb
2 teaspoons butter *or* margarine
Light cream, optional
Cinnamon-sugar, optional

In a mixing bowl, beat eggs lightly; blend in milk. Combine sugar and tapioca; stir into egg mixture. Place bottom pastry in a pie plate; add the rhubarb. Pour egg mixture over rhubarb. Dot with butter. Cover with top pastry. Make slits in top for steam to escape. If desired, brush pastry with light cream. Bake at 425° for 15 minutes; reduce heat to 350°. Bake 35-40 minutes longer or until lightly browned. Sprinkle with cinnamon-sugar if desired. Cool on a wire rack. Store in the refrigerator. **Yield:** 6-8 servings.

STRAWBERRY RHUBARB CRUMB PIE

Paula Phillips, East Winthrop, Maine

1 egg
1 cup sugar
2 tablespoons all-purpose flour
1 teaspoon vanilla extract
3/4 pound fresh rhubarb, cut into 1/2-inch pieces (about 3 cups)
1 pint fresh strawberries, halved
1 unbaked pie shell (9 inches)
TOPPING:
3/4 cup all-purpose flour
1/2 cup packed brown sugar
1/2 cup quick-cooking *or* rolled oats
1/2 cup butter *or* margarine

In a mixing bowl, beat egg. Beat in sugar, flour and vanilla; mix well. Gently fold in rhubarb and strawberries. Pour into pie shell. For topping, combine flour, brown sugar and oats in a small bowl; cut in butter until crumbly. Sprinkle over fruit. Bake at 400° for 10 minutes. Reduce heat to 350°; bake for 35 minutes or until golden brown and bubbly. **Yield:** 8 servings.

BLACKBERRY DUMPLINGS

Liecha Collins, Oneonta, New York
(PICTURED ON PAGE 30)

1 quart fresh *or* frozen (loose-pack) blackberries
1 cup plus 1 tablespoon sugar, *divided*
3/4 teaspoon salt, *divided*
1/2 teaspoon lemon extract
1-1/2 cups all-purpose flour
2 teaspoons baking powder
1/4 teaspoon ground nutmeg
2/3 cup milk
Cream *or* whipped cream, optional

In a Dutch oven, combine the blackberries, 1 cup sugar, 1/4 teaspoon salt and lemon extract. Bring to a boil; reduce heat and simmer for 5 minutes. Meanwhile, in a mixing bowl, combine flour, baking powder, nutmeg and remaining sugar and salt. Add milk; stir just until mixed. (Dough will be very thick.) Drop by tablespoonfuls into six mounds onto hot blackberry mixture; cover tightly and simmer for 15 minutes or until a toothpick inserted in a dumpling comes out clean. Spoon into serving dishes. Serve with cream or whipped cream if desired. **Yield:** 6-8 servings.

BROWNIE PUDDING

Barbara Chamberlain, Lawrenceville, Georgia

SAUCE:
1/2 cup packed brown sugar
1/4 cup baking cocoa
1-1/2 cups boiling water
CAKE:
1 cup all-purpose flour
1/2 cup sugar
1/4 cup baking cocoa
1-1/2 teaspoons baking powder
1/4 teaspoon salt
1 egg, beaten
1/3 cup milk
2 tablespoons butter *or* margarine, melted
1 teaspoon vanilla extract
1/2 cup semisweet chocolate chips
Whipped cream *or* vanilla ice cream

In a saucepan, combine sauce ingredients and keep warm. In a mixing bowl, combine flour, sugar, cocoa, baking powder and salt. In a small bowl, combine egg, milk, butter and vanilla; add to dry ingredients and stir until moistened. Fold in chocolate chips. Pour into a greased 1-1/2-qt. baking dish. Pour warm sauce over batter. *Do not stir.* Bake at 350° for 35-40 minutes or until cake is firm and floats in sauce. Let rest 10 minutes. Serve warm with whipped cream or ice cream. **Yield:** 8-10 servings.

*H*ear eager cheers—instead of groans—with these excellent leftover recipes. Surprise your family with the delicious flavor of leftover turkey and dressing in Turkey Dressing Pie. Next time you have excess mashed potatoes, try tasty Golden Potato Rolls or Potato Puffs. And top off this unique meal with an elegant Pumpkin Trifle.

SECONDS, PLEASE! Clockwise from the top: **Pumpkin Trifle** (p. 73), **Turkey Dressing Pie** (p. 46), **Potato Puffs** (p. 33) and **Golden Potato Rolls** (p. 53).

STRAWBERRY ICE CREAM
Kimberley Whitham, Moscow, Kansas
(PICTURED ON PAGE 50)

6 tablespoons all-purpose flour
3 cups sugar, *divided*
1 teaspoon salt
6 eggs
4 cups milk
1-1/2 pints strawberries, hulled
2 tablespoons lemon juice
4 cups half-and-half cream
2 tablespoons vanilla extract
Red food coloring

In a heavy saucepan and using a whisk, combine flour, 2 cups sugar and salt. Beat in eggs and milk until well blended. Cook over medium heat, stirring constantly, until mixture thickens and coats a spoon (about 45 minutes). Do not boil. Cover with plastic wrap. Allow to cool for at least 2 hours. Meanwhile, in a medium bowl and using a potato masher, crush berries with lemon juice and remaining sugar. Let stand for 1 hour. Pour cream, vanilla, food coloring, egg mixture and berry mixture into an ice cream freezer. Freeze according to manufacturer's directions. **Yield:** 3 quarts.

SOUTHERN BREAD PUDDING
D. Darlene Knight, Bethany, Oklahoma

1/2 cup raisins
1/2 cup hot water
4 eggs
2 cups milk
3/4 cup sugar, *divided*
1 teaspoon vanilla extract
8 slices French bread (1/2 inch thick)
Butter *or* margarine, softened
1 teaspoon ground cinnamon
BUTTER SAUCE:
1/2 cup butter (no substitutes)
1 cup sugar
1/2 cup plus 2 tablespoons heavy cream

Place raisins in a small bowl; pour water over. Let stand for about 10 minutes to soften; drain. In a mixing bowl, beat eggs. Add milk, 2/3 cup sugar, vanilla and raisins. Pour half into a greased 13-in. x 9-in. x 2-in. baking dish. Butter both sides of bread; arrange in a single layer over egg mixture. Cover with remaining egg mixture. Combine cinnamon with remaining sugar; sprinkle on top. Bake at 350° for 30 minutes or until a knife inserted in center comes out clean. Meanwhile, for sauce, melt butter in a saucepan. Add sugar; cook and stir over medium heat for 10 minutes. Remove from the heat

and gradually stir in cream. Return to the heat; cook and stir 8-10 minutes longer or until thickened and golden-colored. Serve warm over a slice of bread pudding. **Yield:** 8 servings.

CRUMB-TOPPED RHUBARB
Betty Combs, De Smet, South Dakota

3 cups diced fresh *or* frozen rhubarb
1 tablespoon all-purpose flour
1/2 cup sugar
1 teaspoon ground cinnamon
1/8 teaspoon salt
TOPPING:
6 tablespoons all-purpose flour
1/2 cup packed brown sugar
1/2 cup quick-cooking *or* rolled oats
6 tablespoons butter *or* margarine, softened

In a mixing bowl, combine rhubarb, flour, sugar, cinnamon and salt. Spoon into a greased 12-in. x 8-in. x 2-in. baking dish; set aside. Combine flour, brown sugar and oats. Cut in butter until crumbly; sprinkle over rhubarb mixture. Bake at 350° for 40 minutes or until lightly browned and bubbly. **Yield:** 6-8 servings.

PUMPKIN TRIFLE
Melody Hurlbut, St. Agatha, Ontario
(PICTURED ON OPPOSITE PAGE)

2 to 3 cups leftover crumbled unfrosted spice cake, muffins *or* gingerbread
1 can (16 ounces) pumpkin (about 2 cups)
1 teaspoon ground cinnamon
1/4 teaspoon ground nutmeg
1/4 teaspoon ground ginger
1/4 teaspoon ground allspice
2-1/2 cups cold milk
4 packages (3.4 ounces *each*) instant butterscotch pudding mix
2 cups whipping cream
Maraschino cherries, optional

Set aside 1/4 cup of cake crumbs for top. Divide remaining crumbs into four portions; sprinkle one portion into the bottom of a trifle bowl or 3-qt. serving bowl. In a large mixing bowl, combine pumpkin, spices, milk and pudding mixes; mix until smooth. Spoon half into the serving bowl. Sprinkle with a second portion of crumbs. Whip cream until stiff; spoon half into bowl. Sprinkle with a

third portion of crumbs. Top with the remaining pumpkin mixture, then last portion of crumbs and remaining whipped cream. Sprinkle the reserved crumbs on top, around the edge of the bowl. Place cherries in the center if desired. Cover and chill at least 2 hours before serving. **Yield:** 12-15 servings.

APPLE CRISP
Gertrude Bartnick, Portage, Wisconsin
(PICTURED ON PAGE 11)

1 cup all-purpose flour
3/4 cup rolled oats
1 cup packed brown sugar
1 teaspoon ground cinnamon
1/2 cup butter *or* margarine, softened
4 cups chopped peeled apples
1 cup sugar
2 tablespoons cornstarch
1 cup water
1 teaspoon vanilla extract
Vanilla ice cream, optional

In a mixing bowl, combine first four ingredients. Cut in butter until crumbly. Press half into a greased 2-1/2-qt. baking dish or a 9-in. square baking pan. Cover with apples. In a saucepan, combine sugar, cornstarch, water and vanilla; cook and stir until thick and clear. Pour over apples. Sprinkle with remaining crumb mixture. Bake at 350° for about 1 hour or until the apples are tender. Serve warm, with ice cream if desired. **Yield:** 8 servings.

QUICK & EASY

PEACHY ANGEL FOOD DESSERT
Lois Walters, Beaconsfield, Iowa

1 prepared angel food cake
2 envelopes (1.3 ounces *each*) whipped topping mix
2 packages (3 ounces *each*) cream cheese, softened
1 cup confectioners' sugar
1 can (21 ounces) peach *or* cherry pie filling

Tear cake into bite-size pieces; set aside. Prepare whipped topping according to package directions; set aside. In a large mixing bowl, beat cream cheese and confectioners' sugar; fold in whipped topping. Add cake pieces; stir gently to coat evenly. Spoon into a 13-in. x 9-in. x 2-in. baking pan. Top with pie filling. Chill until ready to serve. **Yield:** 12 servings.

*F*or those with a sweet tooth, dessert is the focal point of a meal! So when you aim to please the dessert lovers in your family, make sure you have plenty of tasty Almond Rhubarb Pastry on hand. They'll delight in Cream Cheese Rhubarb Pie, and love the taste of light, refreshing Berry Rhubarb Fool.

EVERYTHING'S COMING UP ROSY. Clockwise from lower left: **Spiced Rhubarb** (p. 6), **Cream Cheese Rhubarb Pie** (p. 76), **Rhubarb Pecan Muffins** (p. 57), **Berry Rhubarb Fool** (p. 76), **Rhubarb Chutney** (p. 7), **Rosy Rhubarb Salad** (p. 20), **Rhubarb Pork Chop Casserole** (p. 37) and **Almond Rhubarb Pastry** (p. 77).

RHUBARB CRUMB TART
Rebecca Gairns, Prince George, British Columbia

CRUST:
    1 cup all-purpose flour
    1 teaspoon baking powder
    3 tablespoons confectioners'
      sugar
    1/3 cup butter *or* margarine
    1 egg, beaten
    4 teaspoons milk
FILLING:
    3 cups diced raw rhubarb
    1 package (3 ounces)
      strawberry-flavored gelatin
CRUMBLE TOPPING:
    1/2 cup all-purpose flour
    1 cup sugar
    1/3 cup butter *or* margarine

Preheat oven to 350°. For crust, mix flour, baking powder and confectioners' sugar in a medium bowl. Cut in butter until mixture resembles coarse crumbs. Add egg and milk; stir until a ball forms. Pat into a greased 11-in. x 7-in. x 2-in. baking pan. Place rhubarb in crust. Sprinkle gelatin over rhubarb. In a small bowl, mix topping ingredients together until crumbly. Sprinkle over rhubarb mixture. Bake at 350° for 45-50 minutes. Allow to cool until firm. **Yield:** 12-15 servings.

APPLE ROLY-POLY
Megan Newcombe, Cookstown, Ontario
(PICTURED ON PAGE 40)

    1-3/4 cups all-purpose flour
    1/4 cup sugar
    4 teaspoons baking powder
    1/2 teaspoon salt
    1/4 cup shortening
    1/4 cup butter *or* margarine
    2/3 cup sour cream
FILLING:
    1/4 cup butter *or* margarine,
      softened
    1 cup packed brown sugar
    2 teaspoons ground cinnamon
    6 medium Granny Smith apples,
      peeled, cored and coarsely
      shredded (about 5 cups)
TOPPING:
    2-1/2 cups water
    2 tablespoons brown sugar
    1 teaspoon ground cinnamon
    1/2 cup light cream

In a mixing bowl, combine flour, sugar, baking powder and salt. Cut in shortening and butter until crumbly. Add sour cream and blend until a ball forms. Roll out on a floured surface into a 15-in. x 10-in. rectangle. Spread with softened butter; sprinkle with remaining filling ingredients. Roll up, jelly roll style, start-ing with the long side. Cut into 12 slices. Place slices, cut side down, in a 13-in. x 9-in. x 2-in. baking pan. For topping, combine water, brown sugar and cinnamon in a saucepan. Bring to a boil; remove from the heat. Stir in the cream. Carefully pour hot topping over dumplings. Bake, uncovered, at 350° for 35 minutes or until bubbly. (Center will jiggle when dumplings are hot out of the oven but will set as dumplings stand for a few minutes.) Serve warm. **Yield:** 12 servings.

CREAM CHEESE RHUBARB PIE
Beverly Kuhn, Orwell, Ohio
(PICTURED ON PAGE 74)

    1/4 cup cornstarch
    1 cup sugar
Pinch salt
    1/2 cup water
    3 cups sliced fresh *or* frozen
      rhubarb (1/2-inch pieces)
    1 unbaked pie shell (9 inches)
TOPPING:
    1 package (8 ounces) cream
      cheese, softened
    2 eggs
    1/2 cup sugar
Whipped cream
Sliced almonds

In a saucepan, combine the cornstarch, sugar and salt. Add water; stir until thoroughly combined. Add rhubarb. Cook, stirring often, until mixture boils and thickens. Pour into the pie shell; bake at 425° for 10 minutes. Meanwhile, for topping, beat cream cheese, eggs and sugar until smooth. Pour over pie. Return to oven; reduce heat to 325°. Bake for 35 minutes or until set. Cool. Chill several hours or overnight. Garnish with whipped cream and sliced almonds. **Yield:** 8 servings.

MOM'S LEMON CUSTARD PIE
Jeannie Fritson, Kearney, Nebraska

    1 cup sugar
    1 tablespoon butter *or*
      margarine, softened
    3 tablespoons all-purpose flour
    1/8 teaspoon salt
    2 eggs, *separated*
    1 cup milk
    1/4 cup fresh lemon juice
Peel of 1 medium lemon
    1 unbaked pie pastry (9 inches)
Whipped cream, optional

Using a spoon, cream sugar and butter in a bowl until well mixed. Add flour, salt, egg yolks and milk; mix well. Add lemon juice and peel; mix well. Set aside. In a small bowl, beat egg whites until stiff peaks form; gently fold into lemon mixture. Pour into pie shell. Bake at 325° for 1 hour or until lightly browned and a knife inserted in center comes out clean. Cool. Garnish with whipped cream if desired. Store in the refrigerator. **Yield:** 6-8 servings.

QUICK & EASY

STRAWBERRY ANGEL DESSERT
Mrs. J. Jelen, Minneota, Minnesota

    1 envelope unflavored gelatin
    3/4 cup cold water
    1/2 cup sugar
    1 package (10 ounces) frozen
      sliced strawberries, thawed
    1 carton (8 ounces) frozen
      whipped topping, thawed
    5 cups angel food cake cubes
Fresh strawberries, optional
Fresh mint, optional

In a saucepan, combine gelatin and cold water; let stand 5 minutes to soften. Heat and stir over low heat just until gelatin dissolves. Remove from the heat; add sugar. Stir until dissolved. Stir in undrained strawberries. Chill until partially thickened. Fold in whipped topping. Place cake cubes in a mixing bowl; pour strawberry mixture over cake and mix gently. Pour into an ungreased 8-in. square baking dish. Chill until firm. Garnish with fresh strawberries and mint if desired. **Yield:** 9 servings.

BERRY RHUBARB FOOL
Cheryl Miller, Fort Collins, Colorado
(PICTURED ON PAGE 74)

    3 cups sliced fresh *or* frozen
      rhubarb (1-inch pieces)
    1/3 cup sugar
    1/4 cup orange juice
Pinch salt
    1 cup heavy cream
    1 pint fresh strawberries, halved
Fresh mint leaves

In a saucepan, combine rhubarb, sugar, orange juice and salt. Bring to a boil. Reduce heat; cover and simmer for 6-8 minutes or until rhubarb is tender. Cool slightly. Pour into a blender container; cover and blend until smooth. Chill. Just before serving, whip cream until stiff peaks form. Fold rhubarb mixture into cream until lightly streaked. In chilled parfait glasses, alternate layers of cream mixture and strawberries. Garnish each serving with a strawberry and a sprig of mint. **Yield:** 6 servings.

ALMOND RHUBARB PASTRY

Lois Dyck, Coaldale, Alberta
(PICTURED ON PAGE 75)

PASTRY:
- 3 cups all-purpose flour
- 1 tablespoon baking powder
- 1 teaspoon salt
- 1 cup shortening
- 2 eggs, beaten
- 1/4 to 1/3 cup milk, *divided*

FILLING:
- 1-1/2 cups sugar
- 1/4 cup quick-cooking tapioca
- 6 cups chopped fresh *or* frozen rhubarb

TOPPING:
- 1/2 cup butter *or* margarine
- 3/4 cup sugar
- 2 tablespoons milk
- 1/2 teaspoon vanilla extract
- 1 cup slivered almonds

Combine flour, baking powder and salt; cut in shortening as for pie pastry. Mix eggs and 1/4 cup milk; add to dry ingredients and stir with a fork just until dough clings together. Add some or all of remaining milk if necessary. Shape into a ball. Divide in half. On a floured surface, roll half of dough into a 17-in. x 12-in. rectangle. Transfer to a greased 15-in. x 10-in. x 1-in. baking pan. Combine filling ingredients; sprinkle over dough in pan. Roll out remaining dough into a 15-in. x 10-in. rectangle. Place over filling. Fold bottom edge of dough over top layer of dough; press edges together to seal. For topping, in a saucepan, melt butter; add sugar and milk. Bring to a gentle boil; boil 2-3 minutes, stirring constantly. Remove from heat; stir in vanilla. Spread over pastry. Sprinkle almonds on top. Bake at 400° for 20 minutes; reduce heat to 300°. Bake 30-40 minutes longer or until golden brown. Serve warm or cold. **Yield:** 16-20 servings.

COCONUT CREAM PIE

Vera Moffitt, Oskaloosa, Kansas

- 3/4 cup sugar
- 3 tablespoons all-purpose flour
- 1/8 teaspoon salt
- 3 cups milk
- 3 eggs, beaten
- 1-1/2 cups flaked coconut, toasted, *divided*
- 1 tablespoon butter *or* margarine
- 1-1/2 teaspoons vanilla extract
- 1 pastry shell (9 inches), baked

In a medium saucepan, combine sugar, flour and salt. Stir in milk; cook and stir over medium-high heat until thickened and bubbly. Reduce heat; cook and stir

2 minutes longer. Remove from the heat; gradually stir about 1 cup of hot mixture into beaten eggs. Return all to saucepan; cook and stir over medium heat until nearly boiling. Reduce heat; cook and stir about 2 minutes more (*do not boil*). Remove from the heat; stir in 1 cup coconut, butter and vanilla. Pour into pie shell; sprinkle with remaining coconut. Chill for several hours before serving. Refrigerate leftovers. **Yield:** 6-8 servings.

RAISIN/DATE BREAD PUDDING

Dawn Green, Hopkins, Michigan

- 4 cups milk
- 5 cups day-old bread cubes
- 1 cup sugar
- 8 eggs, beaten
- 1/2 cup butter *or* margarine, melted
- 1/4 cup chopped dates
- 1/4 cup raisins
- 1 teaspoon vanilla extract
- 1/2 teaspoon ground cinnamon
- **Dash salt**
- **Dash ground nutmeg**
- **Additional sugar, cinnamon and nutmeg, optional**
- **Whipped cream, optional**

In a large bowl, pour milk over bread. Add sugar, eggs, butter, dates, raisins, vanilla, cinnamon, salt and nutmeg; stir to mix well. Pour into a greased 13-in. x 9-in. x 2-in. baking dish. If desired, sprinkle top with additional sugar, cinnamon and nutmeg. Bake at 350° for 55 minutes or until golden brown and a knife inserted near the center comes out clean. Serve warm with whipped cream if desired. **Yield:** 10-12 servings.

APPLE DUMPLINGS

Marjorie Thompson, W. Sacramento, California

- 1-1/2 cups sugar, *divided*
- 2 cups water
- 4 tablespoons butter *or* margarine, *divided*
- 1/2 teaspoon ground cinnamon, *divided*
- **Pastry for double-crust pie (9 inches)**
- 6 small to medium apples, peeled and cored

In a saucepan, combine 1 cup sugar, water, 3 tablespoons butter and 1/4 teaspoon cinnamon. Bring to a boil; boil for 3 minutes. Remove from the heat and set aside. Roll pastry into a 21-in. x 14-in. rectangle; cut into six 7-in. squares. Place one apple in the center of each square. Combine the remaining sugar and cinnamon; spoon into center of ap-

ples. Dot with remaining butter. Moisten edges of pastry; fold corners to the center atop apple. Pinch to seal. Place in an ungreased 12-in. x 8-in. x 2-in. baking dish. Pour syrup mixture around apples. Bake at 375° for 45 minutes or until pastry is golden brown and apples are tender. Serve warm. **Yield:** 6 servings.

PINEAPPLE SHERBET

Barbara Libkie, Roswell, New Mexico

- 1 quart buttermilk
- 1 can (20 ounces) crushed pineapple, drained
- 1-1/3 cups sugar
- 1/2 cup chopped walnuts
- 1 teaspoon vanilla extract

In a bowl, combine all ingredients; mix well. Cover and freeze for 1 hour. Stir; return to freezer for at least 2 hours before serving. **Yield:** 6-8 servings.

QUICK RICE PUDDING

Betty Greene, Holland, Michigan
(PICTURED BELOW)

- 1 package (3.4 ounces) instant vanilla pudding mix
- 2 cups cold milk
- 1 cup cold cooked rice
- 1/2 cup raisins
- **Whipped topping**
- **Maraschino cherries**

In a mixing bowl, combine pudding mix and milk; beat for 1-2 minutes until well blended. Stir in rice and raisins. Spoon pudding into individual bowls. Chill. Garnish with whipped topping and a cherry. **Yield:** 6 servings.

Ask Shirley Helfenbein her favorite season, and she doesn't have to think twice.

"Summer has always been my favorite season, since I grew up on a small farm," says Shirley, who now lives in Lapeer, Michigan. "Hard work meant hearty appetites…and there was always lots of farm-fresh food to satisfy them!

"We had a cow to provide rich, creamy dairy products. And I vividly recall the fresh berries, sweet corn and little red potatoes that made such *wonderful* summer meals."

The highlight of each summer week was Sunday supper after church, she recalls. "That was our big meal of the day. Fried chicken was the traditional main course, and all the vegetables were fresh from our garden."

Shirley loved this family feast so much that she frequently prepares it today. In addition to these four dishes, she serves corn on the cob and hot biscuits, both topped with her home-churned butter.

MY MOST MEMORABLE MEAL

All four recipes on this page are from Shirley Helfenbein of Lapeer, Michigan and are pictured on the opposite page.

RED POTATO SALAD

"I REMEMBER digging small red potatoes from the soft warm soil, then gently pushing the plants back into the ground and reminding them to keep on making more potatoes. The new potatoes we brought home were made into this fresh salad."

- 3/4 cup sour cream
- 1/2 cup mayonnaise *or* salad dressing
- 2 tablespoons herb *or* white vinegar
- 1-1/2 teaspoons salt
- 1 teaspoon celery seed
- 6 medium red potatoes (about 2 pounds), peeled, cooked and cubed
- 3/4 cup sliced green onions
- 1/3 cup radish slices
- 1/4 cup chopped celery
- 3 to 4 hard-cooked eggs, chopped

In a small bowl, combine sour cream, mayonnaise, vinegar, salt and celery seed; set aside. In a large bowl, combine potatoes, green onions, radishes, celery and eggs. Add dressing and toss lightly. Cover and chill. **Yield:** 6-8 servings.

PENNSYLVANIA DUTCH CUCUMBERS

"SETTLING IN PENNSYLVANIA, my mom's family adopted some of the cooking and customs of the Pennsylvania Dutch. This is a Dutch dish Mom loved, and today it's my favorite fresh vegetable dish…the blend of cucumbers and tomatoes is wonderful!"

- 3 to 4 small cucumbers
- 1 teaspoon salt
- 1 medium onion, thinly sliced into rings
- 1/2 cup sour cream
- 2 tablespoons vinegar
- 1 tablespoon chopped fresh chives
- 1/2 teaspoon dried dill seed
- 1/4 teaspoon pepper
- Pinch sugar
- Lettuce leaves, optional
- Sliced tomatoes, optional

Peel cucumbers; slice paper-thin into a bowl. Sprinkle with salt; cover and refrigerate for 3-4 hours. Rinse and drain cucumbers. Pat gently to press out excess liquid. Combine cucumbers and onion in a large bowl; set aside. In a small bowl, combine sour cream, vinegar, chives, dill seed, pepper and sugar. Just before serving, add dressing to cucumbers and toss. If desired, arrange lettuce and tomatoes in a serving bowl and spoon cucumbers into the middle. **Yield:** 6 servings.

STRAWBERRY SHORTCAKE

"I CAN still taste the sweet juicy berries piled over warm biscuits and topped with a huge dollop of fresh whipped cream. My father added even more indulgence to this strawberry dessert by first buttering his biscuits."

- 2 cups all-purpose flour
- 2 tablespoons sugar
- 1 tablespoon baking powder
- 1/2 teaspoon salt
- 1/2 cup cold butter *or* margarine
- 1 egg, beaten
- 2/3 cup light cream
- 1 cup whipping cream
- 2 tablespoons confectioners' sugar
- 1/8 teaspoon vanilla extract
- Additional butter *or* margarine
- 1-1/2 quarts fresh strawberries, sliced

In a bowl, combine flour, sugar, baking powder and salt. Cut in butter until mixture resembles coarse crumbs. In a small bowl, combine egg and light cream; add all at once to the crumb mixture and stir just until moistened. Spread batter into a greased 8-in. round baking pan, slightly building up around the edges. Bake at 450° for 16-18 minutes or until golden brown. Remove from pan and cool on a wire rack. In a mixing bowl, beat whipping cream, confectioners' sugar and vanilla until soft peaks form; set aside. Just before serving, split cake crosswise in half; butter bottom layer. Spoon half of the strawberries over bottom layer. Spread with some of the whipped cream. Cover with top cake layer. Top with remaining berries and whipped cream. Cut into wedges. **Yield:** 6-8 servings.

CRISPY LEMON-FRIED CHICKEN

"THIS IS my husband's favorite chicken dish. He loves it done very crispy and well browned. The steps of soaking the chicken pieces in salted lemony water and re-crisping are the secrets to this recipe."

- 2 broiler-fryer chickens (2 to 3 pounds *each*), cut up *or* 16 pieces of chicken
- 3-1/2 teaspoons salt, *divided*
- Juice of 1 medium lemon
- 1 cup all-purpose flour
- 1 teaspoon paprika
- 1/8 teaspoon pepper
- Cooking oil
- 2 tablespoons water

Place chicken in a large bowl; add 3 teaspoons of salt, lemon juice and enough water to cover chicken. Soak in refrigerator overnight. Drain thoroughly. In a paper bag, combine flour, paprika, pepper and remaining salt. Toss chicken pieces in flour mixture; shake off excess. Heat about 1/2 in. of oil in a large skillet. When hot, carefully add chicken and brown lightly on all sides, about 20 minutes. Reduce heat. Add water; cover and cook until tender, about 20 minutes. Uncover and cook until chicken is crisp, about 10 minutes. **Yield:** 6-8 servings.

I grew up in a German Mennonite family," relates Iona Redemer of Calumet, Oklahoma. "It was customary to invite friends or relatives to our home for Sunday dinner.

"Those Sundays were special occasions, so the guests were served this memorable meal. It's one I learned to *love* when I was growing up.

"When I pull out these recipes today, vivid memories come flooding back to me—fond memories of my grandmother and mother, who handed them down through our family.

"Maybe this meal is so dear to my heart because I helped Mother prepare parts of it. We began by baking zwieback (a delicious bread) on Saturday. I can still smell the mouth-watering aroma that filled Mother's kitchen…what a wonderful way to anticipate a house full of guests the next day!

"The rest of the menu included hearty German meatballs, glazed carrots and apple cake. It's my 'Most Memorable Meal'."

MY MOST MEMORABLE MEAL

All four recipes on this page are from Iona Redemer of Calumet, Oklahoma and are pictured on the opposite page.

GLAZED CARROTS

"THE SWEET TASTE of the glaze not only enhances these carrots, but it is very compatible with the rest of the meal. Another great thing about this vegetable dish is that it adds a nice colorful touch to the table. Whenever Mom fixed this dish I was never disappointed!"

> **9 to 12 medium carrots (about 1-1/2 pounds)**
> **4 tablespoons butter *or* margarine**
> **1 to 2 tablespoons lemon juice**
> **2 tablespoons brown sugar**

Peel carrots and cut in half lengthwise. Boil in salted water until tender; drain well. Melt butter in a heavy skillet; add lemon juice and brown sugar and stir until mixture thickens. Add carrots; stir until well glazed and heated through. **Yield:** 6 servings.

APPLE CAKE

"APPLES WERE plentiful in our area, so they were the staple of many of the desserts served at our table. This apple recipe was one of my mom's favorites. Today, it reigns supreme in our family as the choice dessert. Warm or cold, it's a treat every time!"

> **3 tablespoons butter *or* margarine, softened**
> **1 cup sugar**
> **1 egg, beaten**
> **1 cup all-purpose flour**
> **1/2 teaspoon ground cinnamon**
> **1/2 teaspoon ground nutmeg**
> **1/2 teaspoon salt**
> **1 teaspoon baking soda**
> **3 cups diced peeled apples**
> **1/4 cup chopped nuts**
> **1 teaspoon vanilla extract**
> **Whipped cream *or* ice cream**

In a mixing bowl, cream butter, sugar and egg. Stir together dry ingredients; add to creamed mixture (batter will be very thick). Stir in the apples, nuts and vanilla. Spread into a greased 8-in. square baking pan. Bake at 350° for 35-40 minutes or until cake tests done. Serve warm or cold with whipped cream or ice cream. **Yield:** 9 servings.

ZWIEBACK ROLLS

"FRESH ZWIEBACK is baked in many German Mennonite homes to serve to friends who might drop in, or for the weekly Sunday dinner known as Faspa. Instead of butter, we served jelly with our zwieback. Cold sliced meats and cheeses were delicious with these tasty rolls, too!"

 This tasty dish uses less sugar, salt and fat. Recipe includes *Diabetic Exchanges*.

> **1 package (1/4 ounce) active dry yeast**
> **1/4 cup warm water (110° to 115°)**
> **1-3/4 cups milk, scalded**
> **1/2 cup shortening**
> **1/4 cup sugar**
> **2 teaspoons salt**
> **5 to 6 cups all-purpose flour**

Dissolve yeast in warm water; set aside. In a large mixing bowl, combine milk and shortening; stir to melt shortening. When cool, add sugar and salt. Stir in yeast mixture and 3 cups flour; beat well. Add enough of the remaining flour to form a soft dough. Turn out onto a lightly floured board; knead until smooth and elastic, about 6-8 minutes. Place dough in a greased bowl, turning once to grease top. Cover and let rise in a warm place until doubled, about 1 hour. Punch down dough and divide into fourths. Divide three of the pieces into eight pieces each; shape into smooth balls and place on greased baking sheets. Divide the fourth piece of dough into 24 small balls. Make an indentation in the top of each larger ball; press one small ball atop each larger ball. Cover and let rise in a warm place until doubled, about 45 minutes. Bake at 375° for 20-25 minutes or until golden brown. **Yield:** 2 dozen. **Diabetic Exchanges:** One serving (prepared with skim milk) equals 1-1/2 starch, 1 fat; also, 142 calories, 201 mg sodium, trace cholesterol, 23 gm carbohydrate, 3 gm protein, 4 gm fat.

GERMAN MEATBALLS

"THIS WAS one of our favorite main dishes. Since we raised our own pork and beef, the meat we used was always freshly ground. For variety, these meatballs can be cooked with a sweet cream gravy or steamed with tomatoes—but we prefer them with homemade sauerkraut."

> **1 pound ground beef**
> **1/2 pound ground pork**
> **1/2 cup finely chopped onion**
> **3/4 cup fine dry bread crumbs**
> **1 tablespoon snipped fresh parsley**
> **1-1/2 teaspoons salt**
> **1/8 teaspoon pepper**
> **1 teaspoon Worcestershire sauce**
> **1 egg, beaten**
> **1/2 cup milk**
> **2 to 3 tablespoons vegetable oil**
> **1 can (27 ounces) sauerkraut, undrained**
> **1/3 to 1/2 cup water, optional**
> **Additional snipped parsley**

In a mixing bowl, combine first 10 ingredients; shape into 18 meatballs, 2 in. each. Heat the oil in a skillet; brown the meatballs. Remove meatballs and drain fat. Spoon sauerkraut into skillet; top with meatballs. Cover and simmer for 15-20 minutes or until meatballs are done. Add water if necessary. Sprinkle with parsley. **Yield:** 6 servings.

When Belle Kemmerer really wants to "set off some fire-works" with a fantastic Fourth of July feast, she relies on a tried-and-true meal that's become a summer tradition in her family.

"I remember enjoying this wonderful meal at my grandmother's home when I was a child," Belle says. "She served it whenever we got together on the Fourth, so to me, it's become synonymous with our national holiday."

Belle has carried on her grandmother's tradition for her own family in Stanfordville, New York. Everyone's plenty pleased every time she serves this mouth-watering combination.

"My family thinks these dishes taste great, but to me, the real beauty of this meal is that much of it can be prepared ahead of time," says Belle. "That way, the cook can enjoy the holiday, too. Many of my friends have asked for these recipes, and my church included them in its cookbook," she adds.

Whether you prepare Belle's Most Memorable Meal for the Fourth of July or anytime, it's sure to put some real "bang" into a family get-together!

MY MOST MEMORABLE MEAL

All four recipes on this page are from Belle Kemmerer of Stanfordville, New York and are pictured on the opposite page.

CRUNCHY CHEESE POTATOES

"THESE POTATOES are delicious, and they live up to their crunchy name! I make them often since they're easy to prepare and can be made ahead of time. This dish is always 'pretty as a picture' when it comes out of the oven!"

> 1 cup (8 ounces) sour cream
> 1/2 cup milk
> 1 tablespoon minced chives
> 1/2 teaspoon salt
> 1/4 teaspoon pepper
> 6 medium potatoes, peeled and sliced 1/4 inch thick
> 1 cup (4 ounces) shredded sharp cheddar cheese
> 1/2 cup finely crushed cornflakes
> Additional minced chives, optional

In a large bowl, combine sour cream, milk, chives, salt and pepper. Add potatoes and mix thoroughly. Spread in a 15-in. x 10-in. x 1-in. baking pan. Combine cheese and cornflakes; sprinkle over potatoes. Bake at 350° for 50-60 minutes or until potatoes are tender. Sprinkle with additional chives if desired. **Yield:** 6-8 servings.

HONEY BARBECUED SPARE RIBS

"BASTING with the honey-and-oil glaze seals in the goodness of these delicious ribs as they bake to a golden brown. They can be prepared in the oven, or on the grill in a foil packet to keep the meat juicy."

> 3 pounds pork spare ribs *or* pork loin back ribs
> 3 tablespoons lemon juice
> 2 tablespoons honey
> 2 tablespoons vegetable oil
> 1 tablespoon soy sauce
> 1 tablespoon instant minced onion
> 1 teaspoon paprika
> 1 teaspoon salt
> 1/2 teaspoon dried oregano
> 1/8 teaspoon garlic powder

Cut spare ribs into serving-size pieces. Place ribs, bone side down, on a rack in a shallow roasting pan. Cover and roast at 350° for 1 hour. Drain. Combine all the remaining ingredients in a bowl; brush some of the glaze on ribs. Roast, uncovered, 30-45 minutes longer or until meat is tender, brushing occasionally with remaining glaze. **Yield:** 4 servings.

SUMMER SALAD WITH GOLDEN DRESSING

"THE GOLDEN DRESSING for this salad is more than just a salad topping. It's excellent served as a sauce for meat or used as a marinade for vegetables. The touch of curry gives any combination of vegetables a wonderfully tangy taste."

> 1 package (16 ounces) frozen French-style green beans, cooked and drained *or* 1 can (14-1/2 ounces) French-style green beans, drained
> 1/2 cup sliced celery
> 1/2 cup sliced unpeeled cucumber
> 4 radishes, sliced
> 4 medium tomatoes, cut into wedges
> Lettuce leaves
> **DRESSING:**
> 1 hard-cooked egg, chopped
> 1 tablespoon instant minced onion
> 1/4 cup vinegar
> 1/2 cup vegetable oil
> 1/2 teaspoon salt
> 1/8 teaspoon curry powder

In a bowl, lightly toss green beans with celery, cucumber and radishes. Chill. Arrange tomatoes on a lettuce-lined platter. Fill center with vegetables. Combine dressing ingredients; just before serving, pour over salad. **Yield:** 8 servings.

BLUEBERRY PUDDING WITH LEMON CREAM SAUCE

"THIS IS my favorite part of my favorite meal! The 'pudding' really bakes up as a cake, but the delicious lemon sauce crowning each piece has a pudding-like consistency. This dessert is so good I can't resist making it several times during blueberry season...but my family has never complained about having it too often."

> **LEMON CREAM SAUCE:**
> 2 teaspoons cornstarch
> 1/2 cup sugar
> 2/3 cup water
> 2 tablespoons lemon juice
> 1 cup heavy cream
> **PUDDING:**
> 2 cups all-purpose flour
> 1-1/2 cups sugar
> 2 teaspoons baking powder
> 1/2 teaspoon salt
> 1/2 teaspoon ground nutmeg
> 3/4 teaspoon ground cinnamon
> 2/3 cup butter *or* margarine
> 2 eggs
> 3/4 cup milk
> 2 cups fresh blueberries, washed and drained

In a small saucepan, combine the cornstarch and sugar. Stir in water; cook and stir until thickened and clear. Remove from the heat; stir in lemon juice. Cool. In a mixing bowl, whip the cream; fold cooled mixture into cream. Cover and refrigerate until ready to use. For pudding, combine dry ingredients in another mixing bowl. Cut in butter with a pastry blender until particles are the size of small peas. Add eggs and milk and beat on low until thoroughly combined. Spread into a greased 9-in. square baking pan. Sprinkle berries over batter. Bake at 350° for 50-55 minutes or until cake tests done. Serve warm or cold with Lemon Cream Sauce. **Yield:** 9 servings.

MY MOST MEMORABLE MEAL

All four recipes on this page are from Cookie Curci-Wright of San Jose, California and are pictured on the opposite page.

STUFFED MANICOTTI

"THE AROMA of this delicious dish baking in the oven brings back many warm and tasty memories!"

SPAGHETTI SAUCE:
- 1 medium onion, chopped
- 1/2 green pepper, chopped
- 2 garlic cloves, minced
- 3 tablespoons olive oil
- 1 can (29 ounces) tomato sauce
- 3/4 cup water
- 3/4 cup dry red wine *or* water
- 1 teaspoon dried oregano
- 1/2 teaspoon dried basil
- 1/2 teaspoon salt
- 1/4 teaspoon pepper

MANICOTTI:
- 1-1/2 pounds ground beef
- 1/2 medium onion, finely chopped
- 2 garlic cloves, minced
- 1 package (10 ounces) frozen chopped spinach, thawed
- 3/4 cup grated Parmesan cheese, *divided*
- 3 eggs, beaten
- 1 teaspoon dried oregano
- 1/2 teaspoon salt
- 1/4 teaspoon pepper
- 1 package (8 ounces) manicotti, cooked and drained
- 3/4 cup shredded mozzarella cheese

In a saucepan, saute onion, green pepper and garlic in olive oil until tender. Stir in all remaining sauce ingredients; bring to a boil. Reduce heat; cover and simmer for 1 hour, stirring occasionally. Uncover; simmer 10-15 minutes longer or until as thick as desired. Meanwhile, for manicotti, cook beef, onion and garlic in a skillet until the meat is browned and onion is tender. Drain; cool slightly. Squeeze spinach thoroughly to remove excess water; add to the skillet with 1/2 cup Parmesan cheese, eggs, oregano, salt and pepper. Mix well. Refrigerate 1-1/2 cups of the sauce (makes 4 cups) for another recipe. Pour 1 cup of the remaining sauce into a 13-in. x 9-in. x 2-in. baking dish. Stuff manicotti with the meat mixture; arrange over the sauce. Pour another 1-1/2 cups of sauce on top. Sprinkle with the mozzarella and remaining Parmesan. Bake, uncovered, at 350° for 25-30 minutes or until heated through. **Yield:** 7 servings.

ITALIAN GARLIC TOAST

"EVERY Italian meal must have its garlic bread, and this recipe is not only delicious but also attractive."

- 1 unsliced loaf (1-1/2 pounds) French bread
- 1/2 cup butter *or* margarine, melted
- 1/4 cup grated Romano *or* Parmesan cheese
- 2 garlic cloves, minced *or* 1/2 teaspoon garlic powder
- 1/2 teaspoon dried oregano

Paprika

Slice bread lengthwise; place with cut side up on a large baking sheet. In a small bowl, combine butter, cheese, garlic and oregano; brush onto cut surfaces of bread. Sprinkle with paprika. Broil about 4 in. from heat for 2-3 minutes or until lightly toasted. Cut crosswise into 3-in. pieces to serve. **Yield:** 8-10 servings.

GREEN GARDEN SALAD

"THIS DRESSING enhances any kind of greens with a special flavor."

DRESSING:
- 3/4 cup olive oil
- 1/2 cup red wine vinegar
- 2 tablespoons lemon juice, optional
- 2 teaspoons grated Parmesan cheese
- 1 teaspoon dried oregano
- 1/2 teaspoon sugar
- 1/4 teaspoon salt
- 1/4 teaspoon pepper

SALAD:
- 8 to 10 cups torn salad greens
- 1 red onion, sliced into rings
- 1 cucumber, peeled and sliced
- 2 to 3 tomatoes, cut into wedges
- 1 green pepper, sliced into rings

In a jar or bottle with tight-fitting lid, combine all the dressing ingredients; shake well. Chill. Just before serving, combine greens, onion, cucumber and tomatoes in a large salad bowl. Pour desired amount of dressing over salad; toss to mix. Top with the green pepper rings. **Yield:** 8-10 servings (1-1/3 cups dressing).

AUNTIE ANN'S EGGPLANT RELISH

"THIS IS my favorite of Auntie Ann's dishes and one I enjoy making!"

- 1 medium eggplant, peeled and cubed
- 1 medium onion, chopped
- 1 celery rib, chopped
- 1 cup chopped fresh mushrooms
- 1 green *or* sweet red pepper, chopped
- 1 cup pitted ripe olives, sliced
- 4 garlic cloves, minced
- 1 can (8 ounces) tomato sauce
- 1/2 cup water
- 1 teaspoon dried oregano
- 1/2 teaspoon salt
- 2 tablespoons ketchup
- 2 teaspoons red wine vinegar
- 1 teaspoon sugar, optional

Few drops hot pepper sauce

In a Dutch oven, combine the first 11 ingredients; mix well. Bring to a boil. Reduce heat; cover and simmer for 20 minutes or until vegetables are tender. Stir in the ketchup, vinegar, sugar if desired and hot pepper sauce. Cook, uncovered, about 5 minutes longer or until slightly thickened. Cool. **Yield:** 10-12 servings (about 6 cups).

"You don't need to be Irish to get into the St. Patrick's Day spirit," assures Evelyn Kenney of Trenton, New Jersey, "especially at mealtime!"

Evelyn says she likes St. Patrick's Day because it's not a "gift-giving" holiday. Instead, family members and friends can relax and focus on old-fashioned hospitality.

What makes St. Patrick's Day memorable for Evelyn's family is the traditional Irish meal she has served for years on the day for "the wearin' of the green". Along with corned beef and cabbage, there are sauces and beet relish, Irish soda bread and a glazed cake that's right from old Erin's Isle!

These days, Evelyn's children and grandchildren carry on the family tradition she started, sharing this mouth-watering meal with their own friends and family.

Once you've tried Evelyn's tasty recipes, they just may become a St. Patrick's Day tradition in your home, too. Whether or not you're Irish, you'll celebrate this holiday in good taste!

MY MOST MEMORABLE MEAL

All four recipes on this page are from Evelyn Kenney of Trenton, New Jersey and are pictured on the opposite page.

CORNED BEEF AND CABBAGE

"THIS TRADITIONAL Irish dish is perfect not only for St. Patrick's Day, but any time of year."

> 1 corned beef brisket (4 to 6 pounds)
> 2 tablespoons brown sugar
> 2 to 3 bay leaves
> 16 to 24 small potatoes, peeled
> 8 to 12 carrots, halved
> 1 large head cabbage, cut into wedges

Minced fresh parsley, optional

HORSERADISH SAUCE:
> 3 tablespoons butter *or* margarine
> 2 tablespoons all-purpose flour
> 1 to 1-1/2 cups cooking liquid (from brisket)
> 1 tablespoon vinegar
> 1 tablespoon sugar
> 1/4 cup horseradish

SOUR CREAM AND MUSTARD SAUCE:
> 1 cup (8 ounces) sour cream
> 2 tablespoons Dijon mustard
> 1/4 teaspoon sugar

Place brisket in a large Dutch oven; cover with water. Add brown sugar and bay leaves. (If a spice packet is enclosed with the brisket, add it also.) Bring to a boil. Reduce heat; cover and simmer for 2 hours. Add potatoes and carrots. Return to boiling. Reduce heat; cover and simmer 30-40 minutes or until meat and vegetables are just tender. If your Dutch oven is not large enough for cabbage to fit, remove potatoes and carrots and keep warm (they can be returned to cooking liquid and heated through before serving). Add cabbage; cover and cook about 15 minutes or until tender. Discard bay leaves. Remove cabbage and meat. If making Horseradish Sauce, strain and remove about 1-1/2 cups cooking liquid. Let meat stand a few minutes. Slice meat across the grain. Serve with Horseradish Sauce or Sour Cream and Mustard Sauce. Garnish with parsley if desired. **Yield:** 8-12 servings.

Horseradish Sauce: In a small saucepan, melt butter. Blend in flour. Add 1 cup cooking liquid; stir until smooth. Add vinegar, sugar and horseradish. Cook and stir over medium heat until thickened and bubbly. Adjust seasoning with additional vinegar, sugar or horseradish if needed. Thin sauce if necessary with the remaining cooking liquid. **Yield:** about 1-1/2 cups.

Sour Cream and Mustard Sauce: Combine all ingredients in a small bowl. Mix until well blended. **Yield:** 1 cup.

BEET RELISH

"SERVED with corned beef and cabbage, this relish provides an interesting combination of flavors and is a colorful addition to the table."

> 2 cups coarsely shredded cooked beets
> 2 tablespoons chopped red onion
> 2 tablespoons red wine vinegar
> 1 teaspoon sugar
> 2 tablespoons Dijon mustard
> 3 tablespoons vegetable oil

Salt and pepper to taste

Combine all ingredients in a small bowl and blend well. Chill thoroughly. **Yield:** about 2 cups.

IRISH SODA BREAD

"SOME PEOPLE consider bread to be the most important part of a meal...and this bread just might satisfy such folks!"

> 4 cups all-purpose flour
> 1/4 cup sugar
> 1 teaspoon salt
> 1 teaspoon baking powder
> 1 teaspoon baking soda
> 1/4 cup butter *or* margarine
> 3 to 4 tablespoons caraway seeds
> 2 cups raisins
> 1-1/3 cups buttermilk
> 1 egg, beaten

Milk

In a mixing bowl, combine flour, sugar, salt, baking powder and baking soda. Cut in butter until mixture resembles coarse meal. Stir in caraway seeds and raisins. Combine buttermilk and egg; stir into dry ingredients just until moistened. Turn out onto a floured surface and knead lightly until smooth. Shape dough into a ball and place in a greased baking pan. Pat into a 7-in. round loaf. Cut a 4-in. cross about 1/4 in. deep on top to allow for expansion. Brush top with milk. Bake at 375° for 1 hour or until golden brown. **Yield:** 1 loaf.

EMERALD ISLE CAKE

"THIS CAKE is simple to make and provides the perfect finish for an Irish meal."

> 1/2 cup butter *or* margarine, softened
> 1 cup sugar
> 2 eggs
> 1 teaspoon vanilla extract
> 1-3/4 cups all-purpose flour
> 2 teaspoons baking powder
> 1/2 teaspoon salt
> 1/2 cup milk

GLAZE:
> 1 cup confectioners' sugar
> 1 to 2 tablespoons milk *or* Irish whiskey

Green food coloring, optional
Slivered almonds, optional

In a mixing bowl, cream butter and sugar. Add eggs, one at a time, beating well after each addition. Blend in vanilla. Combine flour, baking powder and salt; add alternately with the milk. Beat until smooth. Spread into a greased 9-in. square baking pan. Bake at 350° for 40 minutes or until cake tests done. For glaze, combine confectioners' sugar and milk or whiskey; stir until smooth and fairly thin. If desired, add 1 to 2 drops of food coloring and stir until well blended. Spread glaze over warm cake. Sprinkle with almonds if desired. **Yield:** 9-12 servings.

*N*ot many meals recall the past as well as this one from Anna Baker of Blaine, Washington. But, though it is full of old-fashioned feeling, it's as popular today as ever!

"My home's known as the 'Do Drop Inn'," relates Anna. "I'm delighted with that—the door's always open, and no one needs an invitation to come by and enjoy 'Grandma Baker's goodies'."

And, while family members and friends rate *all* of Anna's dishes as delicious, they readily agree the one she shares here—the meal that she serves at her family's annual reunion—is surely her most memorable. "The combination of aromas that comes from the kitchen while I'm preparing it is so familiar," Anna says, "that everyone always knows 'what's cooking'!"

In addition to these four dishes served at the meal, Anna usually makes a large batch of scalloped potatoes and steams fresh sweet corn from her son's garden. A big green salad makes the meal complete…and oh, so memorable!

MY MOST MEMORABLE MEAL

All four recipes on this page are from Anna Baker of
Blaine, Washington and are pictured on the opposite page.

GREEN BEAN CASSEROLE

"THIS HAS always been one of my favorite 'convenience dishes' because it can be prepared ahead and refrigerated until ready to bake."

- 2 cans (10-3/4 ounces *each*) condensed cream of mushroom soup, undiluted
- 1 cup milk
- 2 teaspoons soy sauce
- 1/8 teaspoon pepper
- 2 packages (16 ounces *each*) frozen whole *or* cut green beans, cooked and drained
- 1 can (6 ounces) french fried onions, *divided*

In a mixing bowl, combine soup, milk, soy sauce and pepper. Gently stir in beans. Spoon half of the mixture into a 12-in. x 8-in. x 2-in. baking dish. Sprinkle with half of the onions. Spoon remaining bean mixture over the top. Bake at 350° for 30 minutes or until heated through. Sprinkle with remaining onions. Return to oven for 5 minutes or until the onions are brown and crispy. **Yield:** 10 servings.

COCOA COLA CAKE

"I GET a great response every time I serve this cake, and I'm forever sharing this recipe! The unusual ingredients make it moist and delicious."

- 2 cups all-purpose flour
- 2 cups sugar
- 1 teaspoon baking soda
- 1 cup butter *or* margarine
- 3 tablespoons baking cocoa
- 1 cup cola
- 1/2 cup buttermilk
- 2 eggs, beaten
- 1 teaspoon vanilla extract
- 1 cup miniature marshmallows

ICING:
- 1/2 cup butter *or* margarine
- 2 to 3 tablespoons baking cocoa

- 6 tablespoons cola
- 3-1/4 cups confectioners' sugar
- 1 cup coarsely chopped nuts

In a mixing bowl, combine the flour, sugar and baking soda; set aside. In a saucepan, bring butter, cocoa and cola to a boil; stir into dry ingredients. Stir in buttermilk, eggs, vanilla and marshmallows; mix well. Pour into a greased 13-in. x 9-in. x 2-in. baking pan. Bake at 350° for 35 minutes or until cake tests done. For icing, combine butter, cocoa and cola in a saucepan; bring to a boil. Remove from heat; stir in confectioners' sugar and mix well. Spread over hot cake. Sprinkle with nuts. Cool before cutting. **Yield:** 8-10 servings.

DINNER ROLLS

"THE AROMA of baked bread makes any house seem so inviting! My family loves the fragrance of these rolls as they bake and has come to expect them whenever I make a special meal."

- 2 packages (1/4 ounce *each*) active dry yeast
- 1/2 cup warm water (100°-115°)
- 1/3 cup plus 1 teaspoon sugar, *divided*
- 1-1/4 cups warm milk (110°-115°)
- 1/2 cup butter *or* margarine, melted and cooled
- 1-1/2 teaspoons salt
- 2 eggs, beaten
- 6 to 6-1/2 cups all-purpose flour

Additional melted butter *or* margarine, optional

In a large bowl, dissolve yeast in warm water with 1 teaspoon sugar. Add milk, butter, salt, remaining sugar, eggs and 3 cups flour; beat until smooth. Stir in enough remaining flour to form a soft dough. Turn out onto a floured surface; knead until smooth and elastic, about 6-8 minutes, adding additional flour as needed. Place in a greased bowl, turning once to grease top. Cover and let rise in a warm place until doubled, about 1

hour. Punch dough down, then turn out onto a lightly floured board. Divide dough in half. Divide each half into 12 pieces. Shape each piece into a ball; place in two greased 13-in. x 9-in. x 2-in. baking pans. Cover and let rise until doubled, about 30 minutes. Bake at 375° for 20-25 minutes or until golden brown. Lightly brush with melted butter if desired and serve warm. **Yield:** 2 dozen.

BEST-EVER MEAT LOAF

"THE COMBINATION of onion, carrot, parsley and cheese—plus the tomato-mustard topping—makes this meat loaf unusually colorful."

- 2 eggs
- 2/3 cup milk
- 3 slices bread, torn into pieces
- 1/2 cup chopped onion
- 1/2 cup grated carrot
- 1 cup (4 ounces) shredded cheddar *or* mozzarella cheese
- 1 tablespoon chopped fresh parsley *or* 1 teaspoon dried parsley
- 1 teaspoon salt
- 1 teaspoon dried basil, thyme *or* sage, optional
- 1/4 teaspoon pepper
- 1-1/2 pounds lean ground beef

TOPPING:
- 1/2 cup tomato sauce
- 1/2 cup packed brown sugar
- 1 teaspoon prepared mustard

In a large bowl, beat eggs. Add milk and bread; let stand a few minutes or until the bread absorbs the liquid. Stir in the onion, carrot, cheese, herbs and seasonings. Add beef; mix well. In a shallow baking pan, shape beef mixture into a 7-1/2-in. x 3-1/2-in. x 2-1/2-in. loaf. Bake at 350° for 45 minutes. Meanwhile, combine topping ingredients. Spoon some of the topping over meat loaf. Bake for about 30 minutes longer or until no pink remains, occasionally spooning some of the remaining topping over loaf. Let stand 10 minutes before serving. **Yield:** 6 servings.

MEALS IN MINUTES

THE RANCH Gail Jenner helps her husband run outside Etna, California has time on its side—the family has raised cattle there four generations.

With three children—17, 14 and 5 —however, time too often is what she *doesn't* have when meals must be made. So Gail's become somewhat of an "expert" at expeditious dishes!

"I love to cook and host fancy dinner parties," she says. "But when my schedule is hectic, planning is everything. To save time, I frequently prepare several meals at once I can simply defrost when I need them."

This menu, though, doesn't require even a moment of advance work.

"My spaghetti's good for feeding ranch hands—or guests who arrive on short notice!" Gail says. "It uses ingredients that are always on hand.

"The salad's also simple—though I like to rub the bowl with fresh garlic for an extra tangy touch!

"To finish off the meal, I put together my sundae. It's one I adapted from a more complicated recipe to fit my need for a quick dessert."

Gail's meal goes from stovetop to tabletop in less than 30 minutes. Try it in your kitchen when time's fleeting...or whenever you want to surprise your family with a new treat!

TOSSED ITALIAN SALAD

1 garlic clove, peeled
6 cups assorted salad greens
1/2 cucumber *or* zucchini, thinly sliced
1 large tomato, cut into wedges
Italian salad dressing

Rub the inside of a salad bowl with the garlic. Add the greens, cucumber or zucchini and tomato. Just before serving, toss with enough salad dressing to coat. **Yield:** 4 servings.

SPAGHETTI WITH EGGS AND BACON

8 ounces spaghetti
1/2 pound bacon
4 eggs, beaten
1/2 cup grated Parmesan cheese
1/2 cup light cream
Additional Parmesan cheese

Cook spaghetti according to package directions. Meanwhile, cook bacon; drain and crumble, then set aside. Combine eggs, Parmesan cheese and cream in a small mixing bowl. Drain spaghetti and return to cooking pan. Stir in egg mixture. Quickly toss and cook until egg mixture is done and coats spaghetti. Stir in bacon and serve immediately with additional Parmesan cheese. **Yield:** 4 servings.

FLORENTINE SUNDAE

1 can (8 ounces) pineapple slices, drained
1 quart orange *or* lemon frozen sherbet
Grated semisweet chocolate
Chopped nuts
Flaked coconut

Place a pineapple slice in the bottom of four dessert dishes. Top with a scoop or two of sherbet. Sprinkle with grated chocolate, nuts and coconut. Serve immediately. **Yield:** 4 servings.

MEALS IN MINUTES

HARVESTTIME has always been "hurry-up time" for South Dakota farm wife Gretchen Kuipers of Platte. Now, her growing family's made the pace at this time of year even a faster one!

"We have two small boys—4 and 2—and they keep me on the move all day long," she remarks. "Most days, I have little time for cooking. So I've come to rely on recipes that can be prepared in 30 minutes or less."

One such three-course standby meal Gretchen's cooked up in her own kitchen not only is quick as can be, it gives tried-and-true ground beef a tasty new zing.

"My Stroganoff Sandwich can easily be prepared at a moment's notice," reports Gretchen. "I often serve it to my husband as a hearty main dish when he comes in from working in the field late in the afternoon.

"The spinach salad's also speedy to prepare—plus, you can substitute other greens for the spinach if you like. Finally, my fruit salad is a convenient dessert all year-round. Our kids *love* it!"

To learn why, try Gretchen's imaginative menu at your house. You're sure to harvest hurrahs...in a hurry!

STROGANOFF SANDWICH

    1 pound lean ground beef
  1/4 cup chopped onion
  1/4 teaspoon garlic powder
Salt and pepper to taste
    1 teaspoon Worcestershire
       sauce
    1 can (4 ounces) sliced
       mushrooms, drained
    1 cup (8 ounces) sour cream

Butter *or* margarine, softened
    1 loaf French bread, cut in half
       lengthwise
    2 medium tomatoes, thinly sliced
    1 medium green pepper, cut
       into rings
    1 cup (4 ounces) shredded
       cheddar cheese

In a skillet, brown beef with onion. Drain. Season with the garlic powder, salt, pepper and Worcestershire sauce. Remove from the heat and stir in mushrooms and sour cream; set aside. Butter the cut surface of the bread. Place it with the buttered side up on a baking sheet; broil until light golden brown. Reset oven to 375°. Spread bread with ground beef mixture. Top with the tomatoes, pepper rings and cheese. Bake for 5 minutes or until the cheese melts. Serve immediately. **Yield:** 6-8 servings.

BACON SPINACH SALAD

    6 bacon strips
    6 cups torn spinach leaves
  1/2 small head iceberg lettuce, torn
    1 bunch green onions, thinly
       sliced

  1/2 cup vegetable oil
  1/4 cup vinegar
    1 tablespoon sugar
    1 teaspoon salt
    1 teaspoon dry mustard

In a skillet, cook bacon until crisp. Drain, crumble and set aside. Place greens and onions in a salad bowl; refrigerate until serving. Combine all remaining ingredients in a jar and shake until well mixed. Just before serving, pour dressing over greens. Toss well to coat. Add bacon and toss. **Yield:** 6-8 servings.

TROPICAL FRUIT DESSERT

  1/2 cup plain *or* vanilla yogurt
    1 tablespoon frozen orange
       juice concentrate
    2 kiwifruit, peeled and sliced
    2 bananas, sliced
    1 can (11 ounces) mandarin
       oranges, drained
Shredded coconut

In a small bowl, combine yogurt and orange juice concentrate. Place fruit in individual dessert bowls. Drizzle each serving with yogurt sauce. Sprinkle with coconut. **Yield:** 6 servings.

MEALS IN MINUTES

AS an ex-farm girl, Jean Brenneman of Cedar Rapids, Iowa enjoys trying out different recipes she comes across in various publications.

As the mother of a 15-month-old baby, however, with a part-time job outside the home to boot, she sometimes needs to improvise on her own! That's where the "Meal in Minutes" Jean shares this time originated.

"After our daughter arrived, our schedule became much more hectic," she notes. "I developed this meal so I could have dinner ready within 30 minutes of getting home from work. Then I can enjoy the evening with my family.

"The recipes all came from different sources. But they blended well when I

"My husband loves this meal—even though I serve it as often as once a week!"

put them together. In fact, my husband says that he *loves* this meal —even though I serve it as often as once a week!"

When she's not scurrying to make up time in the kitchen, Jean relaxes with reading or cross-stitching.

Give her speedy supper a try at your place the next time your cooking has to be extra quick. You never know…if your hungry crew is like Jean's, you may have a new favorite your family will ask for even when meal-making time *isn't* tight!

PARMESAN NOODLES

- 8 ounces wide noodles
- 2 tablespoons butter *or* margarine
- 1/4 teaspoon garlic powder
- 1/4 cup grated Parmesan cheese
- 2 tablespoons minced fresh parsley

Cook noodles according to package directions; drain. Place in a bowl. Immediately add remaining ingredients and toss well. **Yield:** 4 servings.

MARINATED ITALIAN CHICKEN

- 4 boneless skinless chicken breasts
- 1/2 cup Italian salad dressing

Place chicken breasts in a shallow pan; pour dressing over. Marinate for 15 minutes. Place chicken on rack of a broiler pan. Broil for 5-7 minutes on each side or until juices run clear. **Yield:** 4 servings.

SWEDISH CREAM

- 1 package (3.4 ounces) instant vanilla pudding mix
- 1-1/2 cups cold milk
- 1 cup plain yogurt
- 1/8 teaspoon almond extract
- 2 to 3 cups fresh strawberries, raspberries *or* blueberries

In a mixing bowl, whisk together first four ingredients. Place berries in dessert cups and top with cream mixture, or layer berries and cream in parfait glasses. **Yield:** 4-6 servings.

MEALS IN MINUTES

WITH all the plates to fill whenever her family comes visiting, Johnnie McLeod of Bastrop, Louisiana easily could end up spending *hours* cooking.

Instead, she satisfies her clan of 14 with this quick-to-fix summer menu. It goes from start to "Soup's on!" in only 30 minutes—letting Johnnie relax and enjoy her company outside the kitchen!

"An easy meal like this is just what I need," she confirms.

The tasty main course of Johnnie's "Meal in Minutes" has an extra advantage built in—the burgers can be prepared ahead, then refrigerated till it's time to barbecue them.

The corn goes right on the grill with the burgers. And the slaw and fudgy dessert are fast food at its finest also!

Sound good to you, too? Don't hesitate then! Serve this speedy supper to your family without delay…even if you *aren't* cooking for a crowd tonight!

STUFFED BACON BURGERS

1-1/2 pounds ground beef
  1 envelope (1 ounce) dry onion
    soup mix
1/4 cup water
  6 slices (1 ounce *each*) process
    American cheese
  6 bacon strips
  6 hamburger buns, toasted

In a bowl, combine ground beef, soup mix and water; mix well. Shape into 12 thin patties. Place a cheese slice on six of the patties. Cover each with another patty. Pinch edges to seal. Wrap a strip of bacon around each; fasten with a wooden toothpick. Grill for 8-10 minutes, turning once, or until burgers reach desired doneness. Remove toothpicks. Serve on buns. **Yield:** 6 servings.

ROAST CORN ON THE COB

  6 ears fresh sweet corn
  6 tablespoons butter *or*
    margarine
  6 ice cubes
Salt and pepper to taste
Additional butter *or* margarine,
  optional

Remove husk and silk from corn. Place each ear of corn on a piece of aluminum foil. Add 1 tablespoon butter and 1 ice cube. Wrap securely, twisting ends to make handles for turning. Place corn on grill. Cook for 25 minutes, turning once. Season with salt and pepper, and additional butter if desired. **Yield:** 6 servings.

CABBAGE SLAW

  1 medium head cabbage
    (about 2-1/2 pounds)
  1 carrot
  1 cup mayonnaise
  2 tablespoons milk
  2 tablespoons vinegar
  3 tablespoons sugar
  1 teaspoon salt
1/2 to 1 teaspoon pepper
1/2 to 1 teaspoon celery seed

In a food processor or by hand, coarsely chop the cabbage and carrot. In a small bowl, combine the mayonnaise, milk, vinegar, sugar, salt, pepper and celery seed. Stir into the cabbage mixture. Chill until serving. **Yield:** 6 servings.

FUDGE BROWNIE PIE

  1 cup sugar
1/2 cup butter *or* margarine,
  melted
  2 eggs
1/2 cup all-purpose flour
1/3 cup unsweetened baking cocoa
1/4 teaspoon salt
  1 teaspoon vanilla extract
1/2 cup chopped pecans
Whipped cream, optional
Strawberries, optional

In a mixing bowl, beat sugar and butter. Add eggs; mix well. Add flour, cocoa and salt. Stir in vanilla and nuts. Pour into a greased 9-in. pie pan. Bake at 350° for 25-30 minutes or until almost set. Serve with whipped cream and strawberries if desired. **Yield:** 6 servings.

MEALS IN MINUTES

WHEN Dawn Supina, Edmonton, Alberta, has to make tracks in the kitchen, she has time on her side…twice.

"The main course for my favorite 'Meal in Minutes' is actually a classic old dish that my father used to make," Dawn details. "I added the caraway to give it a robust taste. You can add a little bit of leftover meat, too, if you like."

Dawn's dish is "timeless"—or just about so—in another way besides!

"It's so quick and easy to prepare that it can be made at the last minute if necessary," she notes. "I keep all of the ingredients on hand just in case.

"My husband and our two children —5 and 2—like this meal for lunch or for a light supper. So do I! I'm not a 'gourmet' cook, just a very basic one."

Outside the kitchen, this Canadian cook tends to her flower garden. After drying, Dawn uses her floral harvest in wreaths and arrangements.

The other courses in her Meal in Minutes make a pleasing arrangement themselves. The speedy salad is a nice fresh one with ingredients that can be varied based on availability. And the dessert couldn't be quicker or easier. See for yourself sometime soon!

QUICK ITALIAN SALAD

- 1 head romaine lettuce, torn
- 1 medium tomato, cut into wedges
- 1/2 medium cucumber, sliced
- 1 small red onion, chopped
- 1/2 cup cubed mozzarella cheese
- 1/4 cup sliced ripe olives

Bottled Italian dressing

Toss the first six ingredients in a large salad bowl. Pour dressing over all and toss lightly to coat. Serve immediately. **Yield:** 4 servings.

HEARTY CHEESE 'N' TOAST

- 1 tablespoon butter *or* margarine
- 1 tablespoon all-purpose flour
- 2/3 cup milk
- 1 teaspoon Worcestershire sauce
- 1/2 teaspoon dry mustard
- 1 teaspoon whole caraway seeds

Pepper to taste
- 2 cups (8 ounces) shredded sharp cheddar cheese
- 4 to 6 slices white *or* whole wheat bread, toasted
- 4 to 6 slices cooked turkey, chicken, beef *or* ham, optional

Chopped fresh parsley

In a saucepan, melt butter over medium-high heat. Stir in flour to form a smooth paste. Gradually stir in milk. Cook and stir until the mixture is smooth and thickened. Add the Worcestershire sauce, mustard, caraway and pepper. Stir until well blended. Add the cheese; cook and stir over low heat until melted. Cut toast diagonally and place on individual plates. If desired, top each with a slice of meat. Spoon cheese sauce over meat and toast. Sprinkle with parsley. Serve immediately. **Yield:** 4 servings.

SWEET AND CREAMY RASPBERRIES

- 1 pint fresh raspberries
Light cream
Confectioners' sugar
Fresh mint, optional

Place raspberries in individual bowls. Just before serving, pour cream over each serving. Sprinkle with sugar; garnish with mint if desired. **Yield:** 4 servings.

MEALS IN MINUTES

BOTH coming *and* going, busy farm wife Lois McCutchan, Monticello, Missouri, frequently needs to make tracks to put food for the evening meal on the table.

"My husband, Dennis, and I have a 300-acre farm," she explains. "In addition, I work at our local bank, and he's a county commissioner. Many times, I get home from work just as he's coming in from the field and about to go to a meeting.

"Needless to say, I like quick meals. This particular one is such a standby I have it memorized!"

Lois' fast four courses feature basic hearty ingredients—"We're a typical meat-and-potatoes kind of family," she notes.

The Lemon Pepper Steak couldn't be simpler. With the addition of a single easy ingredient, you have a savory seasoned steak. "Sometimes," Lois relates, "since Dennis is an avid sportsman, I'll substitute venison or elk steak as the meat and adjust the broiling time accordingly if necessary."

Cheese and Onion Potatoes cook up crispy to a pretty golden brown…and—talk about saving time—the potatoes don't even need peeling! Citrus Broccoli Toss has a nice tangy taste, and Almond Peach Sundae is a refreshing, no-fuss finish to a filling meal.

Lois hopes that you'll try her Meal in Minutes on your family.

LEMON PEPPER STEAK

    4 T-bone *or* New York strip steaks (1 inch thick)
Lemon pepper to taste

Sprinkle steaks with lemon pepper. Broil in a preheated broiler 3-4 in. from the heat for 5-7 minutes per side or until the steaks reach desired doneness. **Yield:** 4 servings.

CITRUS BROCCOLI TOSS

    2 tablespoons butter *or* margarine
    1 package (10 ounces) frozen cut broccoli, thawed
1-1/2 teaspoons grated orange peel
1-1/2 teaspoons grated lemon peel
Salt and pepper to taste

In a skillet, melt butter over medium heat. Saute broccoli until crisp-tender. Sprinkle with orange and lemon peel, salt and pepper, then toss to coat. Heat through. **Yield:** 4 servings.

CHEESE AND ONION POTATOES

1/4 cup butter *or* margarine
    4 medium unpeeled red potatoes, sliced 1/4 inch thick
    2 tablespoons dried minced onion
Pepper to taste
    1/3 cup shredded cheddar cheese
Chopped fresh parsley

In a skillet, melt butter over medium-high heat. Add potatoes, onion and pepper; toss to coat. Cover and cook, stirring occasionally, until potatoes are tender, about 10 minutes. Uncover; cook until potatoes are browned, about 5-7 minutes. Top with cheese. Cover and remove from the heat; let stand for several minutes. Sprinkle with parsley before serving. **Yield:** 4 servings.

ALMOND PEACH SUNDAE

    1 can (16 ounces) sliced peaches
    1 tablespoon cornstarch
1/2 teaspoon ground cinnamon
1/4 teaspoon ground nutmeg
1/2 teaspoon almond extract
1/4 cup slivered almonds
Vanilla ice cream

Drain peaches and place the liquid in a saucepan. Stir in cornstarch, cinnamon and nutmeg. Cook and stir over medium-high heat until thickened, about 2-3 minutes. Stir in extract, almonds and peaches. Heat through. Serve warm over ice cream. **Yield:** 4-6 servings.